Medieval Academy Reprints for Teaching 33

Medieval Academy Reprints for Teaching

R.I. Moore

THE BIRTH OF POPULAR HERESY

Published by University of Toronto Press
Toronto Buffalo London
in association with the Medieval Academy of America

© Medieval Academy of America 1995
Printed in Canada
ISBN 0-8020-7659-9

First published in 1975 by Edward Arnold Ltd. First published in
the United States of America in 1976 by St. Martin's Press Inc.
This edition is reprinted by arrangement with Edward Arnold Ltd.

Canadian Cataloguing in Publication Data

Main entry under title:

The birth of popular heresy

(Medieval Academy reprints for teaching ; 33)
Includes bibliographical references and index.
ISBN 0-8020-7659-9

1. Heresies, Christian – History – Middle Ages,
600–1500 – Sources.   I. Moore, R.I. (Robert Ian),
1941–   .   II. Medieval Academy of America.
III. Series.

BT1319.B57 1995   273'.6   C95-930644-7

Contents

III A Period of Transition

IV The Triumph of Catharism

Preface

HERESY means choice, and choice implies thought. When Edward Miller invited me to contribute a volume to this series I soon discovered that my notion that I had chosen a neglected topic was a reflection (as such notions so often are) less of the state of scholarly activity than of my own ignorance, and the years that have passed since then have seen a notable improvement in the accessibility of the fruits of that activity to a wider readership. It still seems to me, nevertheless, that the men and causes that have turned out to engage my sympathy and affections with unexpected tenacity ought to occupy a larger place in the view of the early Middle Ages which we teach than they generally do. I hope that I shall have enabled them to speak for themselves: some of them asked for little more.

During the book's preparation Edward Miller's advice, made a daily chore by proximity, was a constant and cheerful inspiration, and Edmund King, James Roy and David Turley must stand as representatives for the host of friends whose patience I abused.

Most of the translations here are original, but I must thank Mrs Marjorie Chibnall and the Oxford University Press for allowing me to use two extracts from her edition of the *Historia Pontificalis*. I would also like to thank Fr Bruno Scott James and Messrs Burns and Oates for permission to reproduce Letter 241 from *The Letters of St Bernard of Clairvaux*. The typing of the manuscript has been paid for by the Research Fund of the University of Sheffield. The dedication acknowledges at last my oldest and greatest debt, and the whole book is a tribute to the tolerance, the patience and the encouragement of my wife.

R. I. MOORE
Sheffield, August 1974

Abbreviations

The following abbreviations are used throughout:

AFP	*Archivum Fratrum Praedicatorum*
Bouquet	*Receuil des historiens des Gaules et de la France*
MGH Epist	*Monumenta Germaniae Historica, Epistolae*
MGH SS	*Monumenta Germaniae Historica, Scriptores*
MGH Script	*Monumenta Germaniae Historica, Scriptores in usum scholarum*
Mansi	J. D. Mansi, *Sacrorum conciliorum nova et amplissima collectio*
PL	Migne, *Patrologia Latina*
RHE	*Revue d'histoire écclésiastique*
RS	Rolls Series

The full titles of other journals and works cited in abbreviated form are given under authors in the bibliography. Scriptural quotations are given in the Douai translation; I have not thought it necessary to identify them or to note where I have expanded the quotation for the sake of clarity.

Bold numerals in the text indicate reference to document numbers.

To my parents

Introduction

THE men and women whose beliefs and activities are recorded in these documents have achieved a precarious immortality. In their own time their doings were recorded only by their enemies, who had over most of them the advantage of literacy, and over all of them the even greater advantage of the support of both ecclesiastical and secular authority. Their enemies have also had the greater part of their posthumous reputation at their command, for the tradition of medieval historical writing has been largely a Catholic one, Roman or not, and where Catholicism has faltered French nationalism, the inspiration of some fine medievalists, has helped to keep at least the Albigensians firmly in the category of those whose failure history does not lament: it is not coincidental that in some circles today a revival of interest in Catharism has accompanied a renewed literary and cultural Languedocian nationalism. On the other hand the apparent incoherence and disreputability of the earlier heretics and the dualism of the later ones has prevented them, perhaps mercifully, from being hailed as important precursors of Protestantism. Protestant and anticlerical historians, of whom the greatest was Henry Charles Lea, have therefore regarded them not as spiritual ancestors to be examined or praised in their own right, but as the immediate inspiration and almost the fortuitous victims of an institution which has commanded so much of their attention, the medieval inquisition. It is only in this century that interest in popular movements of every kind, which has been one of the richest parts of the legacy of Marx and Weber, has directed the attention of social historians to early medieval heresy. More recently still, doubtless for reasons related to current preoccupations with ecumenism, with the place of the laity in the Churches and with the nature of ecclesiastical authority, ecclesiastical historians have begun to treat popular religious movements both seriously and sympathetically, and they have begun to find their way into the textbooks.

The heresies of the eleventh and twelfth centuries fall into two traditions. Their relationship to each other and the sequence and chronology of their respective development are matters of controversy, but their essential qualities are fairly clear. On the one hand are those whose champions, however educated and however motivated, maintained that the Church in their time was not functioning as its founder had meant it to function. They were Christians of a kind familiar at most times since the Reformation who, though they differed widely among themselves, had in common not only a dissatisfaction with the state of the Church, which they shared with most of its greatest leaders, but also a willingness to reject its traditional teachings and customs at the prompting of their personal inspiration. As William the Monk said to Henry of Lausanne, they 'would not bow their presumptuous necks to the yoke of human obedience'. (*See* p. 46.) On the other hand were the Cathars. They called themselves Christians, based their teaching on the parts of the Bible that they recognized, notably the Gospels and the Acts, clothed much of their doctrine in Christian garb, and increasingly as time went on, some historians now argue, drew closer to Christianity in their attitudes and assumptions. But they differed from Christians at a fundamental point: they believed not in one God but in two. The various theologies which they constructed and the differences to which they were led are set out below, most clearly by Rainier Sacchoni (**39**). All their life and teaching was derived from one premise of overwhelming importance, that creation was a dual process: there was a kingdom of good which was immaterial, and a kingdom of evil—the material world—into which their souls had fallen or been led captive, and to which belonged their bodies, the prisons of the evil god. In every material body a soul was immured, and salvation consisted of escape from the flesh. The procreation of the flesh, therefore, and the consumption of its products, meat, milk, eggs, were the perpetuation of the kingdom of evil, to be avoided by those who aspired to good.

Dualism is a very ancient religious tradition, and the dualist mistrust of the flesh and of matter in all its forms is prominent both in Judaism and in Christianity. During the third and fourth centuries AD, as elaborated by the greatest of its exponents, Mani (d. 276) dualism presented perhaps the most potent of all the challenges to the Christianity which was struggling to become the established religion of the Roman world. Augustine of Hippo, for the Middle Ages the most influential formulator of Christian thought, was a Manichee in his youth, and from his anti-Manichean writings the medieval polemicists drew not only their theological analysis of Catharism but also what they believed to be its history (see especially Eckbert of Schonau, p. 89–94). The religion of Mani himself had spread to the borders of China by the eighth century, and still survived there in the twelfth, and in Europe and Asia Minor ideas like his were adopted by the Messalians, the Paulicians, the Bogomils and the Cathars. Whether there was any continuity between these manifestations, or of what kind, are matters of scholarly contention for while some maintain that there was an unbroken tradition of dualism others contest the descent at every point. The debate will continue, because it proceeds not only from the extreme paucity of evidence, but also from profound differences among historians as to how ideas and religious attitudes are generated and transmitted, the resolution of which does not depend upon historical evidence alone.

2

If it is clear that these two heretical traditions were quite distinct, it may be asked how useful it is to treat them as essentially in the same category and as isolated from other religious movements of the age. Certainly their followers regularly disagreed among themselves even to the extent of attracting the attention of authority to them (see Eversin of Steinfeld, **22**) and the Waldensians, who seem to have begun as a group of orthodox laymen dedicated to defending the faith against Catharism, continued to pursue a bitter hostility towards the Cathars long after they had themselves been driven out of the Church. Conversely, there are similarities to be observed between some of the heretical movements and other religious groups of greater respectability. In the twelfth century the definition of heresy was straightforward. A heretical teaching was one which conflicted with that laid down by the Church, and a heretic was someone who not only fell into error, but on being shown his heresy persisted in it. As Robert Grossesteste put it, and his definition was valid for the century before his own, 'a heresy is an opinion chosen by human perception, contrary to holy scripture, publicly avowed and obstinately. defended.' By this measure it is clear that while Henry of Lausanne was a heretic the men of Arras who signed a declaration of faith and were sent on their way in 1025 (**3**) were not: like Peter Abailard, though doubtless for very different reasons, they were willing in the end to acknowledge the authority of the Church. For modern historians, concerned with wider issues than the accuracy of theological statements, the definition may be acceptable but it is not a sufficient delineation of their field of inquiry. It draws far too rigid a line, for instance, between the people described in these documents and the founder of the great monastic order of Fontevrault, Robert of Arbrissel who was nominated by Urban II to preach the first crusade in the Loire valley; described by William of Malmesbury as 'one of the most famous and eloquent preachers of these times', he was indisputably one of the minor heroes of the Church of his day. He fell into no doctrinal error, but his preaching and behaviour are described in terms strikingly similar to those used of Henry by the Le Mans chronicler (p. 34). His official biographer, Baudri of Bourgeuil, said that he 'travelled through the regions and provinces, at first with only a few followers, to sow the seed of the word of God in the streets and at the crossroads . . . joined by many of both sexes, daring to turn away nobody who aspired to God.' A more critical observer, but a respected churchman who knew Robert well, Marbod of Rennes, saw him a little differently, as a bizarre figure 'marching barefoot through the crowds, having cast off the habit of a regular, his flesh covered by a hairshirt, wearing a thin and torn cloak, barelegged, beard tangled, offering a new spectacle to the onlookers since only a club was missing from the outfit of a lunatic,' while his followers 'rushed through the district like a herd, wearing filthy clothes, famous for the thickness of their beards and, it is said, wearing shoes in the countryside but going barefoot in the towns.' Robert's appeal was to the poor: wherever he went he

3

was followed by a motley crowd of thieves, beggars and prostitutes, whom Baudri describes, in a phrase often used by heretics of themselves, as '*pauperes Christi*'; like Henry, though less explicitly, he was suspected of sexual immorality, and like Henry he attacked the vices of the clergy. 'In the sermons that you preach to common crowds,' said Marbod, 'you are not content to reproach the vices of those present, which is proper, but enumerate and calumniate the offences of absent churchmen, not only clerks but even men of high rank, which is improper . . . this is not to preach but to undermine [and will] cheapen the Church in the eyes of the common people.' It is not to be left out of account that like Gregory VII, St Bernard and St Francis, Robert was angered by the very things to which heretics themselves objected: he was no heretic, but he appealed to the same emotions and aspirations of the same people as many of those who were.

Medieval narrative sources are never easy to use. Though they often seem simple and straightforward they are the products of a world of ideas which no modern mind can attempt to inhabit without a struggle. It is pertinent to recall, for instance, that the word 'realist' in the twelfth century bore a meaning directly opposite to that which is usually attached to it today: a realist believed that for every idea there was a corresponding reality. Thus St Anselm could prove the existence of God by arguing that, since he could only be defined as 'that than which no greater can be conceived,' he must exist because if he did not a greater being could be conceived with all the same attributes plus that of existence. To us this only proves that it would be nonsense to believe in a God without also believing in his existence, but to Anselm and most of his contemporaries the 'existence' of the idea 'proved' that of the reality. It was with this real world that historical writing was concerned. 'All these chroniclers,' as John of Salisbury put it, 'have had a single purpose: to relate noteworthy matters, so that the invisible things of God may be clearly seen by the things that are done, and men may by examples of reward or punishment be made more zealous in the fear of God and the pursuit of justice.' Medieval chroniclers, of course, did not succeed in living up to their principles with any more success than modern historians do, and did not always resist the temptation to report the fascinating, if by these standards trivial, happenings of the mundane world of being. Nevertheless for them the line between what did happen and what should have happened, between the fact and what it symbolized was blurred, and the modern reader must bear in mind the possibility that he is presented with a description not of what happened, but of the meaning of what happened. He must be willing to consider whether Tanchelm or Henry of Lausanne really seduced their female followers, or were the kind of men whose character seemed to be truthfully described by the assertion, whether the process of seducing souls was not more vividly represented by the parallel, but after all less heinous process of seducing bodies.

The regular allegations that heretics flouted Catholic sexual morality will serve to illustrate another assumption on which these narratives were written which may not be immediately obvious. It was taken for granted in the early Middle Ages that the imbalance of the humours which caused bodily illness might also manifest itself in moral forms, and therefore that disease and sin were directly related to each other, and could be classified accordingly. The Carolingian writer Rhabanus Maurus, who expounded this theory in his *De Universo*, said, 'Leprosy is the false teaching of heretics, and lepers are heretics blaspheming against Jesus Christ.' The comparison between heresy and leprosy which is so regularly made in these documents, therefore, is not a casual metaphor, but the expression of the conviction that the two conditions were the moral and the physiological expressions of the same disorder. That conviction was strengthened by numerous similarities between them. Leprosy (a portmanteau label which was applied to any disease that showed unpleasantly on the skin, through boils, ulcers, rashes and desiccation) was increasing rapidly at this time, though it is not true that it was brought to Europe for the first time by the crusaders. Like heresy, it appeared suddenly and unpredictably, spread rapidly, was very rarely cured, was passed from parents to children, and showed itself most unpleasantly and alarmingly among the poor who, finding themselves excluded from the communities to which they had belonged, settled in the squalid and isolated encampments which became leper villages, or wandered through the countryside in bands causing terror by their appalling appearance and desperate conduct. The persistent, though mistaken, belief that leprosy is contagious gained ground rapidly in the later part of the twelfth century, and it was also believed that lepers were exceptionally lascivious, and that the disease was sexually transmitted. Since syphilis was among the disorders known as *lepra* this latter belief had, of course, some foundation in fact. Hence the presumption that heretics behaved immorally and might make converts by seduction was entirely consistent with the prevailing analysis of the nature of heresy itself.

Since we still live in a world which does not hesitate to attribute the most spectacularly orgiastic behaviour to almost any group which deliberately sets itself in opposition to accepted values, the invocation of these considerations in order to explain the scandal-mongering of the chroniclers may seem unnecessary. Nevertheless this serves to illustrate three qualities of medieval historical writing which its lively and circumstantial nature makes it easy to forget. The chroniclers had little conviction of historical change, a deep respect for the *auctoritates* upon whom they would rely in preference to their own knowledge and perceptions, and the assurance of the Church that heresy was always to be regarded as a reassertion of ancient error long since condemned. It followed that they were often ready to supplement their own knowledge of the particular episode which they reported with information and analysis derived from other reports of other heretics, in their own or ancient times. Since they wrote, or tried to write, from a divine and timeless, rather than a human and temporal perspective they did not always think it necessary to make it clear when they were doing so. Truth is unchanging, and a Manichee is always a Manichee. And since, like those of all historians, their thought and writing was in fact the product of a particular time and its mental climate, it was often affected by assumptions about the operation of the human and natural worlds which have vanished into obscurity. The common coinage of historical criticism, which talks of the 'honesty' and the 'prejudices' of its sources, is scarcely adequate for a full understanding of them.

The inconsistency between the assumption that heretics reasserted ancient errors and the regular condemnation of their opinions as 'novelties' is only apparent. A novelty was not, in the modern sense, something that had never happened before, but something which had superfluously been added to the teaching of the Church and the orthodox interpretation of the scriptures. Nevertheless, heresy was a new phenomenon in the emergent civilization of western Europe in the central Middle Ages, and the reaction of contemporaries who found it not only shocking but unnatural is still widely expressed. It had been almost, though not quite entirely unknown since the conversion of the Lombards from Arianism in the later part of the seventh century, and that lacuna no doubt encouraged the acceptance as fact of the vision which orthodox writers from St Augustine onwards nourished, and which many cherish today, of a Christendom in which one clear truth is proclaimed by the Church and recognized by all men of good will. Just as contemporaries were led by such a premise to attribute the appearance of heterodoxy in their time to alien influence and to the revival of the ancient errors of Mani and Arius, modern writers have devoted much attention to the 'origins' of medieval heresy. Yet in the perspective of two thousand years heresy—which is derived from the αἱρεσις (choice), and which from some points of view is only another name for diversity of opinion—is a normal element of western Christian civilization. Christianity is a comprehensive and complex creed which depends on the exposition and interpretation of a great body of enormously various writings and of a long and tangled tradition. Historically its great characteristic has been a capacity for adaptation to the needs of the most diverse groups and attitudes, as a glance at South Africa or Ireland today will make clear. The ancient, the medieval and the modern Churches have all been habitually divided up to and beyond the point of schism by disputes over doctrine which have covered the whole range of intellectual sophistication from the crudest to the most dazzling, and which have given stimulus to, and received it from, every conceivable kind of social division, whether between imperialist and particularist, lord and peasant, countryman and townsman, or rich and poor. The period which we call the Dark Ages was wholly exceptional in the degree to which orthodoxy went unchallenged from within. Even then Catholic harmony did not reign over an undivided Europe. The challenge of those centuries was the challenge of the old religions, which were a long time a-dying, and whose threat was carried back into the heart of Christian Europe by the new barbarian invasions of the ninth and tenth centuries. Conversely as Christianity did become established, in Northumbria in the seventh century, in Germany in the eighth or at a more sophisticated level in the Carolingian Empire in the ninth, diversities of belief and practice rapidly began to become matters of controversy which emphasizes the point that, though no regular or coherent tradition of heresy either learned or popular emerged at that time, its potentiality was inherent in the religion itself.

Christianity preserved and enriched the tradition of classical learning upon which European civilization is based, and did so because it needed that tradition with its ability to create, to analyse and to expound ideas to preserve the vitality of its own religious function. If Christianity was to be a religion for all classes, as Gregory VII wanted it to be, it could not hope to reserve to some of them the qualities of adaptability and controversy upon which it was founded. In the first instance at least, therefore, the renascence of popular heresy ought to be regarded, as that of intellectual heresy long has been, as part of the emergence of European civilization which we call, more generally, the renaissance of the twelfth century. Heresy and the disposition towards it are an integral part of the European inheritance, not an optional extra.

To say this is not to dispense with the need for explanations, but this collection is not a substitute for the history whose absence more than one reviewer has lamented in recent years. Nor is it intended, in the tradition of the most famous of all collections of medieval sources, Stubbs's 'Charters', to illustrate or justify my own views. Its goal is to provide as nearly as possible a complete collection of the main sources for each of the four themes presented: the first signs of popular dissent in the eleventh century, the emergence of a relatively coherent evangelical anticlericalism in the twelfth, the beginning of the infiltration of western heterodoxy by eastern dualism in the 1140s, 50s, and 60s, and the establishment and early organization of the Cathar Churches in southern France and northern Italy which finally precipitated the Albigensian crusade and prepared the way for the inquisition. I have tried to present each group of documents in such a way as to enable, even to compel, my readers to form their own conclusions without being dominated by mine, and have therefore preferred relatively complete documentation of some incidents to representation of all. Much is omitted—the almost complete exclusion of the Waldensians will be particularly noticed—but in consequence it has been possible to include everything of any significance about Henry of Lausanne, and the complete treatises of Rainier Sacchoni and Anselm of Alessandria. Much that I have left out may be found in *Heresies of the High Middle Ages* by Walter L. Wakefield and Austin P. Evans, a much more ambitious collection which appeared after my own selection and translations were complete, but with whose versions of many of the texts I have been grateful to be able to compare my own.

I Eleventh-Century Origins

EXCEPT for the isolated cases of the schoolmaster Vilgard of Ravenna and the peasant Liutard of Vertus, near Châlons-sur-Marne, both described by Ralph Glaber (trans. Wakefield and Evans, pp. 72–3), the passages which follow note all the known incidents of popular heresy in the eleventh-century West, as well as that of Ramihrdus of Cambrai, who, although he was not a heretic, is usually thought to have had much in common with those who were. The tendencies which they show towards the rejection of the authority of the Church and some of its sacraments, and towards personal austerity, used to be thought, for instance, by Lea and Runciman, to show that the Bogomils, who had become established in the Balkans during the tenth century, were now carrying their heresy into western Europe. In 1944 R. Morghen argued that there is no evidence of such a connection, and that these incidents, and therefore the origins of medieval heresy, should be regarded as the consequences of social change, and of the growing impetus towards religious reform, especially as it was fostered by the expanding monastic movement within the West itself. His view, which is conveniently restated in *Hérésies et sociétés* pp. 121–34, and in *Revue Historique* (1966), was powerfully criticized, notably by A. Dondaine in *Rivista di storia della chiesa in Italia*, (1952), but has increasingly gained acceptance: the debate is examined more fully by R. I. Moore in *History* (1970).

This discussion in turn has revealed disagreement about the relationship of eleventh-century heretical movements in the West not only with those of other places, but also with those of other times. Against the general opinion that the beginning of the tradition of popular heresy is here, Russell maintains that enough evidence of similar sentiments and impulses can be detected in earlier periods to justify the view that 'medieval dissidence began in the eighth, not the eleventh century' (*Dissent and Reform*, p. 247), while I have argued that the eleventh-century incidents are so diverse in place, in time and in kind that the continuous history of popular heresy cannot really be said to begin until after the Gregorian reform, with the movements that are described in Chapter II of this book. But this question, like that of the connection of these incidents with Bogomilism, should be regarded as only one aspect of the general problem of the relationship of heresies and heretical movements not only with each other but also with social, religious and intellectual development in general, which is the theme of *Hérésies et sociétés*, and of C. N. L. Brooke's 'Heresy and Religious Sentiment: 1000–1250'. G. Cracco, 'Riforma ed eresia in momenti della cultura Europea tra X e XI secolo', regards the heresies as one manifestation of a movement towards deliberate reliance on personal inspiration, or as Ratherius of Verona put it, the *Deus interior*, as opposed to the institutional and formal tradition of Carolingian Christianity, which he finds widely expressed in the religious thought of the tenth and eleventh centuries. Like C. Violante, 'La pauvreté dans les hérésies du XIe siècle en occident', he helps to place the heretics more precisely in the context of the development of the apostolic ideal which contributed so greatly to the movements of monastic and ecclesiastical reform, and is classically described by M. D. Chenu, 'Moines, clercs et laics au carrefour de la vie évangélique' (English translation in *Nature, Man and Society*). Much less is known about the social background of these incidents, but Janet L. Nelson, 'Society, theodicy and the origins of heresy', poses some challenging questions. The Patarenes of Milan, who disrupted the city in the cause of religious reform especially between 1056 and 1075 were not heretics, but have much in common with some of them: their history is outlined by J. P. Whitney, *Hildebrandine Essays*, pp. 143–57, and there is an important recent discussion by H. E. J. Cowdrey of 'The Papacy, the Patarenes and the Church of Milan', in *Transactions of the Royal Historical Society* (1968).

1 Adhémar of Chabannes: early heresies in the Languedoc

The chronicle of Adhémar of Chabannes, written in Angoulême in the 1020s, is one of our most reliable sources for events in southwestern France in the early eleventh century. These paragraphs are from Book III, *MGH SS* IV, 138, 143, 148.

c. 1018 Manicheans appeared in Aquitaine, leading the people astray. They denied baptism, the cross, and all sound doctrine. They did not eat meat, as though they were monks, and pretended to be celibate, but among themselves they enjoyed every indulgence. They were messengers of Antichrist, and caused many to wander from the faith.

c. 1022 At this time ten canons of Orléans, who had seemed to be more religious than the others, were proved to be Manicheans. When they refused to return to the faith King Robert ordered them first to be deprived of priestly orders, then expelled from the Church and finally burned by fire. They had been led astray by a peasant who claimed that he could give them great strength and who carried about with him dust from dead children which quickly made anyone who came into contact with it into a Manichee. They worshipped the devil who appeared to them on one occasion in the guise of an Ethiopian, and on another as an angel of light, and brought down money for them every day. In obedience to him they secretly rejected Christ, and in private committed sins and crimes which it would be sinful even to mention, while in public they pretended to be true Christians.

Some Manicheans, were discovered and destroyed at Toulouse, and messengers of Antichrist appeared in various parts of the West, concealing themselves in hideouts and corrupting men and women whenever they could.

A canon of Orléans, a chantor named Theodatus, had died in this heresy, according to trustworthy witnesses, three years before, though he had seemed to be religious. After this was proved his body was taken from the cemetery by order of Bishop Odalric, and thrown into waste ground. The ten who were burned along with Lisois,—a man whom the king had once loved for his apparent holiness—did not fear the fire. They promised to emerge unharmed from the flames, and laughed as they were bound in the centre of the pyre, but almost at once they were reduced to ashes so completely that no trace of their bones could be found.

c. 1020   At this time Duke William summoned a council of bishops and abbots to Charroux, to wipe out the heresies which the Manicheans had been spreading among the people. All the princes of Aquitaine were present, and he ordered them to keep the peace and respect the Catholic Church.

2 The Synod of Orléans, 1022

A full list of the fragmentary and contradictory sources for this episode, the first case of burning for heresy in the medieval West, is given by J. B. Russell, *Dissent and Reform*, pp. 276–7, n. 24. Among them this account, by Paul of St Père de Chartres, the house in which Aréfast later became a monk, is probably the least inaccurate: it is taken from his *Gesta Synodi Aurelianensis*, Bouquet, X, 536–9. There are various estimates of the number burned: compare Adhémar of Chabannes above, with John of Fleury, who says that it was 'fourteen of the higher clergy and of the more respectable laity of the city', (Bouquet, X, 498).

Too many of those who have discussed the significance of the orgies which Stephen and Lisois are here alleged to have conducted, including the present writer, have overlooked the very close similarity between this passage and stories retailed about the early Christians. Gibbon, in the sixteenth chapter of the *Decline and Fall*, tells one almost identical from Justin Martyr; it is repeated by Guibert of Nogent about the heretics whom he examined at Soissons c. 1114 (p. 28), and was commonplace in the thirteenth century.

I think it worthwhile to record for posterity how Aréfast, with the help of God, and his own admirable native cunning, detected a wicked heresy which was active in the city of Orléans and was spreading its vicious and deadly poison through the provinces of Gaul, and had it thoroughly crushed. Aréfast was a relation of the counts of Normandy, polished in speech, cautious in counsel and sound in morals, and therefore highly regarded as an emissary both to the king of France and to other nobles. In his household he had a clerk named Heribert who went to study in the city of Orléans. Though his visit should have been adequately occupied in discovering true authors, he fell blindly into the pit of heresy. In the city there lived two clerks, Stephen and Lisois, who were widely famed for their wisdom, outstanding in holiness and generous with alms. Heribert sought them out and in a short time had become their docile disciple: intoxicated by them with a deadly draught of evil disguised by the sweetness of the holy scriptures, he was demented, ensnared by a diabolical heresy, and believed that he was skilled in divinity and had ascended the citadel of wisdom.

When he returned home, he was anxious to convert his lord, whom he loved dearly, to the path of error. He approached him gradually, with subtle phrases and said that Orléans shone more brightly than other cities with the light of wisdom and the torch of holiness. His words revealed to Aréfast that he had strayed from the path of righteousness. He immediately informed Count Richard and asked him to write to King Robert to tell him of the disease that was lurking in his kingdom before it should spread any further, and to ask the king not to deny Aréfast himself whatever help he needed to root it out. Thunderstruck by this news, the king instructed Aréfast to go to Orléans at once with his clerk, and promised him every assistance.

When he set out at the royal command, Aréfast went first to Chartres, to consult the venerable Bishop Fulbert, but as it chanced he was away on a mission to Rome. He unfolded the plan of his journey to a wise clerk named Everard, sacristan of the church of Chartres and asked for his advice on the project—where he should draw the line of battle, and with what weapons he should provide himself against such a range of devilish and deceitful arts. Everard wisely advised him to seek the help of the Almighty every morning, to go to church, devote himself to prayer and fortify himself with the holy communion of the body and blood of Christ. Thus protected by the sign of the cross, he should proceed to listen to the wickedness of the heretics, contradicting nothing that he should hear them say, and pretending that he wished to become their disciple, while he quietly stored everything away in his heart.

Aréfast followed this advice, and when he reached Orléans, took communion every day and, fortified by prayer, went to the house of the heretics as though he were a simple disciple coming to hear their teaching. At first they taught him by citing texts from the holy scriptures, and by employing certain figures of speech. When they saw that he listened carefully, as a perfect pupil should, they put to him, among other metaphors, the image of a tree in a wood: 'We regard you,' they said, 'as a tree in a wood, which is transplanted to a garden, and watered regularly, until it takes root in the earth. Then it is stripped of thorns and other excess matter, and pruned down to the ground with a hoe, so that a better branch can be inserted into it, which will later bear sweet fruit. In the same way you will be carried out of this evil world into our holy company. You will soak in the waters of wisdom until you have taken shape, and armed with the sword of the Lord, are able to avoid the thorns of vice. Foolish teachings will be shut out from your heart and you will be able with a pure mind, to receive our teaching, which is handed down from the Holy Spirit.'

He received everything they told him with exclamations of thanks to God, until they thought that they had converted him to their heresy. Then, feeling secure, they revealed the depths of their wickedness to him, disguised in the words of the holy scriptures. They said, 'Christ was not born of the Virgin Mary, he did not suffer for men, he was not really buried in the sepulchre and did not rise from the dead,' to which they added, 'there is no cleansing of sin in baptism, nor in the sacrament of the body and blood of Christ administered by a priest. Nothing is to be gained from praying to the holy martyrs and confessors.'

When these doomed and wretched men had spewed these and other abominable sentiments from their festering bellies Aréfast replied, 'If these things which you have spoken of offer no chance of salvation to men, as they hope, I must press you urgently to tell me what does offer hope. Otherwise my soul, which you have brought to doubt, will soon fall into the ruin of despair.'

'There is no doubt, brother,' they answered, 'that until now you have lain with the ignorant in the Charybdis of false belief. Now you have been raised to the summit of all truth. With unimpeded mind you may begin to open your eyes to the light of the true faith. We will open the door of salvation to you. Through the laying of our hands upon you, you will be cleansed of every spot of sin. You will be replenished with the gift of the Holy Spirit, which will teach you unreservedly the underlying meaning of the scriptures, and true righteousness. When you have fed on the heavenly food and have achieved inner satisfaction you will often see angelic visions with us, and sustained by that solace you will be able to go where you will without let or hindrance, whenever you want to. You will want for nothing, for God, in whom are all the treasures of wealth and wisdom, will never fail to be your companion in all things.'

Meanwhile the king and Queen Constance had come to Orléans, as Aréfast had asked, with a number of bishops, and on the following day, at his suggestion, the whole wicked gang was arrested by royal officials at the house where they met, and brought before the king and queen and an assembly of clerks and bishops at the church of Ste Croix.

Before we come to the disputation, I must tell those who have not heard how these people confected the meal which they called heavenly. They met on certain nights in the house which I have mentioned, each holding a light in his hand, and called a roll of the names of demons, like a litany, until suddenly they saw the devil appear among them in the guise of some wild beast. Then, as soon as they saw that sight, the lights were put out and each of them grabbed whatever woman came to hand, and seized her to be put to ill use. Without regard to sin, whether it were a mother, or a sister, or a nun, they regarded that intercourse as a holy and religious work. On the eighth day they lit a great fire among them, and the child who was born of this foul union was put to the test of the flames after the manner of the ancient pagans, and burned. The ashes were collected and kept with as much reverence as the Christian religion accords to the body of Christ, to be given as a last sacrament to the sick when they are about to depart this life. There was such power of diabolic evil in this ash that anyone who had succumbed to the heresy and tasted only a small quantity of it was afterwards scarcely ever able to direct his mind away from heresy and back to the truth. It is enough to speak of this only briefly, so that Christians should beware of this nefarious device, and will be sure not to imitate it. But I have digressed; I will return to the burden of my story, and if the barbarity of these infidels is treated hastily it is because a fuller discussion of it might disgust a sensitive reader.

When they were brought before the king and the assembly of bishops Aréfast addressed the king first:

'My lord, I am a knight of your faithful vassal Richard, count of Normandy, and do not deserve to be held bound and chained before you.'

'Tell us at once,' the king replied, 'how you come to be here, so that we may know whether you should be kept in chains as a criminal or released as an innocent man.'

'I heard of the learning and piety of those who stand before you with me in chains,' answered Aréfast, 'and came to this city in the hope of profiting from the example of their good works and teaching. That is why I left my own country and came here. Let the bishops who sit with you decide and judge whether I committed any crime in that.'

To this the bishops replied, 'If you tell us the nature of the wisdom and piety which you have learnt from these men, we will have no difficulty in reaching a conclusion.'

'Your majesty,' said Aréfast, 'order them to repeat before you what they taught me. When you have heard it you may decide whether they are worthy of praise or should be condemned to death.'

When the king and the bishops ordered the heretics to explain the principles of their faith these enemies of all truth spoke for one another, but would not open a path into the foulness of their heresy. Just as the more a snake shrinks in the hand, the more easily it can escape, so the harder they were pressed the more elusively they seemed to evade the truth. Then Aréfast, seeing that they were playing for time, and trying to cloud over their views with a shield of words, turned to them and said:

'I thought that you were teachers of truth, not of falsehood, so long as I saw that you taught me your doctrine, which, you claimed, brings salvation steadfastly, and promised that you would never deny it, even if it meant sustaining punishment, or enduring death itself. Now I see that your promises are forgotten. Through fear of death, you want to be dissociated from your doctrines, and you count it little to leave me, your former disciple, in danger of death. The royal command should be obeyed, and the authority of so many bishops respected, so that I may know whether any of the things which I have learnt from you are contrary to the Christian religion, and which of them, in their judgement, should be followed, and which rejected. You taught me that nothing in baptism merits forgiveness of sin; that Christ was not born of the Virgin, did not suffer for men, was not truly buried, and did not rise from the dead; that the bread and wine which seem to become a sacrament on the altar in the hands of priests through the operation of the Holy Spirit cannot be turned into the body and blood of Christ.'

When Aréfast had finished speaking, Bishop Guarin of Beauvais questioned Stephen and Lisois, who seemed to be leaders in the heresy, whether they held and believed these things as Aréfast had reported them. They had prepared themselves a dwelling with the devil in hell, and replied that he had remembered accurately, and they did hold and believe those things. The bishop said that he believed that Christ was born of the Virgin—which is possible—and that he suffered in human form for us, and then defeated death and rose again on the third day, and in his Godhead, to teach us that we too might be reformed and rise again.

They replied with the tongues of snakes, 'We were not there, so we cannot believe that these things are true.'

'Do you believe that you yourselves had human parents, or not?' asked the bishop. When they replied that they did he continued, 'If you believe that you were procreated by your parents when you did not exist before, why do you refuse to believe that God was born of God without a mother before time, and born of the Virgin by the shadow of the Holy Spirit within the limits of time?'

'What nature denies is always out of harmony with creation.'

'Before anything was done by nature, do you not believe that God the Father through the Son made everything from nothing?'

To this these aliens from the faith replied, 'You may tell all this to those who are learned in earthly things, who believe the fabrications which men have written on the skins of animals. We believe in the law written within us by the Holy Spirit, and hold everything else, except what we have learnt from God, the maker of all things, empty, unnecessary, and remote from divinity. Therefore bring an end to your speeches and do with us what you will. Now we see our king reigning in heaven. He will raise us to his right hand in triumph and give us eternal joy.'

From the first until the ninth hour of that day everyone put forward various arguments to make them renounce their errors, and they resisted with the obstinacy of iron. Then they were all commanded to put on the holy vestments of their order, and immediately stripped of them again with full ceremony by the bishops. At the king's command, Queen Constance stood before the doors of the Church, to prevent the common people from killing them inside the Church, and they were expelled from the bosom of the Church. As they were being driven out, the queen struck out the eye of Stephen, who had once been her confessor, with the staff which she carried in her hand. They were taken outside the walls of the city, a large fire was lit in a certain cottage, and they were all burned, with the evil dust of which I have spoken above, except for one clerk and a nun, who had repented by the will of God.

3 The Synod of Arras, 1025

The most difficult problem raised by the *Acta Synodi Atrebatensis* (*PL* 142, col. 1271–1312) is that of the identity of Bishop R., to whom the prefatory letter is addressed. Of the two possible candidates, Roger I of Châlons (1018–42) is preferred by J. M. Noiroux, 'Les deux premiers documents concernants l'hérésie aux Pays-Bas', *RHE* XLIX (1954), 842–55, and Reginard of Liège (1025–36) by J. B. Russell, 'A propos du synode d'Arras', *RHE* LVII (1962), 66–87.

The *Acta* contains, in addition to the prefatory letter, almost 20,000 words, of which by far the greater part is concerned neither with the proceedings of the synod nor with any account of the actions or beliefs of the accused, but with the criticisms expressed by Bishop Gerard of a number of beliefs which this report does not say that the heretics professed: the discrepancies are examined and possible reasons discussed by Russell, *Dissent and Reform*, pp. 21–7. The likeliest explanation is that this is not an unadorned account of an episode which Gerard chose to use as the occasion of a general polemic. For this reason, the length and tediousness of his remarks apart, I have excluded his oration, translating only the beginning and end of the account, which directly concern the heretics (col. 1269–72, 1311–12).

Even when I recall your outstanding shrewdness and insight it does not greatly surprise me that wicked men, bewitched by the spirit of error, conspired to propagate the madness of evil doctrine, but I am astonished that when you examined them they were able to dissimulate effectively enough to deceive you. For, as you know, I have reported to your holiness that such people were living in your dioceses, and supported it with sound evidence. When they fabricated the appearance of religion because they were afraid of being punished you let them go, uncondemned and unpunished. It is obvious that this will make it very much easier for them to convert simple folk, for if they have been formally investigated, and no reason has been found to punish them, there seems to be no reason to hesitate to listen to them. Certainly the people whom they sent to our district as missionaries put up a strong resistance and dissimulated stubbornly when they were caught. They could not be made to confess by any manner of persuasion until some of those whom they had imbued with the evil of their heresy were taken, and partially explained their teaching to us. After this those who falsely claimed to follow the teaching of the apostles and the Gospels said that the ceremony of baptism and the sacrament of the body and blood of Christ were nothing, and should be avoided, unless taken for the sake of deception; that penance does not help us towards salvation; that married people cannot aspire to heaven, and other things which are set out in his pamphlet. I am sending it to you so that you will not listen to their bogus religion and artificial words.

The Synod

In the year of our Lord 1025, the eighth indiction, Gerard, bishop of Cambrai-Arras, happened to have spent Christmas and Epiphany at Cambrai, in the course of his itinerary, so he proceeded to his seat at Arras. While he was attending to his ecclesiastical business there he was told that some heretics from Italy had imported a new sect into the diocese, and were trying to pervert the precepts of the Gospels and the apostles. They claimed a certain righteousness by which alone, they insisted men could be purified: there was no other sacrament in the Church but this, through which they had been able to approach salvation. The bishop ordered them to be found and brought before him. When they heard that they were to be questioned they prepared to escape, but were discovered by the bishop's officers, and dragged into his presence. He was very busy hearing other cases, and inquired briefly about their faith. He got the impression that they avowed false doctrine, and ordered them to be kept in custody for three days, and that on the following day the monks and clerks should observe a fast, so that by divine grace they might be restored to a recognition of the Catholic faith.

On the third day, a Sunday, the bishop in full regalia, accompanied by his archdeacons bearing crosses and copies of the Gospels, processed to St Mary's church with a great crowd of clerks and of the populace to hold a synod. The whole of the appointed psalm, 'Let God arise and let his enemies be scattered', was sung. Then, when the bishop was seated in his court with the abbots, religious and archdeacons placed around him according to their ranks, the men were taken from their place of confinement and brought before him. After addressing a few words to the people about them, the bishop asked, 'what is your doctrine, your discipline and your way of life, and from whom have you learnt it?'

They replied that they were followers of an Italian called Gundolfo. They had learned from him the precepts of the Gospels and the apostles, and would accept no other scriptures but this, to which they would adhere in word and deed. Since it had come to the bishop's ears that they abhorred the ceremony of holy baptism, rejected the sacrament of the body and blood of Christ, denied that penance profited the sinner after confession, denied the authority of the Church, condemned legitimate matrimony, saw no virtue in holy confession and held that nobody after the time of the apostles and martyrs ought to be venerated, he began to question them on these points. 'How do you reconcile your belief in the precepts of the Gospels and apostles with preaching against them?' he asked. 'For the Gospel tells us that when Nicodemus, a ruler of the Jews, confessed that Jesus came from God because of the signs and miracles that he performed, the Lord immediately answered that nobody could gain the kingdom of Heaven by this confession alone, unless he were born again of water and the Holy Ghost. It follows therefore, from the words of Jesus himself, that you must either wholly accept the mystery of regeneration, or go against the words of the Gospel.'

To this they replied, 'Nobody who is prepared to examine with care the teaching and rule which we have learnt from our master will think that they contravene either the precepts of the Gospels or those of the apostles. This is its tenor: to abandon the world, to restrain the appetites of the flesh, to earn our food by the labour of our own hands, to do no injury to anyone, to extend charity to everyone of our own faith. If these rules are followed baptism is unnecessary; without them it will not lead to salvation. This is the height of righteousness, to which there is nothing that baptism can add when every rule of the Gospels and apostles is observed in this way. If anyone says that baptism is a sacrament we would deny it on three grounds—first, that the evil life of the minister cannot be a vehicle for the salvation of him who is baptized; second, that the vices which are renounced at the font may be resumed later in life; third, that the child who neither wills it nor concurs with it, knows nothing of faith and is ignorant of his need for salvation, does not beg for rebirth in any sense, and can make no confession of faith: clearly he has neither free will nor faith, and makes no confession of it.' . . .

[Gerard harangues the assembly at great length.]

The day was now wearing to a close, and the lord bishop said to those who had come to listen to the proceedings, 'There are other things, brothers, which I ought to say to strengthen you in your faith, but in case I oppress you with a great burden of words let that suffice. Keep your faith unstained, and remember the words of the apostle Paul, "In the last times some shall depart from the faith, giving heed to spirits of evil and doctrines of devils, speaking lies in hypocrisy and having their conscience seared; forbidding to marry, to abstain from meats which God hath created to be received with thanksgiving by the faithful." '

When the bishop had spoken, those who a little while before had thought themselves invincible by words, incapable of being swayed by any manner of argument, stood stupified by the weight of his discourse, and the evident power of God, as though they had never learned any better argument. Speechless, they could only reply that they believed that the sum of Christian salvation could consist in nothing but what the bishop had set out. To this the bishop answered, 'If you believe this, set aside the wickedness of your unbelief, and join us in condemning this heresy and its authors.' Then the bishop and all those present, abbots, archdeacons and clerks, with the support of the people, said: 'We condemn and anathematize this heresy and all who profess it, which today has been found conspiring against the Holy Catholic Church; which holds baptism and the washing away of the stain of original sin and actual sin to be profitless—claims that the punishment of sin cannot be ameliorated through penance; says that the Holy Church of God is nothing, and the holy altar and sacrament of the body and blood of the Lord no more than can be observed with bodily eyes, and rejects it; and condemns lawful matrimony. We confess according to the faith of the Gospels and the tradition of the apostles that there is no salvation except through the water of regeneration; as the Lord said, "Unless a man be born again of water and the Holy Ghost he cannot enter into the kingdom of God." We confess that the sins which men commit after baptism at the prompting of the devil and their own wills are not only mitigated by penance, but may be accorded divine grace, as we see from the purification of Mary Magdalene, the justification of Zachaeus, the restoration of Peter after his betrayal, and the reception of the brigand into paradise.

'We believe that Holy Church is the common mother of all the faithful, and that nobody may join her in heaven who has not belonged to her on earth. We confess that the sacrament of the body and blood of the Lord is our pledge of redemption, of which the Lord said, "Except you eat of my flesh and drink of my blood you shall not have life in you", and "my flesh is meat indeed and my blood is drink indeed." Of this body and blood, he also said, "Take ye and eat. This is my body", and "drink ye all of this; for this is my blood." We acknowledge that this is undoubtedly the same flesh that was born of the Virgin, suffered on the cross, rose from the tomb, was exalted in the heavens, and sits in the glory of his father's majesty. He who does not believe in this, the birth, the suffering and the burial of Christ, will not share with Christ the blessing of the resurrection. This mystery may be sanctified in no other way than as God ordained through Moses, on the holy altar. The Lord and his disciples and the apostle of the gentiles gave licence for marriage and ordained it to be observed by those to whom it is permitted. Anyone who does not endorse this Catholic rule can have no place among the faithful.'

The men who shortly before had adhered to heretical unbelief did not fully understand these words, which were spoken in Latin. Through an interpreter they heard the sentence of excommunication and the exposition of the profession of faith in the vernacular. They confessed with a solemn oath that they abjured what had been condemned, and believed what is believed by the faithful. To confirm this attestation of their faith each of them wrote a sign of the cross, like this †, so that at the Last Judgement the sign would present them for salvation if they had preserved their faith, or consign them to chaos if they had betrayed it. In this way, by the grace of God, all of them repented, and returned to their families with the blessing of the bishop.

4 The Heretics of Monforte, c. 1028

There is no convenient study of this episode, which is described by Landulf Senior, *Historia Mediolanensis* II, *MGH SS* VIII, 65–6, but the general background of popular religious conflict in northern Italy is well discussed by C. Violante, *Hérésies et sociétés* pp. 171–97, and by H. E. J. Cowdrey, 'The Papacy, the Patarenes and the Church of Milan'.

At this time Archbishop Aribert, travelling round Italy and visiting almost all the suffragan bishops of the diocese of Milan reached Turin with a large retinue of good clerks and brave soldiers. He stayed there for some time and, as befitted his position, delivered advice from the prophets and the apostles to the bishop, clergy, and people of the city. He heard that a new heresy had recently been established in the castle above the place called Monforte, and immediately ordered one of the heretics from the castle to be brought to him, so that he could have a trustworthy account of it. When the man came before him he was prepared to answer every question with alacrity, eager for death, happy to end his life with the most serious punishments. When Aribert saw how steadfast he was he began to ask him, methodically and carefully, about the life, morals and faith of the heretics. He called for silence, and Gerard, thus given leave, began to speak.

'I am grateful to Almighty God, Father, Son and Holy Ghost that you want to question me so carefully. He who has known you from the loins of Adam grant that you may live and die with him, and reign with him in glory through the ages. Whatever your motive in asking about the faith of myself and my brothers, I will answer. We value virginity above everything. We have wives, and while those who are virgins preserve their virginity, those who are already corrupt are given permission by our elder (*nostro majori*) to retain their chastity perpetually. We do not sleep with our wives, we love them as we would mothers and sisters. We never eat meat. We keep up continuous fasts and unceasing prayer; our *majores* pray in turn by day and by night, so that no hour lacks its prayer. We hold all our possessions in common with all men. None of our number ends his life except in torment, the better to avoid eternal torment. We believe in and confess the Father, Son and Holy Ghost. We believe that we are bound and loosed by those who have the power of binding and loosing. We accept the Old and New Testaments and the holy canons, and read them daily.'

Gerard expounded these and other views that seemed both serious and deplorable with great sophistication. Aribert realizing with each word he spoke how cunning and shrewd he was in his wickedness, directed him to clarify the opinions of himself and his friends, and in particular to make it clear exactly what they believed about the Father, Son and Holy Spirit.

To this Gerard replied cheerfully, 'I mean by the Father eternal God, who created all things and in whom all things come to rest. I mean by the Son, the soul of man beloved by God. I mean by the Holy Spirit the understanding of divine wisdom, by which all things are separately ruled.'

'What have you to say, my friend, of our Lord Jesus Christ, born of the Virgin Mary by the word of the Father?'

'Jesus Christ of whom you speak is a soul sensually born of the Virgin Mary; born that is to say, of the holy scriptures. The Holy Spirit is the spiritual understanding of the holy scriptures.'

'Why do you marry if it is not to have children? How are men to be born?'

'If all men married without corruption the human race would increase without coition, as the bees do.'

'Where do we find absolution from our sins? From the pope, or from a bishop, or from any priest?'

'We do not have the Roman pontiff, but another one, who daily visits our brothers, scattered across the world. When God gives him to us spiritually we are given complete absolution from our sins.'

'How do you end your lives in torment?'

'We rejoice to die through torment inflicted on us by evil men; if any of us is dying naturally his neighbour among us kills him in some way before he gives up the ghost.'

Silently the astounded Aribert listened carefully to all this, while the spectators shook their heads. Then he asked Gerard whether he believed in the Catholic faith held by the Roman Church, in baptism and in the Son of God born in flesh of the Virgin Mary, and that his true flesh and true blood are sanctified by the word of God through the Catholic priest, even if he is a sinner. Gerard replied, 'There is no pope but our pope, though his head is not tonsured, and he is not ordained.'

When it was thus clear what their faith was, the truth was apparent, Aribert sent a large body of soldiers to Monforte, and took all of them that he could find into custody. Among them the countess of the castle was taken, as a believer in this heresy. He took them to Milan and laboured to convert them to the Catholic faith, for he was greatly concerned that the people of Italy might become contaminated by their heresy. For, whatever part of the world these wretches had come from, they behaved as though they were good priests, and daily spread false teachings wrenched from the scriptures among the

peasants who came to the town to see them. When the leading layman of
the town heard of this a huge funeral pyre was set alight, and a holy cross
erected nearby. Against Aribert's wishes the heretics were brought out, and
this decree ordained, that if they wanted to embrace the cross, abjure their
wickedness, and confess the faith which the whole world holds, they would
be saved. If not, they must enter the flames, and be burned alive. So it was
done: some of them went to the holy cross, confessed the Catholic faith, and
were saved. Many others leapt into the flames, holding their hands in front
of their faces, and dying wretchedly were reduced to wretched ashes.

5 Wazo of Liège: heresy at Châlons and Goslar

After the relative abundance of the 1020s we know little of the spread of heresy in the
rest of the century. The Council of Rheims in 1048 excommunicated 'the new heretics
who have appeared in Gaul and their associates' (Mansi, XIX, col. 742), but there is no
indication of who or where they were, or what their heresy was. At Goslar in 1052
certain heretics were brought before the Emperor Henry III by Godfrey of Upper
Lorraine. 'Among other wicked Manichean doctrines they condemned all eating of
animals, and with the agreement of everybody present he ordered them to be hanged,
to prevent the disease of their heresy from spreading widely and infecting more people.'
(Heriman of Reichinau, *MGH SS*, V, 130; Duke Godfrey's part is mentioned by Lam-
pert of Hersfeld, *ibid.*, 155). Before the Council of Rheims we know only of the group
discovered between 1043 and 1048 by Bishop Roger II of Châlons-sur-Marne, and
mentioned here by Anselm, in his *Gesta episcoporum*. . . . *Leodiensis, MGH SS*, VII,
226–8. For Wazo of Liège, one of the more sophisticated ecclesiastical thinkers of his
time, see E. de Moreau, *Histoire de l'église en Belgique*, II, 34 sqq., and for discussion of
the views he expresses here, Maisonneuve, pp. 99–100, and Russell, *Dissent and Reform*,
pp. 38–40.
   'The example of St Martin of Tours' to which Anselm refers, was of vigorous
opposition to the first execution of a heretic by the secular power, that of Priscillian
in 385 AD, and to the practice of the commissioners who were sent to Spain to hunt
his followers of identifying them to the paleness of their faces, which was regarded as
evidence of abstention from meat. (Sulpicius Severus, Life of St Martin, trans. F. R.
Hoare, *The Western Fathers*, pp. 133–7).

After Wazo became bishop he received many letters which he accepted respectfully, and answered humbly whatever they asked him. Different people sought
out the advice of our distinguished bishop on many problems, and none of
them was kept waiting, or denied a wise answer to his question. One of them
was the bishop of Châlons who had occasion to consult his lordship about a
menace to the souls of his flock which he described in his letter. He said that
in one part of his diocese some peasants who followed the perverse teaching of
the Manichees were holding secret meetings. I do not know what outrages and
obscenities they solemnly repeated. They falsely claimed that by the imposition

of hands they had been given the Holy Spirit, which they alleged (to strengthen faith in their heresy) had been sent by God only through their heresiarch Mani, as though Mani himself were the Holy Spirit: hence they fell into the blasphemy which, according to the voice of truth, can be forgiven neither now or hereafter. Bishop Roger said that they make anyone they can join their sect, abhor marriage, shun the eating of meat, and believe it profane to kill animals, presuming to assimilate to their heresy the words of the Lord in the commandment which prohibits killing. He claimed that if uncouth and ignorant men become members of this sect they immediately become more eloquent than the most learned Catholics, so that even the pure argument of the truly wise almost seems to be conquered by their fluency. He added that he was more worried about their daily corruption of others than about their own damnation. The anxious prelate therefore sought the advice of our wise bishop about how he should deal with these people and whether the sword of the secular power should be turned against them, since if they were not exterminated their festering might infect the whole people.

This is our bishop's reply:
'The heresy of the people you write about is clear. It was discussed of old by the fathers of the Church, and rebutted by their brilliant arguments. Even if we leave aside the insane blasphemy of their claim to the Holy Spirit, your lordship will see what traps they fall into by misunderstanding the Lord's commandment, "Thou shalt not kill." If they do not understand this as a prohibition only of the killing of men how do they think that they can legitimately eat at all? According to their interpretation such things as corn, vegetables and wine are forbidden: from being seeds entrusted to the ground they take on the nature of life, and cannot serve human uses unless they are killed by being deprived of their power of growth. Without resort to secular writings we may find this attested by the psalmist when he says, "And he destroyed their vines with hail", and by the apostle, "Senseless men, that which thou sowest is not quickened, except it die first"; and by the Lord, "Unless the grain of wheat falling into the ground die itself remaineth alone." It follows that what can be said to have been killed by incidental causes must be said to have lived. They cannot have it both ways: either "thou shalt not kill" is to be taken, in the Catholic way, as referring only to men, and we may kill animals quite legitimately, or if they deny this we are guilty, according to this article of their heresy, if we take bread, vegetables, and other such things, because they cannot be adapted to human needs except by being killed in their own way.

'The Christian religion abhors this view and finds these heretics guilty of the Arian sacrilege. Nevertheless we must imitate our Saviour, gentle and humble in heart, who "came not to contend nor cry out", but to bear insults, indignities and blows, and in the end, death on the cross: we must put up with such people as these because, as St Gregory says, Abel would not have found grace but for the malice of Cain, and the juice of grapes would not flow into wine if they were not trodden underfoot. [*Moralia* 75.] Hence it is clear how our merciful and magnanimous Lord, who does not judge sinners at once, but calmly waits for them to repent, would have us treat these people. We hear from the Gospel, when he expounds the parable on the wheat and the tares to his disciples—or rather teaches us through them—"He that soweth the good seed is the son of man. And the field is the world. And the good seed are the children of the kingdom. And the tares are the children of the wicked one. And the enemy that sowed them is the devil. But the harvest is the end of the world, and the reapers are the angels." What is signified by the servants who want to pluck out the tares as soon as they appear if not the order of preachers? Do they not want to separate the good from the bad in the Church as though they are seeking to uproot the tares from the wheat in the field? But the Lord restrains their zeal with the discernment of fatherly authority and says, "No, lest perhaps gathering up the tare you root up the wheat also together with it. Suffer both to grow until the harvest, and in the time of the harvest I will say to the reapers: Gather up first the tares, and bind them into bundles to burn, but the wheat gather ye into my barn." What do these words mean but that the Lord extends his patience towards those whom his preachers want to condemn as wandering into heresy, because those who are tares today may be converted tomorrow, and become wheat? The fervour of spiritual zeal which burns in your breast for the souls deceived by the fraud of the devil urges you that it must be your duty as one of his servants to try to purge the corn field of tares with the hoe of justice, lest the good be corrupted by the bad. Yet we ought not to act prematurely, or before the proper time. We must obey the divine command. In thinking that we do justice in punishing wrongdoers we might disguise impiety as a kind of severity and rush to judgement before him who does not want the death of sinners, or rejoice in the condemnation of the damned, because he knows how to lead sinners to repentance through patience and farsightedness. We have heard the words of our creator: let the judgement of the arena cease. We should not try to drag them from this life with the power of the secular sword when we know that God the creator and redeemer wishes them to be spared so that they may draw back from the snares of the devil in which they are held captive, to return to his will. Therefore it behoves us to leave these things to the last harvest of the head of the house himself, and to whatever he commands his harvesters to do with them, just as we must look forward with fear and trembling on our own behalf. Some of those who seem tares in the field of this world may turn out to be wheat in that harvest, and it is possible that God may make those whom we now think adversaries in his path superior to us in the heavenly fatherland. We read how Saul was the most savage among those who stoned the protomartyr Stephen, and how, to him

B

who was once a persecutor the martyr apostle later rejoiced to give first place.

'We must always remember that we who are called bishops do not receive the sword of the secular power in ordination, and are anointed to bring life, not death. Of course you must take action against these heretics; you must deprive them, as you well know, of the Catholic communion, and proclaim publicly to everybody, the advice of the prophet, "Go out of the midst of them: touch no unclean thing" of their sect, because "he that toucheth pitch shall be defiled with it." '

In this way the man of God strove to follow the example of St Martin of Tours, and restrain the usual hasty frenzy of the French from stirring up any kind of cruelty, because he had heard how heretics had been identified only by the paleness of their faces, as though anybody who was pale was undoubtedly a heretic, and how many Catholics had been killed as a result of this hysterical mistake.

Given this, when such clear arguments and biblical authority cannot be fairly or reasonably contradicted, anyone can see how reprehensibly they behaved at Goslar, when some members of this sect were captured. They were rightly excommunicated, after much discussion of their beliefs, for their stubbornness in heresy, but they were sentenced to be hanged as well. I have most diligently tried to find out what passed at this discussion, and can discover no justification for the sentence except that the heretics refused to obey the order of the bishop to kill a chicken. I cannot refrain from pointing out that if Wazo had been there he would not have consented to this sentence: he would have followed the example of St Martin, who interceded for the Priscillianists condemned by edict of the Emperor Maximus after they had been wickedly misrepresented by a council of fawning priests, courageously preferring to risk damage to himself than not to urge that the heretics should be saved. I say this not because I want to conceal the errors of the heretics, but because it can be shown that such a decree nowhere receives the approval of the divine law.

6 Ramihrdus of Cambrai: trial and death

Gerard II, who succeeded to the bishopric of Cambrai in September 1076, found himself in conflict both with the pope, because he accepted investiture from the emperor, and with the citizens of Cambrai, in one of the earliest communal uprisings. There is no direct evidence that Ramihrdus was connected with either dispute, but the possibility is usefully discussed by A. H. J. Cauchie, *La querelle de l' investiture* I, 1–18, II, 74–6, 124–6, and A. Vermeesch, *Les communes dans le nord de la France*, pp. 88–9.

This part of the Chronicle of St André de Castres, *MGH SS* vii, 543, was probably written c. 1133.

After this the bishop happened to visit the town of Lambres which was under his jurisdiction, and stayed there for a short time. While he was there it was reported to him that a man named Ramihrd had been preaching against the faith in the nearby village of Schere, and had found many followers of both sexes to accept his teachings. He immediately inquired into the man's life and teaching, decided that he ought to answer the charges, and ordered him to be brought to his seat at Cambrai, where they could be discussed in full. On the appointed day he was brought before a group of abbots and learned clerks and questioned about the Catholic faith. But when the bishop told him to confirm what he had said by taking communion he refused, saying that he would not accept it from any of the abbots or priests, or even from the bishop himself because they were up to the neck in simony and other avarice. Everyone was greatly angered by these words, they denounced him as a heresiarch, and the meeting adjourned. But certain of the bishop's servants, with many others, led him out and took him—not reluctantly, but without fear, and, they say, prostrate in prayer—to a hut which they set on fire. Many of those who had been his followers took away some of his bones and ashes for themselves. In some towns there are many members of his sect to this day, and it is thought that those who make their living by weaving belong to it.

7 Ramihrdus: the reaction of Gregory VII

A fuller translation of this letter, from the *Registrum* of Gregory VII, ed. Caspar, *MGH Epist* II, 1, 328–9, may be found in E. Emerton, *Select Correspondence*, pp. 116–18. Whether Bishop Geoffrey did investigate the death of Ramihrdus, or with what consequence, is unknown, but three months later the pope informed his legate, Hugh of Die, that Gerard of Cambrai had confessed to receiving his See uncanonically, resigned it, and been restored: *Registrum* 331–4; Emerton, 118–20.

To Geoffrey, bishop of Paris,

... We have also heard that the people of Cambrai have burnt a certain man because he dared to say that simoniacal and unchaste priests ought not to celebrate mass, and that their offices ought to be avoided. This seems to us a dreadful thing, and if it is true he ought to be avenged with all the rigour of canonical severity, and we order you as our brother carefully to investigate the truth of the matter. If you find that they have impiously committed this outrage you will not distinguish between the originators of the crime and their accomplices in cutting them off from entrance into church, and from its communion. Take care to inform us by letter as quickly as possible what you are able to discover of the truth of this affair.

Furthermore, we ask you, and urge you strongly, to let all your colleagues and fellow bishops throughout France know by apostolic authority that they are to forbid priests who will not give up fornication to perform any office at the holy altar, and to preach the same thing yourself in every place or meeting. If you find the bishops sluggish in this matter, or if those who unworthily presume to usurp the name and office of the priestly order are intransigent because of their crimes, you are to forbid the people to attend their services any more, in the name of St Peter, and by our apostolic authority, so that they will be defeated in this way, and forced to reform their lives and return to the purity of religious continence. Do these things so that, with God's help, the Holy and Universal Mother Church may know that you are her faithful minister, working with us in our apostolic responsibility, and permit us, as we greatly desire it, to rejoice in the freedom and fruitfulness of our priestly office now, and confidently look forward to doing so, through the mercy of God, in the future.

II An Age of Anticlericalism

IT is now widely agreed that the appearance over most of western Europe from the beginning of the twelfth century onwards of heretical leaders whose bitter criticisms of the Church aroused great popular enthusiasm is intimately associated with the upheavals which followed the papal reform programme of the later eleventh century. But few would endorse the opinion of Fliche (*Histoire d'l'église*, 9.1, pp. 91–2) that the reform forced people to choose 'between the basest passions of the flesh and the moral teaching of the Church.' On the contrary it seems that the vigorous publicity which Gregory VII and his circle gave to the vices of the clergy and to the consequences of the involvement of the Church in the feudal structure of western Europe, coupled with their failure to change the situation at least as it affected the lower clergy, must be counted an important cause of the growth of heresy. Disappointment at the slow pace of reform was a common sensation. Robert of Arbrissel became a popular preacher, and later the founder of Fontevrault, c. 1100, after he failed as archpriest in the dioceses of Rennes to persuade the parish priests to give up their concubines. Other monastic leaders, like Robert of Molesmes, the founder of the Cistercian Order, Bernard of Tiron, and Geoffrey the second abbot of Savigny, left unreformed Benedictine houses because they were dissatisfied with what they regarded as the laxity of their lives, and in doing so some of them gave their conscience priority over their vow of obedience.

At the same time the willingness of Gregory VII to call upon the people for direct assistance in his campaign to reform his own hierarchy, to invite the laity to judge their priests and the lower clergy their superiors, as he did in the case of Ramihrdus, can only have stimulated popular activity. Although the difference between his instruction that the masses of uncelibate priests should be boycotted and the contention of most of the heretics mentioned in the following pages that they were invalid is theologically crucial, the distinction was slight to the uneducated, and could rapidly disappear in practice. Similarly many of the complaints made by Tanchelm, Henry of Lausanne and Peter de Bruys against the wealth of the Church were echoed by the great monastic reformers who were their contemporaries, and St Bernard was not much less pessimistic than Arnold of Brescia about the consequences of the temporal power of the papacy, 'successor not to Peter but to Constantine', for its ability to perform its spiritual function. Such considerations as these are expanded in the works of Walter Wakefield, J. B. Russell, and C. N. L. Brooke.

The increase of heresy was naturally accompanied by an increasing anxiety on the part of the Church. It was still the responsibility of the bishop to deal with the heretic in his own diocese, and the measures which he adopted, officially at least, were not severe. But there was an increasing determination to control preaching, and the Church began to legislate against popular heresy. The council over which Calixtus II presided at Toulouse in 1119 enacted this canon

> We condemn, and exclude from the Church as heretics those who, under the guise of religion, reject the sacrament of the body and blood of Christ, infant baptism, the priesthood and other ecclesiastical orders, and condemn the ties of legitimate matrimony, and require them to be constrained by the secular powers. Their defenders shall be subject to the same penalties until they recover their senses. (Mansi, XXI, col. 226–7.)

One of the best known episodes of popular heresy in the period is omitted from this selection. In c. 1114 Guibert, abbot of Nogent, examined a group which had been discovered near Soissons, led by Clement of Bucy (*De vita sua*, translated as *Self and Society in Medieval France* by J. F. Benton, pp. 212–14, and Wakefield and Evans, pp. 132–4). He concluded, as his education naturally prompted him to do, that they must be Manicheans, and his description of the orgies in which they were alleged to indulge is strikingly similar to that of the clerks of Orléans in 1022. They rejected baptism, the mass and marriage, and after Clement had been subjected to the ordeal by water they were seized from imprisonment by a mob and burned. Their heresy had, apparently, no especially distinctive features, and the interest of the story lies chiefly in the clarity with which it shows how instinctively an intelligent churchman of this period looked for the source of disaffection in the revival of ancient error rather than in modern grievance or innovation.

8 Tanchelm: Letter of the canons of Utrecht, 1112–14

Tanchelm is one of the best known of early heretical leaders, and there are good discussions of him by Russell, *Dissent and Reform*, pp. 56–68, 265–9 (on sources), and 282–3, and Cohn, *The Pursuit of the Millennium*, pp. 46–53. Before he became active as a preacher he visited Rome as the agent of Robert II of Flanders (1093–1111), who was anxious to have certain areas transferred from the diocese of Utrecht to that of Thérouanne, where his own influence was greater. Tanchelm was killed c. 1115, 'by a blow on the head delivered by a priest while they were in a boat.' (Continuation of Sigebert of Gembloux, *MGH SS* VI, 449, translated by Wakefield and Evans, *Heresies of the High Middle Ages*, p. 101.) The letter is translated from *Acta Sanctorum*, June, 832–3.

To her lord and venerable father Frederick, archbishop of Cologne, the humble church of Utrecht. . . .

We send you our thanks, reverend father, because you have taken pity on us with fatherly solicitude, and checked the attacks of our Antichrist, who has upset and blasphemed against the Church of Christ. He raised his voice to the heavens, and dared to excite a heresy against the sacraments of the Church which was long since refuted by its fathers. Swelling with spiritual pride (which is the root of all heresy and apostasy) he maintained that the pope, and archbishops, priests and clerks are nothing; hacking at the columns of the Church of God, the very rock of our faith, it was Christ that he presumed to divide. He maintained that the Church consisted only of himself and his followers; the Church which Christ received from his Father, 'Gentiles for his inheritance and the utmost parts of the earth for his possession' was to be a Tanchelmite dominion.

Therefore, holy father, support us in our afflictions now. Ward off the predecessor of Antichrist who is coming ahead of him by the same road, in the very footsteps that he will follow. He first mixed his evil potion in the coastal region, where the population is backward and infirm in the faith. He began to spread his errors gradually through women both old and young, freely exploiting their intimacies and secret conversation by sleeping with them. Through them he ensnared their husbands also in the trap of his wickedness. After that he moved out of the shadows and bedrooms, and began to preach from the rooftops, giving sermons in the open fields, surrounded by huge crowds. He used to preach as though he were a king summoning his people, as his followers crowded around him carrying swords and flags like royal insignia. The deluded populace listened to him as though he were an angel of God.

He was more like an angel of Satan, urging that the Churches of God should be thought of as brothels; that the office of priests at the altar is worthless— they should be called pollutions rather than sacraments. He said that the efficacy of the sacraments proceeded from the merits and holiness of the ministers, in spite of the words of St Augustine: 'The Lord Christ sent out a traitor (who was called a devil, and could not keep faith before he betrayed the Lord even over the Lord's purse) to preach the kingdom of Heaven with the other apostles, to show that the gifts of God come to those who receive them in faith, even if he through whom they are received is a very Judas', or, as Augustine also said, 'Should the merits of the giver and the receiver be considered in the receiving of the sacraments? Then let it be God's merit in giving and my faith in receiving. For me two things in this are certain: God's goodness and my own faith. But if you intervene, how can I know anything for certain? Let me say that I trust in God. For if I trust in you how can I be sure that you have done nothing evil that night?' Denouncing these and other such opinions, this blasphemer urged the people not to receive the sacraments of the body and blood of Christ, and not to pay their tithes to the ministers of the Church, in which they were easily persuaded. This view he emphasized so much because he preached what he knew the people would welcome either for its novelty or because they were already predisposed to it.

The wretched man became so arrogant in this train of wickedness that he began to say that he was God, arguing that Christ was God because he had the holy spirit, and that he was not inferior, or less like God, since he also had received a plenitude of the holy spirit. He made such play with this presumption that some people worshipped the divinity in him. He was able to distribute his bath water to the fools, to be drunk as a benediction, as though it were a holy and efficacious sacrament which would assure the salvation of body and soul. Later he devised another novelty. He ordered an image of St Mary— the mind recoils from repeating it—to be brought into the middle of the crowd. Then he walked over to it, and joining hands with the image, used it as proxy in marrying himself to St Mary. He would sacrilegiously give tongue to the usual sacrament and solemn words of marriage, and then say, 'There, beloved followers. I have married the Blessed Virgin. Let us have the cost of the betrothal and the wedding.' Placing one purse in the left, and one in the right hand of the image, he would continue, 'Let the men put their offerings in this purse, and the women in the other. I will see now which sex shows the greater generosity towards me and my wife.' Sure enough, the deluded people rushed upon him with gifts and offerings. The women showered him with earrings and necklaces, and by this monstrous sacrilege he made a great deal of money.

We hear that you have arrested a certain blacksmith named Manasses with the other scoundrel. Following the example of his wicked master he founded a sort of fraternity commonly called a gild. It was composed of twelve men, representing the twelve apostles, and a woman as St Mary. They say that she used to be led round the twelve men one by one and joined with them in foul sin, a gross insult to the Holy Virgin, as a sort of confirmation of their fraternity. There is also a priest named Everwacher, who deserted the sacerdotal dignity to attach himself to this wicked men, and followed him to Rome when he tried to have the coastal area which is a quarter of our see attached to the diocese of Thérouanne, in the kingdom of France. This would have detracted from your grace and we rejoiced at his failure. The same priest, Tanchelm's champion in everything, fell upon the tithes of the brothers of the church of St Peter, and drove the priests themselves from their church and altar by force of arms. His crimes are endless my lord; we must leave out many of them from this short letter. It is enough to sum them up by saying that he has brought holy things into such contempt that the more holy the Church the more it is despised.

Therefore father we beseech and beg you in God who by his divine mercy will not let his Church be exposed to this peril any longer and has placed these men in your hands. Do not let them slip. If that should happen we assure you and testify without ambiguity that our church would suffer irreparable damage and enormous loss of souls. For in truth our church will come to serious harm if these men should escape; as the apostle has it, their words crawl like crabs, and destroy the souls of simple people by their blandishments. And now, for this very object, our Antichrist has disguised himself as a monk, following the example of the chief whose tool he has made himself, and turned himself into an angel of light so that he may mock more safely, and cunningly assume a false appearance of holiness. We ask you, my lord, to move with just indignation against these underminers of the Church. . . . So we pray to God that your holiness will do something about these things to relieve our church, which has been tried for so long.

9 Tanchelm: The Life of St Norbert

There are two versions of the *Vita Norberti*. This extract is taken from (A), which is generally accepted as the earlier (c. 1155, *MGH SS* 690–1). (B) attributes the susceptibility of the citizens of Antwerp to heresy to the corruption and venality of their only parish priest, and adds (as is the way of redactions) some details of Tanchelm's sexual excesses which are more picturesque than plausible.

At that time a very dangerous heresy appeared at Antwerp, a large and populous place. A heretical preacher of extraordinary subtlety and cunning, named Tanchelm, found there a good opportunity for his activities. He was so wicked, and such an enemy of the Christian faith, and of all religion, that he would allow no respect of bishops and priests, and denied that the sacraments of the body and blood of our Lord Jesus Christ were of any assistance towards eternal salvation. He led many of the people of those parts into his errors, and they believed him in everything so firmly that some three thousand armed men used to follow him about, and no prince or magnate would resist him or kill him. He dressed in gilded clothes, and glittered because of the gold twisted into his hair, and the many ornaments which he wore. He won over the good will of his hearers with lavish festivity as well as persuasive words. It was quite fantastic; they used to drink his bath water, or carry it off to be kept as a relic. His followers willingly associated themselves with him in many other wickednesses and detestable blasphemies, to such a degree that the evil pestilence could not be rooted out even after the death of the heretic himself.

In the same town there was a community of twelve clerks, who were driven by the persistence of this heresy to hand over their church to Norbert and his companions, through the agency of the bishop, in the hope that the merits of his preaching would raise the curse of the stubborn pestilence, and the light of truth flood in again after the shadows of ignorance had been driven away. Norbert took over the church, and the clerks built themselves another in the town; both churches remain made over to the service of God, until this day. So it was that the people who had been fraudulently led astray by that wicked man were led back to the way of truth and righteousness by the pious preacher Norbert and his companions.

10 Heretical priests at Ivois, c. 1120

The only ground for suspecting that this incident belongs to the last years of the reign of Archbishop Bruno of Trier (1102–24) is the position that it occupies in the *Gesta Treverorum* (*MGH SS* VIII, 193–4) which normally observes chronological sequence. There is no other medieval account.

Dominic William was told to pronounce the canon of the mass clearly because it would normally be spoken quietly, and therefore perhaps slurred, by the priest: it was called the *actio* because it was the moment when divine judgement would be exercised on an imposter.

At this time there were some heretics at Ivois in the diocese of Trier, who denied that the substance of bread and wine blessed on the altar by priests is truly transformed into the body and blood of Christ, and that the sacrament of baptism helps infants to salvation, and professed other heresies which I would think it wrong to hand down to posterity. Four of them were discovered, two priests and two laymen. One priest was called Frederick, and the other had two names, Dominic William, and the laymen were called Durand and Amalric. While the archbishop was reviewing their case and expounding Christian doctine to them Amalric escaped, and Durand confessed that he had been a party to the crime, and swore on the relics of the saints that he would not persist in it.

The priest Frederick not only did not deny his heresy when he was summoned to a hearing, but claimed that he did right to profess it. To him Archbishop Bruno said, 'As a teacher of the faithful you ought to have preached sound doctrine to everybody, not assertions of unfaithfulness. Yet it is as clear as day that you have lied to the faithful. St Augustine says, "It is not ordained that Christ should be eaten with the teeth. Christ wished this bread and wine to be mystically made his flesh and blood, by the consecration of the Holy Spirit, and eaten daily for the sake of the spiritual life of mankind, so that just as he was created without coition, as true flesh from the Virgin, by the Holy Spirit, in the same way his body should be mystically created from the substance of the bread and wine." In his letter *On the Catholic Faith* he says, "Hold firmly and never doubt that children may attain salvation through the sacrament of faith which is holy baptism even though they cannot believe, or do penance of their own will for the original sin in which they are steeped before they have attained the age of understanding." '

These and other passages from sacred writings were cited, and those of the faithful who were present called upon him, and urged him to return to the Christian faith. When he refused and obstinately insisted on sticking to his infidelity the whole crowd pronounced the sentence of the Lord, 'If he will not hear the Church let him be to thee as the heathen and the publican', and added, 'Let him be deprived of his rank and condemned.' In the excitement he saw a chance to escape, slipped through the bystanders, and got away. Accordingly, when the search for him had failed, he was condemned, under the canon, 'Let whoever will not come to a hearing when he is summoned be sentenced in his absence.'

The other priest, the one who had two names to obscure the wickedness of his infamy, was now asked whether he was a disciple of this heresy. He maintained that he had never confessed or acknowledged it. There were witnesses who claimed that they had chanced across a meeting of these heretics and found him taking part in it. He, afraid that if he were convicted he would be deprived of the rank of priest, said that he would be willing to undergo the most severe trial to purge this suspicion. Everybody approved of this suggestion, and he was ordered to celebrate a mass, and to chant the holy canon, which is called the *secreta* or *actio* in a loud voice, since anyone who were to presume to defile this mystery of the precious body and blood of Christ would be sure to be judged by him. He went through the mass, and just as he was about to reach the communion the bishop interrupted him with this invocation: 'If you have dared to say impiously that the lifegiving sacrament of our salvation which you hold in your hand is not the true body and blood of Christ I forbid you, in its presence, to receive it. If your belief is not that, but the Catholic one, take it.'

He took it, but I do not think it wrong to claim that the gift of redemption entered his mouth to his own damnation. In the anxiety induced by his trial he prayed to almighty God with a contrite heart, promising to do penance for what he had been charged with, and promising to be more careful in future, and was released from his present trouble. But when he returned to his own way of life he was not afraid to break his promises, and resumed the heresy which he had abjured more stubbornly than before, forgetting that the more patiently God, that just, firm and long-suffering judge, puts up with offences the more severely he judges them in the end. In consequence he descended from evil to evil, as it is written, 'he that is filthy, let him be filthy still,' for he was misled by the spirit of fornication, and soon afterwards was taken in adultery, and met a death worthy of his wickedness.

11 Henry of Lausanne: at Le Mans, c. 1116

Although Henry is the best documented of the heretical leaders of the early twelfth century nothing is known of him before his appearance at Le Mans beyond the assertions of St Bernard nearly thirty years later, from which the two epithets, 'Henry of Lausanne' and 'Henry the Monk', by which he is usually known are derived.

The fullest examination of Henry's career is that of Manselli, *Studi sulle eresie*, and in English, that of Russell, *Dissent and Reform*, pp. 68–74. This account of his sojourn at Le Mans is from the *Gesta Pontificum Cenomannensium*, Bouquet, XII, 547–51. It should be noticed that Le Mans was the scene of one of the earliest communes in France in 1070, on which see R. Latouche in *Mélanges Louis Halphen*.

At about this time a hypocrite appeared in the neighbourhood whose behaviour, perverted morals and detestable teaching showed that he deserved, like a parricide, to be punished with scorpions. He was a wolf in sheep's clothing, with the haggard face and eyes of a shipwrecked sailor, his hair bound up, unshaven, tall and of athletic gait, walking barefoot even in the depths of winter, a young man always ready to preach, possessed of a fearful voice. His clothes were shabby, and his life eccentric: he had lodgings in the houses of the town, his home in the doorways, and his bed in the gutters. But why go on? His reputation for unusual holiness and learning rested not on the merit of his character but on falsehood, not on his morals or piety, but on rumour. Women and young boys—for he used both sexes in his lechery—who associated with him openly flaunted their excesses, and added to them by caressing the soles of his feet and his buttocks and groin with tender fingers. They became so excited by the lasciviousness of the man, and by the grossness of their own sins, that they testified publicly to his extraordinary virility, and said that his eloquence could move a heart of stone to remorse, and that all monks, hermits and canons regular ought to imitate his pious and celibate life. They claimed that God had blessed him with the ancient and authentic spirit of the prophets, and he saw in their faces, and told them of sins which were unknown to others.

When this man's reputation began to grow in our area the people, with characteristic frivolity and predictable consequences, were delighted. They longed for his meetings all day and every day, so that they could know his heresy better and become more closely entangled in it. They often seek most eagerly what will do them most harm. As time passed it got worse. Deciding to tame our people with his snake-like speech, he sent to the bishop two disciples who resembled him in their dress and way of life, just as our Saviour had sent his people ahead of him. When they reached the outskirts of the city on Ash Wednesday, the whole people, longing for the wickedness that was offered to them, received them as though they were angels of the lord of the universe. They carried a standard in the way that doctors bear staves, a cross with wrought iron fixed at the top, and their bearing and manner suggested some sort of penitent. The bishop, a man of great piety, received them gently and devoutly. Not anticipating the wiles of the Trojan horse, he greeted them cheerfully and generously, and although he was about to set out for Rome ordered his archdeacons to allow the false hermit Henry (for that was the heretic's name) to enter the city peacefully and preach to the people.

When he entered the city the mob in its usual way applauded the novelty, preferring the unknown to the familiar. Was it surprising? They believed that his righteousness was even greater than his fame which was constantly inflated by gossip. Blinded by his schism and faction, and by personal corruption, many of the clerks pandered to the mob and prepared a platform from which the demagogue could address the crowds of people who followed him. When he spoke to them, with the clerks sitting weeping at his feet, his speech resounded as though legions of demons spoke through his open mouth. He was certainly remarkably eloquent. His words stuck in the minds of people just as freshly taken poison when it has been forced into the limbs spreads its strength through the vitals and, with inexorable hatred of life, twists and bends to attack them unceasingly.

His heresy turned the people against the clergy with such fury that they refused to sell them anything or buy anything from them and treated them like gentiles or publicans. Not content with pulling down their houses and throwing away their belongings, they would have stoned and pilloried them if the count and his men had not heard of their wicked and vicious exploits, and suppressed them by force instead of by reason, for a monster admits no argument. Some of the clerks who were left in the city, William D'Osell, William who-won't-drink-water [*Qui-non-bibit-aquam*] and Payn Aldricus obtained access to him one day to negotiate with him, and were viciously beaten and had their heads rolled in the filth of the gutter; they were scarcely able to escape alive from the attack of these brutal people, and when they did get away their departure had the appearance of flight. Once they had been caught they would not have escaped from the danger at all if they had not found shelter with the count and his knights, for as we have said the count resisted the heresy of the city, and did not shrink from the defence of the clerks.

The clerks, since they did not dare to address the heretic in person, sent him the following letter

Our Church received you and your friends peaceably and honourably when you came dressed as a sheep, concealing the wiles of a hungry wolf underneath. In thought and deed it treated you with brotherly charity, expecting that you would advise the people faithfully on the salvation of their souls, and sincerely sow the seed of the word of God in their hearts. You have perversely returned anger for peace, slander for respect, hatred for charity, curses for blessings, and have presumed to disturb the Church of God with your heresy. You have sown discord between clergy and people, and repeatedly incited a seditious mob to attack Mother Church with swords and clubs. You have offered us the kiss of Judas and called us and all clerks heretics, to our public injury. Worse still you have said pernicious and infidel things against the Catholic faith, which a faithful Christian would shudder to repeat. Therefore, by the authority of the one and undivided Trinity, and of the whole orthodox Church, of St Mary mother of God, of St Peter the prince of the apostles, and his present vicar Pope Paschal, and of your bishop Hildebert, we forbid you and your associates in your evil and damnable heresy to preach again anywhere in the diocese of Le Mans, in private or in public, or to presume to propagate your perverse and absurd teachings. If you defy this authority and open your evil jaws once more then by the same authority we excommunicate you and all your accomplices, followers and associates, and he whose divinity you have not ceased to contravene will have you delivered on the day of judgment to eternal damnation.

He would not accept the letter, but William Musca delivered it to him in person. The people who were standing around threatened to kill him, because he bravely heaped reproaches on Henry in public so that he could be seen. Henry nodded his head at each sentence of the letter, and replied in a clear voice, 'You are lying.' If it had not been for the count's steward, under whose protection he had come, William would not have returned to the church alive.

After this he summoned a sacrilegious meeting at the church of St Germain and St Vincent, where he pronounced a new dogma, that women who had not lived chastely must, naked before everybody, burn their clothes and their hair. No one should accept any gold or silver or goods or wedding presents with his wife, or receive any dowry with her: the naked should marry the naked, the sick marry the sick, and the poor marry the poor, without bothering about whether they married chastely or incestuously. While they followed his instructions he admired the beauty of the women, and discussed which ones had fairer skin or better figures than the others. In spite of this the people subjected their every wish and deed to his command.

If he wanted it, gold and silver flowed to him in such quantity that he seemed to be the sole master of everybody's wealth. He accepted a great deal openly, but spared his greed in case he should seem avaricious. All the same he kept a lot for himself and gave very little for the clothes which, as we have said, had been burnt. On his advice many of the young men married the corrupt women, for whom he bought clothes to the value of four *solidi*, just enough to cover their nakedness. But the true judge destroyed the work of the heretic, and showed that this was the sort of tree that produces leaves rather than fruit. The young men who had married worthless women at his behest were soon driven by the poverty or debauchery of their wives to flee the city, leaving the women destitute, and while the men coupled with others in adultery the women whom they had left behind hoped to remarry illegally. Of those who entered into matrimony at his urging, and there were many of them, neither men nor women showed fidelity or respect towards their spouses. None of the women who had promised to renounce fornication when they destroyed their clothes were able to restrain themselves, and adding to their crimes daily they relapsed into a worse condition than ever.

After he had behaved in this way for some time the scoundrel heard that the bishop, who, as we have said, had made a journey to Rome, was returning and withdrew to the village of St Calais. He stayed there and in other towns nearby, and far from desisting from his wickedness daily discovered some new iniquity. On the holy day of Pentecost, when the true faithful devote the whole day to divine offices this most evil of men, accompanied by a young clerk whose evidence later revealed his wantonness, went secretly at night to the house of a certain knight, and there caroused all day until mid-day in bed with the mistress of the house. Neither the fear of God nor shame before men could moderate his lasciviousness, until he had blazoned the enormity of his crimes to people far and wide.

When the bishop entered the city on his return, surrounded by a great retinue of his clerks, he made the sign of the living God over his people, and blessed them with fatherly solicitude. But they blasphemed bitterly, and rejected his episcopal sign and benediction.

'We want none of your ways,' they cried. 'We don't want your blessing. Bless the dirt! Sanctify filth! We have a father, a bishop and defender greater than you in authority, fame and learning. These wicked clerks of yours here opposed him, and contradicted his teaching. They have hated it and rejected it as sacrilege because they are afraid that their crimes will be revealed by his prophetic spirit. They wrote letters attacking his heresy and his bodily unchastity. Their sins will be speedily turned against them when they presume so audaciously to forbid his heavenly preaching of the word of God.'

The bishop took pity on the errors and ignorance of his people, and bore the insults which they hurled at him calmly, praying that God would restrain this mixture of heresy and excitement and prevent it from creating a schism in his Church. God allowed a sudden fire to burn down a large part of the suburbs of the city, so that temporal loss might cause them to cast aside their evil beliefs, and call upon his holy name, the name of the living God.

A few days later the bishop went to the heretic and by divine authority brought his impiety under control. The bishop opened their conversation by asking how he had made his profession, but he did not know what a profession was, and kept silent. Trying again, the bishop asked what orders he had, and he replied, 'I am a deacon.' 'Well then,' said the bishop, 'tell us whether you have been to mass today.' 'No.' 'Then let us recite the morning hymns to the Lord.'

When they did so Henry showed himself ignorant of the daily office. Then to make his ignorance absolutely clear, the bishop began to sing the usual psalms to the Virgin, and Henry knew neither the lines themselves nor the sequence. So, blushing furiously, he revealed what kind of life he had led, the worth of his teaching, and the extent of his presumption. He was only a vagabond, quite without knowledge and wholly given to lechery, who had been attracted by the idea of preaching to the people, and showing them portents.

When Henry's frivolity and impiety had been established the bishop forbade him by his apostolic authority to remain any longer within the bishopric, and told him to take himself off somewhere else and leave us alone. Thus convicted by the bishop's efforts he fled to disturb other regions and infect them with his poisonous breath, unless his reputation should precede him. Hildebert took every precaution to calm by reason and humility the popular fury which Henry had seditiously stirred up against the clergy, for the people had become so devoted to Henry that even now his memory can scarcely be expunged, or their love for him drawn from their hearts.

12 Henry: two repentant converts

Hildebert of Lavardin *Epistola* II, 24, *PL* 171, col. 242. This is Hildebert's only reference to his encounter with Henry. The letter which precedes this one (*ibid.*, col. 237-42) has been thought by Dieudonné and others, including Russell, pp. 70, 284 n. 16, to be addressed to Henry. As P. von Moos, *Hildebert von Lavardin*, p. 325, points out, the thesis is supported by neither the matter nor the manner of the letter: the suggestion that it was directed to Roscelin is much more plausible.

To all archbishops and bishops, Hildebert, humble bishop of Le Mans.

The bearers of this letter, Cyprian and Peter, set aside the aspiration of their spirits and descended into the valley of death by following a false prophet named Henry, and in following him maltreated themselves. This Henry is a senior servant of the devil, the famous esquire of Antichrist. Our brothers attached themselves to him when he simulated religion in his dress and learning in his words, until his evil life and heretical teaching became obvious to them. When they saw that the paths he followed were not those of righteousness they left him and came back to us—into whose diocese he had carried his disease so effectively that a clerk could scarcely guard his freedom even within the walls of the church. With God's help, after many tribulations, we made the viper sound off before us, and disclose the wretchedness of his life and the poison of his teaching. Since then these two have thrown off the cloak of seduction and the angel of darkness, and returned to our advice, which they have zealously embraced. Therefore, my brothers, I write you this fraternal letter so that if these two young men should chance to enter your diocese they will not suffer on account of this episode: rather rejoice because 'he who was dead is come to life again, was lost and is found.'

13 Henry: the Council of Pisa, 1135

The source of this document is the *Gesta Pontificum Cenomannensium*, Bouquet XII, 554.

s.a. 1134 The false hermit of whom we have already written again began to spread the germ of his heresy in remote places, and to corrupt the Church of God with the stain of his wickedness.

He adapted many of the sayings and writings of the prophets to his purpose, and expounded a perverse doctrine which a faithful Christian ought neither to repeat nor examine.

By the mercy of God, who 'hath had regard to the humble, and hath not despised their petition', Henry was taken by the archbishop of Arles, and brought before Pope Innocent [II] at the Council of Pisa. There he was again convicted, and by agreement labelled a heretic, and imprisoned. But later he was allowed to go away to another region, where he found new opportunities for evil and founded a new sect. He has created so much disturbance that soon Christians will scarcely enter the doors of the Churches: they reject the holy mystery, refuse offerings to the priests, first fruits, tithes and visits to the sick, and withdraw their habitual piety. But we had better avoid these matters, and turn to something else. . . .

14 Henry: St Bernard prepares his mission

St Bernard, Epistola 241, *PL* 182, col. 434–6; translated by B. Scott James, *The Letters of St Bernard of Clairvaux*, pp. 388–9.

This letter announces the mission which St Bernard undertook to the Languedoc in 1145, in the company of Geoffrey of Chartres and the papal legate Alberic of Ostia, to combat heresy in the area: *see* Vacandard, *Vie de St Bernard*, II, 224–41: W. Williams, *St Bernard of Clairvaux*, pp. 337–45.

1 We have heard and known of the great evils which the heretic Henry inflicts every day on the Church. He is now busy in your territory, a ravening wolf in the guise of a sheep. But, according to the indication given by our Lord, we can tell what sort of man he is by his fruits. Churches without people, people without priests, priests without the deference due to them, and Christians without Christ. The Churches are regarded as synagogues, the holiness of God's sanctuary is denied, the sacraments are not considered sacred, and holy days are deprived of their solemnities. Men are dying in their sins, and souls are everywhere being hurled before the awsome tribunal unreconciled by repentance, unfortified by communion. The grace of baptism is denied, and Christian children are kept away from the life given by Christ. Although Christ cries out: 'Suffer little children to come unto me', children are nevertheless kept away from salvation. Does God, who has 'multiplied his salvation so as to save man and beast', withhold his mercy only from the innocent? The Saviour became a child for the sake of children, why grudge him to them? This is devilish jealousy, this is the jealousy which brought death into the world; or does this man think that the Saviour does not want children because they are children? If this is the case, then it was for nothing that the mighty Lord was born a child, not to say scourged, spat upon, crucified and done to death.

2 How can this man be a man of God who thus acts and teaches against God? It is shocking that he should be heard by so many, and have such a large following who believe in him. Unhappy people! At the voice of one heretic you close your ears to all the prophets and apostles who with one spirit of truth have brought together the Church out of all nations to one faith in Christ. Therefore the divine oracles are deceived and the eyes and hearts of those who believe what they said to have been fulfilled are also deceived. With what stupendous and more than Jewish blindness does this man alone either close his eyes to the clear truth or, because he resents its fulfilment, by some diabolical art persuade stupid and foolish people to ignore the obvious facts in front of them, and believe that the prophets were deceived, the apostles were in error; that the whole world even after the shedding of Christ's blood, is going to perdition; and that the riches of God's mercy and his grace to the world are only for those who follow him? Because of this, although weak in body I have taken the road to those parts which this boar is ravaging without anyone to resist it or save them. When he was chased from France for his wickedness, the only territory open to him was yours. Only under your protection could he ferociously ravage Christ's flock. But whether or not this is in keeping with your honour, you alone must judge. Yet it is no wonder that the cunning serpent has deceived you, since he has 'the appearance of godliness, but denies the power thereof'.

3 Now hear what sort of man he is. He is an apostate who, having abandoned the monastic habit (for he was once a monk), has returned to the world and the filth of the flesh, like a dog to its vomit. Ashamed to live amongst kinsmen and those who know him, or rather not permitted to do so on account of his monstrous crimes, he has girded himself and taken the road to where he is not known, becoming a vagabond and fugitive on the face of the earth. When he began to seek a living he sold the Gospel (he is an educated man), scattering the word of God for money and preaching so that he might live. If he is able to secure something over and above his keep from simple people or some elderly women, he squanders it in gambling or more shameful ways. Frequently after a day of popular adulation this notable preacher is to be found with prostitutes, sometimes even with married women. Inquire if you like why he left Lausanne, Le Mans, Poitiers, and Bordeaux. There is no way at all

of return open to him in any of these places, because of the foul traces he has left behind him. Do you really hope to collect good fruit from such a bad tree as this? He fouls the land in which he is and makes it stink in the nostrils of the whole world, because, according to the words of the Lord, 'a bad tree cannot bring forth good fruit.'

4   This, as I have said, is the cause of my coming. But I do not come now on my own, I am drawn both by the summons and the plight of the Church, to see if the thorns and evil things of that man can be uprooted from the field of the Lord while they are still young, not by my hand, for I am nothing, but by the hands of the holy bishops who are with me, and also with the help of of your right hand. The chief amongst the bishops is the venerable bishop of Ostia, sent by the Holy See for this very purpose. He is a man who has done great things in Israel and by him the Lord has given victory to the Church on many occasions. It must be your concern, most excellent sir, to receive him honourably and those who are with him; and, so that the good work which such a great man has undertaken on your behalf and on behalf of your people, shall not be in vain, give him all the help you can according to that power which you have received from above.

15 Henry: St Bernard's mission, 1145

The *Vita Prima* of St Bernard contains three accounts of his mission of which this letter, (*PL* 185, col. 410–16) written while it was still in progress, is the fullest and most circumstantial. To it the others add that Henry had once been a Black Monk (*ibid.*, col. 427), and that 'when he fled and went into hiding he found the roads so well blocked and the footpaths so carefully watched that he was safe hardly anywhere, and was captured and brought to the bishop in chains. (*ibid.*, col. 313.) This is the last we hear of him.

On his return Bernard wrote to the people of Toulouse congratulating them on the success of his mission, and warning them not to 'receive any outside or unknown preacher, unless he be sent by the supreme pontiff, or have permission to preach from your bishop.' (Epistola 242, *PL* 182, col. 436; translated by B. Scott James, *The Letters of St Bernard*, pp. 389–91.)

The question of how many separate groups of heretics are revealed by Geoffrey's letter, and who they were, is also important. The thesis that the *Ariani* and the *Textores* were Cathars, and the first to be recorded in this area, is expounded by E. Griffe, *Les débuts de l'aventure cathare en Languedoc*, pp. 21–52; Y. M. J. Congar, 'Arriana Haeresis', pp. 450–56, and R. I. Moore, 'St Bernard's Mission to the Languedoc in 1145', do not agree.

To his dear master Archenfred and to both chapters, brother Geoffrey.

I know well by experience that with you my dear master verbal subtleties will avail me nothing. The son over whom you watched more tenderly than others, and held more dear not because you thought him worthy but because you knew his weakness, can hide nothing from you. From you I can hide nothing, for you receive as freely those who are not fluent in words, agreeing with the apostle that 'the kingdom of God is not in speech but in power.' Why waste words? You know my love for you. You know how I need the prayers of you and your flock. You are not ignorant of either my love, or my need. I shall be silent therefore about myself, for I know that I write to one who knows me. Rather, remembering how anxious you and everybody at Clairvaux were when we left, what doubts were entertained about the Abbot's journey, I shall write of what is much more important, of what we have seen and heard, and thereby console you.

As we approached Poitiers the abbot became so unwell that he began to regret having undertaken the burden of this journey. But there, to his great relief and my own, he had a vision in which a voice sang, 'And the house was filled with the odour of the ointment'. The song continued for several verses each ending with the same words, 'And the house was filled with the odour of the ointment'. It later became clear how wrong we were in our first interpretation of the significance of this. Another day when the abbot was resting a new song was put in his mouth, 'The just shall rejoice in the Lord', and he often lay awake thinking about it. At Poitiers, where we spent the night, he was walking alone with a candle when the candle was blown out, and the abbot of Charlieu saw him walking on without a light. Later he admitted that the candle was lighted again by a certain sound, and it was burning when he came to us.

Something which happened in Bordeaux deserves to be called a miracle. The stubborn clerks were persuaded to allow the introduction of canons regular into the cathedral, though they had resisted it to the point of being excommunicated for seven years. Because of this the archbishop had been exiled from his seat for five years, leaving the church empty, and they had resisted his return violently. The hatred of the people for the archbishop was so great that when we entered the town they reviled us all, because we were his supporters. But the living and potent word of God moved them more than those who knew the great complexity and sad history of the affair had dared to hope.

At the village of Bergerac a nobleman who was seriously ill came to him, and from that moment, as we learned later, he recovered. Another native of the place, poor and destitute now praises the name of the Lord: he had for long been so weakened by illness that he could not work, but after he had followed us for a few days and eaten bread blessed by the abbot he recovered his health and strength.

In Cahors one of the bishop's servants lost the sight of an eye after a blow on the head, and recovered it at a sign from the abbot. Another man there drank water which he had blessed, and it seemed to him as though a whole jar of water had been thrown over his head: from that moment he recovered from a fever which had troubled him for seven years.

How can I depict the enthusiasm of the people of Périgueux? They nearly smothered him, so that he had to leave the town surreptitiously. In Tolouse he was received at first devoutly enough; after a few days it was more than enough, and after a few more it was tremendous. There were only a few in the city who favoured the heresy, some of the weavers [*de textoribus*], whom they called *Ariani*. A great many of these supported the heresy in the city, including some of its most prominent citizens. Not long before our arrival they had persuaded one of the rich men of the city and his wife to go to a village which was full of heretics, leaving their property and their young son behind them, and the pleas of their neighbours could not persuade them to return. He was called Henry; they were called *Ariani*; and the people promised that nobody would give them any support thereafter unless they came forward for public debate. It would take a long time to recount the flight of Henry and the hiding places of the *Ariani*. The *Ariani* in the city fled when they heard of the portents and miracles that were taking place. Their supporters renounced them, and we believed that the city was wholly free of the infection of heresy. Some of the knights promised to drive them out and not to support them in future. To make sure that this would not be infringed by anybody who might be bribed by the heretics, judgement was pronounced that the heretics, their supporters, and anybody who gave them any help would not be eligible to give evidence, or seek redress in the courts, and nobody would have any dealings with them either socially or commercially. We set out in pursuit of Henry, but wherever we went he fled further.

The abbot spoke in the villages which he had led astray; his comrades willingly testified their faith in eternal life in the hearing of the people. Some of the knights we found obstinate, not, it seemed to us, through error, but through greed and evil will. They hated clerks and enjoyed Henry's jokes, and what he told them gave them a reason and an excuse for their malice. All of them however, now said that they would support him no longer, because he had fled from debate with the abbot. Judgement was pronounced against him and his patrons. It was made clear to everybody what a wicked life he had led, and how at the Council of Pisa he had renounced the heresies which he was now preaching, and had been handed over to the abbot, from whom he had received letters to enable him to become a monk at Clairvaux. We believed that with God's help his evil would soon be stopped. A land led astray by so many heretical teachings needed a great deal of preaching, but the abbot did not think that he could perform such a task, and was afraid that it would be a great burden to his brothers. This, I believe, was the mistake we made about the line of the chant that he had heard which I mentioned above.

Having received many letters from Clairvaux, the abbot is returning as quickly as he can, and we hope that you will see him soon after the octave of the Assumption [22 August]. If only we realized what a great, what an inestimable gift God has given us in our holy father, a faithful guardian, a powerful protector, a good shepherd, full of grace and strength before God and the ages! I have good reason to know how in humility he keeps his powers carefully hidden, for the sick are always cured after his departure, so that though they are cured nobody praises him. He has admitted that if necessary he would rather risk danger to himself than fail to provide for their salvation.

In the church of St Sernin in Toulouse, where we were staying, there was a canon regular named John who was very skilled in medicine. He had been ill in bed for seven months he told us, and since Easter he had wasted so much that he was expected to die at any time. His calves were so thin that they were no fatter than a boy's arms. The muscle of his right thigh in particular was so withered that he had not been able to bend his knee since Easter. The poor man lay half alive, always at the point of death, without the strength even to get up to go to the lavatory. Because of his smell and of his weakness he had been put out of the monastery and lodged in the town, because the canons could not abide his presence. He begged to be placed near the abbot, and six men carried him on a couch to the room next to that in which we were staying. The abbot visited him there, and he confessed his sins and begged for his recovery and health. The abbot blessed him and left the room, and I went with him. As he walked he thought aloud to himself, saying like a faithful servant, 'Lord they are seeking a sign, and we can make no progress without one. How long will you hide from them?' Immediately the clerk sprang up and ran after us, and we had hardly got back to our own room when we saw him following us, walking, as he said himself, not by his own strength but by divine grace. From there he went to church, giving thanks to God, and the brother sang a 'Te Deum' with him. Nobody who did not see it would credit the devotion with which he kissed the abbot's feet.

We were told of a boy seven years old languishing in the arms of his mother, who did not know what was wrong with him. When he came back after being blessed by the abbot he immediately vomited up a large stone, which many people saw, and recovered from that moment. In the same city he gave light by the sign of the cross to an old man who had lost the sight of one eye. He did the same for a boy who was blind in both eyes. There was a woman in the city who suddenly felt a pain in her head, and said that she would not eat until she came to the man of God. Her husband compelled her to eat, but she choked on the first piece of bread, and her constricted throat was entered by a demon. For three days she could not eat or drink anything, and then she was presented to the abbot, and received blessed bread and water from his hand. The abbot told her to pass the night in a chapel near us so that he could visit her secretly, without fuss. During the night she began to shout vehemently. Sometimes it was the woman talking, and sometimes the demon, sometimes her tongue moved to the right side of her mouth, and sometimes to the left, as the person who was talking changed. The demon said, in the hearing of all those who were standing around, that he would not leave her until the abbot came, until the little abbot came. Thus warned the abbot visited her in a dream, and left her in peace, whom he had found in such agony. Immediately afterwards he celebrated a mass, gave her holy communion, and sent her home safe.

He cured three people in Toulouse, whose hands were twisted with the fingers folded back and three more in the neighbourhood. A girl was brought to him while he was collecting an offering. He made a sign with his hand, took her fingers, and opened them quite easily. He did the same for two others, though with one of them, being embarrassed by the presence of the bishops, he opened the hands a little way, and then handed the man over to a Templar who was there to finish the job. He cured another case of this kind in a child at Damesières, in the presence of the bishop of Angoulême, who expressed astonishment that when the abbot made a sign with his hand and dismissed him he was cured as though at the striking of a note, and his fingers began to open. On the same occasion he made a deaf man hear and a dumb one speak. He cured a fifth cripple at the village of Verfeil, that seat of Satan, who was the son, unless I am mistaken, of one of the worst of the heretics. He performed a sixth cure at the village of St Paul. Some of the legate's servants would have been forced by serious illness to stay in this foreign land if he had not cured them with the divine medicine of blessed bread.

In the city of Albi he performed a miracle greater even than these, which are not to be despised. The people of this city, we had heard, were more contaminated with heresy than any others on our route. It was so bad that when the legate arrived, two days before us, they came out to meet him on donkeys, beating drums, and when the signal was given to call the people together for mass scarcely thirty came. Two days later the people welcomed the abbot with great joy, but he had heard so much of their wickedness that he was reluctant to accept their devotion. Next day, St Peter's, [1 August], so many people came to listen to the word of God that the great church would not hold them. The abbot addressed them thus:

'I have come to sow, but I find the field already sown with wicked seed. But you are a reasonable field: you are, after all, God's field. I will show you both seeds, and you can decide which to choose.'

He began with the sacrament of the altar, and carefully expounded each point that the heretic preached, and what the true faith said about it. Then he asked them which they would choose. The whole people began to execrate and decry the wickedness of the heretic, and joyfully to receive the word of God and the Catholic faith. 'Repent,' said the abbot. 'Each of you is contaminated. Return to the unity of the Church. So that we can know which of you has repented and received the word of life, raise your right hand to heaven as a sign of Catholic unity.' All raised their right hands in exultation, and so he brought his sermon to an end. And so too I end this letter. Farewell.

16 Henry: the debate with the monk William, 1133–5

This account is edited by R. Manselli, *Bulletino dell'Instituto storico Italiano* (1953), pp. 36–62. It is a complete edition of a Paris manuscript to which is added one section from another version of the debate preserved at Nice to which I have given the heading 'Prayers for the dead'.

R. Manselli held that the debate probably took place between the death of Peter de Bruys, (1132–3), and the Council of Pisa, and discussed the possibility that William was William of St Thierry, the friend of St Bernard and enthusiastic hunter of heresy, for which the evidence is circumstantial and inconclusive. The account is the fullest we have of the opinions of a popular heretic at such an early date, and while it is a pity that William is so much less concerned to report Henry's arguments than his own, in doing so he offers a typical example of the kind of response which the Church made to charges brought against it by such opponents. There is no indication to whom the letter is addressed. In order to avoid confusion, quotation marks signifying direct speech are omitted after the first three paragraphs. Unless otherwise indicated, William is speaking.

After I left your distinguished company I had a great argument with the heresiarch Henry. I have written a careful account of the dispute for you so that if this brute should chance to descend upon your region you will know that he has been convicted of heresy by many good reasons and arguments, and will be sure to keep him away from the doors of your Church.

I approached him with these words: 'I would like to know under whose obedience you preach, who has charged you with this mission, and what scriptures you have read, since you are propounding things which are so wicked and contrary to our faith.'

'If you ask about obedience,' he replied, 'I profess obedience to God, not man. If you ask me about my calling, I was sent by him who said, "Go, therefore, teach ye all nations." He charged me with my task who said, "Love thy neighbour as thyself." I accept the New Testament and my teaching is based upon it. If you bring arguments against me from Jerome or Augustine, or other doctors, I will grant them some force, but they are not necessary for salvation.'

Obedience To this I said: It astonishes me that you will not bow your presumptuous neck to the yoke of human obedience when the apostle said, 'Be ye subject therefore to every human creature for God's sake' and, 'Let every soul be subject to higher powers. For there is no power but from God', and again, 'Obey your prelates and be subject to them.' In the book of Kings when Saul kept the best from the conquered city for sacrifice the prophet Samuel said to him, 'Why did you not obey me and spare the city? Know that obedience is better than sacrifices. It is like the sin of witchcraft to rebel:

and like the crime of idolatry to refuse to obey.' Jesus Christ, whose teaching
you pretend to follow, clearly showed us the virtue of obedience when he
said, 'I come not to do my own will, but the will of him that sent me', and
of him you must admit that he obeyed his father even to the point of death.
All this confounds your pride in preaching without being under obedience
to a bishop, and quibbling that bishops ought not to be obeyed because they
are men. As for the text which you so impertinently abuse, that it is better to
obey God rather than men, nothing in the sentence constitutes in any way a
denial of all obedience. It uses the adverb *rather* comparatively, not exclusively.

Callings I will take your views on callings and on being charged with duties
separately. Whether you seek among the greatest or the humblest preachers
you will find none who preaches without being called and chosen for his
office. God the Father sent his Son. The Son, Jesus Christ, sent his apostles
according to the texts 'As the Father hath sent me, I also send you', and 'Behold
I send you. . . . And he sent them two and two before his face.' The apostles
in their turn chose others and sent them. So, as I have said, you will find
nobody who has assumed the office without a calling and ordination. St Paul
preached the faith according to the order, 'How shall they believe in him of
whom they have not heard? And how shall they preach unless they be sent?'
The Lord himself says in the Gospel, 'All others, as many as have come, were
thieves and robbers.' He said not, 'that have come', and thus showed that no
one should be received unless he has been sent, so it is absurd to argue that
you have been called or chosen by the words, 'Go, teach', and 'Love thy
neighbour as thyself.' Was that a general command or an individual one?
If it was general it applies to everybody. If it applies to everybody a raving
old man or wretched peasant, even the deaf and the dumb, would be compelled by this order to preach. And if that is the case St Paul was wasting his
time when he enumerated the divisions of grace of the Holy Spirit and need
not have bothered to say, 'Ascending on high, he led captivity captive; he
gave gifts to men. And when he ascended above all the heavens he gave some
apostles, and some prophets, and other some evangelists, and other some
pastors and doctors, for the work of the ministry, for the edifying of the body
of Christ.'

Let me show the absurdity of your argument again. Ought one to preach
to man or to non-man? It would be ridiculous to preach to non-man. Yet
since it is said, 'Preach the Gospel to every creature' you cannot object that
only man is specified by name. All the same it remains true that one ought to
preach only to men. If, therefore, all men were preachers, according to your
two clumsily chosen precepts, it is obvious what inconveniences would follow.
What about the faithful and prudent servant whom the Lord has placed at the
head of his family to give them food in this world? When he has made a
profit on his talent he will carry the interest on his money back to the Lord.

The writings of Jerome, Augustine and others When you say that the writings of Jerome, Augustine and others do not lead us to salvation I wonder in what sense you mean it. If you mean by 'they do not lead to salvation' that they do not confer salvation you are right. In that sense not even the words of the Gospels lead to salvation, which is conferred only by divine grace. But if you mean that they do not lead to salvation in the sense that they do not teach us how to attain salvation you plainly lie, because they do. If therefore you refuse to listen to them you cut yourself off from the unity of the Church, and show that you are a schismatic. At the approach of the Lord you will not join the crowd of the faithful in strewing branches from the trees, not understand with Solomon 'the nails deeply fastened in' [i.e. the words of the wise, Ecclesiastes 12. 11]. You will do great injury to the Church in thus condemning so arrogantly her doctors and prelates. But since it is evident that you are sunk in your own ideas and your foolish heart is in darkness we will turn now to the wicked propositions which you have stated.

Children who die before maturity Your argument that children who die before they reach the age of discretion will be saved denies original sin, and so falls into the Pelagian heresy. You say, 'It is wicked to condemn a man for the sins of others, according to the texts, "The soul that sinneth, the same shall die: the son shall not bear the iniquity of the father", and "every one shall bear his own burden."' These words are true, but they do not support the Pelagian heresy, for they refer to *actual* sin, not to *original* sin. If you would deny original sin, listen to St Paul: 'Wherefore as by one man sin entered into this world and by sin death; and so death passed upon all men, in whom all have sinned.' Through Adam's transgression everything has been weakened and corrupted as the penalty of his sin. We come from the loins of Adam, and little particles of him have flowed into us from him. This flow of corruption is called sin, because it is the punishment for the original sin. It is not surprising that sin is borne down to the whole mass of people from its beginning in the loins of Adam: we may observe the same phenomenon in both animate and inanimate things by rational experience, as when a whole flock in a field is infected with mange by one animal, or all the branches and parts of a tree are infected by one diseased root, so that the tree dies, or one infected grape passes its discolouring to another.

The antidotes of original sin are clear in natural law, and in both the old and the new law. We know that in natural law it is gifts and offerings, for it is said, 'The Lord had respect to Abel, and to his offerings', and in the old and the new law respectively it is circumcision and baptism. Hence it is clear that there is original sin in children. If you argue that children have no original sin, that they have not sinned in Adam, you must show authority and reason for the view that if they die without baptism they can be saved without the death of Christ. The apostle says, 'All we who are baptized in Christ Jesus are baptized in his death.' By denying baptism you deny the necessity of benefiting from the death of Christ, and show yourself clearly a Pelagian heretic.

On the other hand if you argue that children have inherited original sin from Adam, which is true, but that they can be saved without the purification of baptism, you incur the error of Vincentius Victor, whom Augustine condemned with irrefutable arguments. I challenge you to answer me by bringing forward any principle by which you can defend your heresy. Do children die of their own free will or from necessity? If they die of their own free will they must have the power of giving and taking life, which only Christ has. If they die of necessity it must be through either actual sin or original sin. It cannot be through actual sin, because actually they have not sinned, since they have not attained the age of reason. Therefore it follows that they are held by original sin. If they have not sinned in Adam sin has not entered them through Adam, and therefore neither has death through sin. Therefore, if they die because of original sin it is proved that they have original sin: otherwise they would die for no reason, for death is the punishment of sin. If they incur original sin when they are born, or rather when they are conceived, how can they lose their original sin, which is washed away in baptism, without being baptized? If, or rather because, you cannot answer that you admit the necessity of baptism. As Augustine says, 'If children are not baptized, although they are held in lesser sin, whoever claims that without baptism they can die unpunished, both misleads and is misled.' Again, let me convince you from the clear authority of the Gospels. When children are born they must be born again, for the Lord says, 'Ye must be born again', and in the same place that those who are not baptized cannot be born again 'Unless a man be born again of water and the Holy Ghost, he cannot enter into the kingdom of God.' If this perilous fate, inherited from Adam by carnal generation, is to be avoided, there must be regeneration of the spirit through Christ; otherwise, as I have said, original sin will still be present.

To this Henry replied: If, as you say, original sin is washed away in baptism, and if death is a punishment for original sin, why do the baptized die? When the Gospel says, 'He that believeth and is baptized shall be saved; but he that believeth not shall be condemned', how can you maintain that baptism is possible without faith? He who has not yet attained a state of being able to believe or not to believe cannot believe. For the view that some may be saved without being baptized I can cite these authorities: 'Suffer the little children to come unto me, for of such is the kingdom of God'; and, on the occasion when Jesus called to a child and set him in the midst of them, he said, 'Unless you be converted and become as little children, you shall not enter into the kingdom of heaven.' By his authority, therefore, you should admit that those children, if they died without baptism, were to be saved. And at that time children were not baptized.'

I answered him thus: Truly your wickedness in interpreting holy writ so perversely will find you out. Since 'There must be heresies in the Church so that when they are proven they may be made manifest', I commit you to that judgement in which impiety is destroyed. Any faithful Catholic would find it easy to refute the authorities which by misinterpretation you have adduced for your heresy. When the Gospel says, 'He that believeth and is baptized shall be saved' etc. it is the truth, but it is impossible to be baptized or to please God without faith. Everything which does not spring from faith is sin. Children are baptized in the faith of those who baptize them, in the faith of their parents, in the faith of the whole Church. If you sincerely desire to understand you will find many authorities in the Gospels for the proposition that it is possible to be saved in the faith of others. You will dispute this no longer when you have listened to Luke's words on how, when the men who were carrying the paralytic could not make their way through a large crowd, 'they let him down through the tiles, and when he saw their faith' (note that the Evangelist says *their*, not *his*) 'he said: Man, thy sins are forgiven thee.' Thus the paralytic was freed not only from his affliction but from his sins, not by his own faith, but by that of those who carried him. In the same way the faith of parents can be handed down to their children, as in the case of the woman of Canae who showed by her faith that her child deserved to be cured. So the faith of the baptizers and of the whole Church may avail, as the Gospel shows.

I can also prove quite easily that the point which you make about the children in support of your heresy is not valid. You have interpreted this story, which Jesus Christ used to advocate humility, to support your madness. Obviously you contradict yourself, since you try to reduce all those who have been baptized to the status of those who have not been baptized. For if the children were unbaptized—which you assert without any authority—it would have been impossible to declare that they could enter the kingdom of Heaven in that condition. Your reasoning excludes all the baptized from the kingdom of heaven; it excludes the apostles and martyrs, and everybody else who has been baptized. There is no need to demonstrate the absurdity of that.

Therefore stop worrying about how and why children bear original sin. If you do not understand this believe it so that you may understand, [*crede ut intelligas*] so that you are not misled by the insoluble questions about the incarnation of the soul which Augustine raises in his *Expositio genesi ad litteram*, and the treatise which he wrote for Jerome *De anima humana*. There he discusses whether souls, being born individually, individually come into being anew, because, as he says, the question ought to be asked in case anyone should think that he denies that the souls of children need to be set free. Don't stand around asking how a man fell into a pit unless you know some means of getting him out of it again. Don't ask by what justice or for what reason a man falls into a pit of sin at his incarnation when many arguments of the Gospels, the apostles, and the saints confirm that he can get out of it again by the regeneration of water and the Holy Spirit.

As for your question why death remains in the baptized after sin has been forgiven, though death is the punishment for sin, and why a Christian is not born of a Christian, I can only say that I understand the reason given by many authorities to be that one should not persist with this question, since the contrary does not seem true to men of good understanding. It is not inconsistent to forgive sin while retaining the punishment for it. Death remains in the baptized lest men should be baptized for no other reason than to attain the felicity of immortality, if that were given in baptism. If immortality followed from baptism people would rush to be baptized for that alone, because they saw Christians enriched with the blessing of immortality, and not to obtain the other Christian felicities, but in order to be able not to die. Christ could have done this for the faithful, so that they need not experience the death of their bodies, but if he had the happiness of the flesh would have been increased, and the fortitude of the faith correspondingly diminished. Nobody living this life, which will become a blessed one after death, could find grace through Christ's strength while despising his death. On this point master Anselm, in his *Cur Deus Homo*, uses the appropriate example of the son who has injured his father, when the father forgives the sin, but does not remit the punishment. Similarly a Christian is not born of a Christian for this reason, that it is not birth, but rebirth that makes a Christian. Men are cleansed of their sins not by being born, but by being born again. Hence whoever is born of purified men is born again, and by that is purified himself. In this way the faithful remove from their children and parents from their sons, infidelity which they do not have themselves, as though it were chaff from corn, or the circumcision of the foreskin. And now we have talked enough about this problem to satisfy a sensible man.

There ought to be no baptism with oil and chrism   Now let us move to another problem. You say, 'the Gospel does not require baptism to be with oil and chrism.' Why do you babble so foolishly, as though every institution which serves the Christian religion must be found in the Gospels, and the apostles and their successors had not initiated many things which are not found in the Gospels? Jesus said, 'I have yet many things to say to you: but you cannot hear them now. But when he, the spirit of truth, is come, he will teach you all truth.' These words give us to understand that the Holy Spirit, who made things clear to them so that they could understand the scriptures and teach the whole truth, suggested many things to them which he desired to have observed and believed in the Church. So why say that this or that 'is not a precept of the Gospel'? I don't know what you mean by precept. Properly speaking precepts are things without whose observance nobody can be saved, as for instance, certain orders and charges about marriage, or prohibitions, as of killing. Therefore if you say, 'Because it is not a precept of the Gospels baptism is possible without oil and chrism' you speak the truth, but do not thereby dispense with the anointing with oil and chrism. It is wicked to undermine what is sanctioned by the holy fathers for the honour and edification of the Church.

If you say that what is not a precept of the Gospels is not good or should not be done, you obviously lie: the authority of both Old and New Testaments shows that it is good, and should be done. Paul says, 'Is any man sick among you? Let him bring in the priests of the Church and let them pray over him, anointing him with oil in the name of the Lord.' In the Old Testament kings and priests are anointed with chrism, and we are anointed today to show ourselves 'a chosen generation, a kingly priesthood', according to the text 'and hast made us to our God a kingdom and priests.' When the patriarch Jacob set up a stone as a title he poured oil over it. From all this it is clear that the anointing with oil and chrism is a sign and symbol of invisible anointing which must be given in baptism by the Holy Spirit, even though it is not mentioned in the Gospels. If it were to be held that there ought to be no baptism because it is not to be found in the Gospel, then by the same argument there should be no marriage, because that is not mentioned in the Gospel either. There is no command to marry, only permission. The apostle says, 'It is good for a man not to touch a woman. But for fear of fornication, let every man have his own wife.' Nor could it be argued that unction becomes visible in baptism, because we read that the Holy Spirit has been given in visible form. We read of our Saviour himself that the Holy Spirit descended on him in corporal form, and nobody doubts that it was given to the apostles in tongues of fire, or to Moses at the baptism of the Israelites in the form of a cloud. As the apostle says, 'I would not have you ignorant, brethren, that our fathers were all under the cloud. And all in Moses were baptized, in the cloud and in the sea.' This and other sacraments are all concealed under a symbol and form, and called sacraments because they are signs of sacred things.

The body of Christ is not conferred by unworthy ministers Now we reach your third proposition, that 'the body of Christ is not conferred by unworthy ministers.' In this I see your impiety clearly. Under this pretext you are trying to undermine and drive from the Church the institution of the sacrament which strengthens man's body and sustains his spirit. When you say, 'Mass may be sung, and the body of Christ may be consecrated, if he who does it is found to be worthy', you postulate a chimera, a man who will never be found, for there is nobody who is without sin, not even a child of one day old. For all have sinned, and do need the glory of God. You seek the impossible; you are trying to pull down the pillar of our faith, and like the Arians and other heretics, you do not hesitate to tear the garment of Christ.

Listen to the words of authority on your heresy:

No stain of any kind can pollute the divine sacraments which cleanse all cognitive beings, just as the rays of the sun cannot be contaminated by drains and sewers. It should be realised that when evil men administer the good they hurt only themselves, just as a lighted torch may show up a flaw in the man who holds it, and yet cast light for others. Therefore receive the mysteries of Jesus Christ, which cleanse in the faith of Christ, from any priest with confidence. The faith is of the receiver, not the giver, for the holy scriptures say that baptism is perfect in every soul, and the body of Christ perfect in every priest [Nicholas I]. In the Holy Catholic Church the service of the body of Christ is no better from a good priest and no worse from a bad priest, because it is conferred not by the merit of the consecrator, but by the word of the Creator and the power of the Holy Spirit [Paschasius Radbert].

Just as the material of the sacraments has three parts, so the way in which it ought to be consecrated depends on three things: on the rank of priest, in which you are in error; on the place, for there can be no true sacrifice outside a Catholic Church, though you claim that there can be when you preach in the fields and meadows; and on the word of the Holy Spirit, in whose virtue the materials of bread and wine are turned into the body and blood of Christ, which according to you cannot be done by an unworthy minister. As I have said, there are three ways of taking it, because the material of the eucharist is either sacramental, or real, or both. It is merely sacramental to the wicked, for even if they receive it as a visible part of the body of Christ the bread cannot be united with heaven, because they have no true faith or love. It is real only to the good, because even if they do not consume the visible flesh of Christ in the sacrament they lead the bread to heaven with their faith and love, and are there joined with it. The eucharist therefore is death to some who cannot touch the bread of life, and life to others whom it makes one with the word of life. In the spiritual feast these things need to be considered: faith, thought, understanding, love, emulation and cohesion. A mouthful of bread is a portion of faith, and thought follows it to seek the truth and ponder it. Then understanding gives birth to a mental picture, the picture nourishes love, and love leads to emulation. Emulation produces cohesion, when the spirit which aspires to God becomes one with him, and by this meal the spirit of man is cleansed and strengthened. Because you neither understand nor believe all this you will be removed from this communion.

That the consent of the persons involved alone makes a marriage [It should be remembered throughout this discussion that the dissolution of a marriage did not permit the remarriage of either party. On marriage at this time see Fliche and Martin, 8, pp. 464-7.]
Let us turn now, if you can recall it, to your error on the sacrament of marriage. You say, 'the consent of the person involved alone makes a marriage, without any ceremony, and a marriage thus contracted cannot be dissolved by

the Church for any reason except adultery.' In this you err grossly. You fail to understand that there are three institutions of marriage, three causes, and three benefits, and corresponding to these, three things stand in the way of marriage, three things make it, and three can dissolve it, and each of these follows from the others.

The first institution was created in paradise before the fall by the authority of Adam and the Lord, in the words, 'a man shall cleave to his wife.' The second institution was by the precept of the apostle when he said, 'for fear of fornication let every man have his own wife.' The third institution is that of the modern fathers, which says that marriage is consecrated, unless it is between relatives. These institutions differ not in the nature of marriage, but according to different times and human conditions. The first reason for marriage is the propagation of children, the second the avoidance of fornication, and the third love. It confers three benefits: faith, the hope of offspring, and that it is a sacrament. Three things pertain to this: modesty, fruitfulness, and the indissoluble union of Christ and the Church. Three things prevent the contracting of the sacrament: vows, holy orders, and consanguinity. Three things make it: the manifest consent of legal parties, the love of children, and the intention of each to keep faith with the other until death. Augustine says, 'If any of these things is lacking I do not see how we can call them to their wedding.' Three things may dissolve the marriage: honest agreement, fornication, or impotence. These proceed from three things: illness, defect, or weakness of the limbs. Therefore it is not the contract between the parties which makes the marriage, as you contend so foolishly, but a clear agreement involving the direction of each life and the love of persons between whom it is legitimate, directed towards procreation. Hence the law says, 'Marriage is the joining of a man and a woman who may lawfully do so, involving the habits of each life, a perpetual interlocking of divine and human law.' Such a contract may not be dissolved, as I have said, except because of either adultery or impotence.

Priests of the present day have not the power of binding and loosing Since you don't know what makes, impedes or dissolves a marriage, I will give up arguing about it with you, and deal with the priests and bishops against whom you rant. You claim that 'modern priests have not the power of binding and loosing, because they have been deprived of it by their sins.' How can you rave so insanely? How can you talk of modern priests as though priests have had different powers at different times? Did they not sin before as they do now? Priests differ from bishops only in that bishops have the additional powers of ordaining clerks, dedicating churches, consecrating chrism, and laying-on hands. That is for one reason only, that if all priests were given such power it might make them insolent, dissolve the bonds of obedience, and give rise to scandal. All priests, of both higher and lower orders, act in the place of Jesus Christ and of the bishop when they call the erring to repentence, and cure them with the medicine of prayer. 'God indeed was in Christ, reconciling the world to himself, and he hath placed in us the word of reconciliation.'

You claim that sinners cannot reconcile the world, and cannot bind and loose. Listen to what the authorities have to say to you, learn how and when the power of binding and loosing was given to priests, and that they do not lose it by sinning. Jesus Christ, true man and true God, had particularly and uniquely among men the power of binding and loosing. He justified the impious, gave life to the dead, and had the power to send body and soul into Gehenna. Because he is overhead, the overlooker [*episcopus*] of our souls, he did not wish to leave us orphans, and made Peter and the other disciples his vicars, committing to them the keys of the kingdom of heaven. For when Peter said, 'Thou art Christ, the Son of the living God,' he replied, 'Thou art Peter, and upon this rock I will build my church. And whatsoever thou shalt bind upon earth, it shall be bound also in heaven: and whatsoever thou shalt loose upon earth, it shall be loosed also in heaven.' And, in case you should think that this was given to Peter alone, St Matthew says in another place, 'Amen I say unto you, whatsoever you shall bind upon earth shall be bound also in heaven: and whatsoever you shall loose upon earth shall be loosed also in heaven.' And after Christ rose from the dead he said, 'As the Father hath sent me, I also send you.' And when he said this he breathed on them and said to them, 'Receive up the Holy Ghost. Whose sins you shall forgive, they are forgiven them: and whose sins you shall retain, they are retained.'

The disciples, since they could not live until the end of time, received others whom they charged with their powers and their mission. When the Apostle Peter felt the approach of death he selected Clement as his successor, and told him, 'I have called you alone to preach the word of the Lord, through which men may reach salvation. Your words will be received with reverence, because they will know that you have been designated a preacher of the truth. And whoever you bind on earth will be bound in heaven.' Admit, therefore, that the authority of Peter—unless you despise even that—was given not only to the apostles, but also to their bishops, priests and vicar. Christ made it plain that they had this power when he raised Lazarus from the dead and left his loosing to the apostles for it was a greater thing to release him from the bandages in which he was bound than to raise him from the dead. St Paul used this power against the Corinthian who had defiled his father's bed when he said, 'I, indeed, absent in body but present in spirit, have already judged . . . to deliver such a one to Satan.' He had the power of binding over a fornicator. He had the power of loosing when he wrote, 'To whom you have pardoned anything, I also. For, what I have pardoned, if I have pardoned any thing, for your sakes have I done it in the person of Christ.'

You will also find in many authorities that this power is not lost through sin, unless a man is deprived of his orders by judicial procedure. Peter, when he was head of the Church, sinned by denying his lord and master in the Passion,

C

and abandoned him at the voice of a single maid-servant. Judas sinned when he was one thief among twelve men, a traitor who conspired against his master. Yet neither of them lost their apostolic dignity by these sins.

Here Henry interrupted: Peter repented and made expiation with his tears. Judas, because he sinned secretly, was forgiven, and not deprived of his power.

I replied: In the same way I judge you out of your own mouth. If our priests sin secretly and repent, if they are not accused and deposed, as I have said by a proper judgement, they must be forgiven, and not deprived of the powers that have been given to them. Therefore give up your raging against priests and show reverence towards them, for as the scriptures say, they are worthy of a double dignity. Accept too that those who are called greater priests must receive greater reverence. In many places in the Gospels—or do you deny the Gospels?—Jesus Christ commanded us to honour them. He said of them, 'He that heareth you heareth me: and he that despiseth you despiseth me', and we are told in the psalms, 'Touch ye not my anointed, and do no evil to my prophets.'

The Gospels do not require us to go to a priest for penance Let us turn your chapter about penance. You say, 'The Gospels do not require us to go to a priest for penance, because the Apostle James says, "Confess therefore your sins one to another." ' He says not 'Confess to priests', but 'Confess one to another.' You lie; this is proved by the authority of the Gospels, and confession to priests is therefore necessary. If our sins make us sons of wrath, 'vessels fitted for destruction', penitence must make us sons of reconciliation, and vessels fit for glory. There cannot be reconciliation except through a mediator. We know the priest as a mediator who acts in place of Christ, who was uniquely and especially the mediator between God and man. Therefore we must confess to priests.

If we confess our sins to peasants and illiterates we disobey the apostle who says, 'If therefore you have judgements of things pertaining to this world, set them to judge who are the most despised in the Church', and goes on to say, 'Is it so that there is not among you any one wise man that is able to judge between his brethren? Know you not that we shall judge angels? How much more things of this world?' These words show that if judgement of secular affairs should be kept from idiots and illiterates, it is far more important that they should not have spiritual judgement over souls, especially when this involves fixing a penalty for a particular sin; otherwise I may be judged by a man who is not capable of it, when he ought to be thoroughly versed in holy knowledge, and the whole discipline of the Church. As Persius says, 'Public law and human nature alike maintain the rule that ignorance of the law debars its enforcement. It is against reason and instinct to allow a man to do what he nullifies by doing it.'

Your example from James has no force, and indeed, if you consider its context, tells against you. When the apostle commands the priests of the Church to pray over the sick and anoint them with oil he adds, 'and the prayer of faith shall save the sick man.' How that is to be done is shown in the next verse, 'Confess your sins one to another.' In other words according to the apostle the confession is to be made to the priest who is saying the prayers. Remember also the words of Christ to the cured leper, 'Go, shew thyself to the priest and offer for thy cleansing according as Moses commanded.' And in the book of Leviticus the law about leprosy is described like this, 'If a man shall have in his head or in his beard a bald patch which remains bald, or a dark patch or sore on his skin and flesh, he shall be shown to the priest, and according to his judgement shut up for seven days, and then adjudged either clean or unclean.' Now tell me, if you can, whether Christ thought that he was sending a cured or an uncured leper to the priest? One cannot say that he thought he was uncured, when he knew that he was cured. But if he knew that the leper was cured, and still sent him to the priest, why do you say that the Gospels do not tell us to go to a priest for penance? For we should understand that his leprosy was nothing but the spots of various sins. Therefore the leper was ordered to go to the priest because it was necessary for him to confess his sins. Perhaps you will argue that it was Christ who cleansed his leprosy, not the priest. That is true; nevertheless he ordered him to show himself to the priest.

You too are a leper, scarred by heresy, excluded from communion by the judgement of the priest, according to the law, bare-headed, with ragged clothing, your body covered by an infected and filthy garment; it befits you to shout unceasingly that you are a leper, a heretic and unclean, and must live alone, outside the camp, that is to say outside the Church. However, that is enough about your heresy; let us continue with our business.

Bishops and priests ought not to have money or benefices You say, 'Bishops and priests ought not to have money or benefices', which confirms your rage against priests. Since you set your mouth against the heavens like this, tell me what you mean by 'they ought not to have benefices.' If you mean that they are not obliged to, that there is no command that they should have them, you are unquestionably right. If, on the other hand, you mean that they should not have them, in the sense that it is not permitted to them, that they are damned if they have them, the Gospels and many other authorities prove you wrong. The Gospel says of Judas that 'he was a thief, and having a purse, carried the things that were put therein', and therefore there was something in the purse. Now if he had a purse, and indeed since he had it, he had it either legitimately or illegitimately. If he had it legitimately it was proper that he should have it; if illegitimately, why was it not thrown away? If it was not, it follows that since it was permitted to him, as a disciple and companion of our Lord, it must also be permitted to our priests. The Gospel also tells you how Joseph of

Arimathea, a rich and noble disciple of Jesus, and Nicodemus, went to the tomb of Christ by night, and bought for it 'a mixture of myrrh and aloes, about an hundred pound weight'. They could not have bought that if they had no possessions. In the Acts, 'As many as were owners of lands or houses sold them, and brought the price of the things they sold. And laid it down before the feet of the apostles.' Therefore the apostles and their companions had money. The Gospel shows clearly that the disciples had money when it speaks of Jesus, tired from the journey, sitting by a well and talking to a Samaritan woman while 'his disciples were gone into the city to buy meats.' Could they have done so without money?

When Paul, by whose authority bishops are ordained, wrote to Timothy about bishops he said, 'If a man desire the office of a bishop he desireth a good work', and commended hospitality to them among other virtues. If one ought to be hospitable, one must be permitted to have a place to put a guest, and the means of looking after him. Can you define, by reason and authority, the limits of what and how much a bishop should be allowed for this purpose? If you can't you must admit that bishops are permitted to have many honours and a lot of money, and indeed that they need them. The sin of avarice is committed not in possessing, but in wanting to possess. As David says, 'If riches abound, set not your heart upon them', and the apostle, 'as having nothing and possessing all things'. I think that is a sufficient reply to your pernicious teaching on this point.

The ring, mitre and pastoral staff I do not wish to discuss the appurtenances of priests with you, or the pastoral ring and staff, all of which are sanctioned by authority for the sanctification and regulation of Christian life, or the significance of the array of vestments, the flashing jewels and glittering gold, or what their origins were. There is no need to justify them and I do not want to argue about these things with you, because there is no doubt that they add to the honour, status and righteousness of the Church. It is said of them, 'The queen stood on thy right hand in gilded clothing; surrounded with variety.' You, since you are not of the Church and do not love the Church, cannot say with the psalmist, 'I have loved, O Lord, the beauty of thy house.' Give up your perverse discontent.

Churches should not be made of stone or wood In your first chapter you say that churches should not be made of either wood or stone. I would like to know whether you will allow them to be made of something else, or of nothing. If you say nothing you contradict the Gospel. When Christ ejected the traders and merchants from the temple he said, 'My house shall be called the house of prayer', and when he said house he meant church, which is nothing but his house. If there are to be churches you must concede that they have to be made of stone or wood or some other materials. We also read that

Solomon built a temple for the Lord, and that the apostles built churches and basilicas.

You are trying to subvert and disturb the house of God, and the beauty, condition and laws of the Church. Let those who disturb us be confounded. 'He shall bear the burden, whosoever he be.' Your preaching crawls furtively, like a crab. Though you please me greatly be cursed, for you know not the law. The hidden waters are sweeter, and the hidden bread softer, 'the lips of a harlot—that is a heretic—are like a honeycomb dropping, and her throat is smoother than oil. But her end is bitter as wormwood, and sharp as a two-edged sword.' Foul scorpion, minister of Antichrist, in you 'the mystery of iniquity already worketh; only that he who now holdeth do hold, until he be taken out of the way.' Since, 'they also who are approved will be made manifest among you', I flee from your vile doctrines, and leave you to the judgement of him 'in whose spirit the wicked one shall be killed.'

Prayers for the dead Your point, 'that no good can be done to the dead, for they are all either damned or saved as soon as they die', is clearly heretical. On this Christ said, 'whosoever shall sin against the Father and the Son it shall be forgiven him: but he that shall sin against the Holy Ghost, it shall not be forgiven him, neither in this world, nor in the world to come.' Tell me if you can why Jesus Christ, who did not waste words, made this distinction, that they would not be forgiven either in this world or in the world to come? If you cannot the Catholic Church will teach you, even if you are unwilling to learn. Certain sins are cancelled out in the next world by the gifts of friends and the prayers of the faithful, as well as by the fires of purgatory. The apostle puts it clearly when he says, 'For other foundation no man can lay but that which is laid, which is Christ Jesus. Now, if any man build upon this foundation, gold, silver, precious stones, wood, hay, stubble: every man's work shall be manifest. For the day of the Lord shall declare it, because it shall be revealed in fire. And the fire shall try every man's work, of what sort it is. If any man's work abide, which he hath built thereupon, he shall receive a reward. If any man's work burn, he shall suffer loss: but he himself shall be saved, yet so as by fire.' The fire of the Last Judgement lasts until those who are to be saved have been purged. Faith, and the authority of the holy father, and of all who have lived before us in the Church of God, alike confirm that alms, and prayers, and sacraments of the body of the Lord benefit the souls of the dead by truly confessing in this world the wicked condition in which they left it. The true and authentic history of the Maccabeans confirms that the ancients believed the same thing before the incarnation of Christ. It tells how the great Juda, who fought to death for his faith, collected a large quantity of money and sent it to Jerusalem to be offered for the sins of the dead, who at that time benefited as much by the sacrament of circumcision as they do now from the regeneration of baptism. If you think carefully and reverently about the resurrection you will see that it is neither vain nor superfluous to pray for the release of the dead from their sins. Augustine believed this, and defended it in the book which he dedicated to Bishop Paulinus. On the question of whether it was of benefit to those buried in the basilicas he said, 'what is offered for the dead by their faithful friends and relations benefits those among them who showed when they were alive that they would deserve the benefits when they were dead'; and elsewhere, 'We do not believe that our care for the dead will avail, unless we express it solemnly with masses, or prayers, or alms'; and, in his sermon at St Peter's, 'I would show how you can purge the souls of the dead. Pray daily for your dear ones.'

See then how many great authorities protest against your impiety. The Bible says, 'In the mouth of two or three witnesses every word shall stand.' Are you alone to be believed in preference to Christ, the apostle Paul, Judas Maccabaeus, Augustine, and the many others whose authority I have shown against you?

17 Peter de Bruys: the teachings of the Petrobrusians

Peter the Venerable's *Tractatus contra Petrobrusianos* (ed. James Fearns, *Corpus Christianorum, Continuatio Mediaevalis* X, (1968); also *PL* 189. col. 719–850), which is our only substantial source of information on Peter de Bruys and his followers, is too long to be included in full, but the prefatory letter (*ibid.*, pp. 3–6) sets out most of what we know of the teachings of the Petrobrusians. Its date has often been disputed, the most important question being whether it was written before or after the Council of Pisa in 1135. Giles Constable, *The Letters of Peter the Venerable*, II, 285–8, gives full references and advances a strong case for the date c. 1139–40; the same view is taken by Dr Fearns, 'Peter von Bruis', *Archiv fur Kulturgeschichte* XLVIII, 1968, which with R. Manselli *Studi sulle eresie del secolo xii* is the fullest discussion of the Petrobrusians. Despite the evident similarity of their teaching Manselli's conclusion that Peter the Venerable exaggerates the closeness of any relationship between Peter and Henry of Lausanne is now generally accepted. This point must qualify the very interesting argument of Marcia L. Colish, 'Peter of Bruys, Henry of Lausanne, and the facade of St Gilles', *Traditio* 28 (1972), 451–60.

To the lords archbishop of Arles and Embrun, and the lords bishop of Die and Gap, Brother Peter, abbot of Cluny.

Recently I wrote a letter to you which argued against the heresies of Peter de Bruys, but I have not sent it until now because important business has prevented my mind from composing, and my pen from writing. I send it to your lordships now so that you can pass it on to the heretics against whom it was written, and also to Catholics to whom it might be of some use. I send it to you because this stupid and sacrilegious heresy has killed many souls and infected more in and around your diocese. With your active help the grace of God will remove it little by little from your regions. It has moved, or so I hear, into places close to you: you have chased it from Provence and it now makes ready its snares in Gascony and that neighbourhood. Sometimes hiding in fear, sometimes gathering courage to come forward, it deceives and corrupts whom it can, passing its deadly poison hither and thither. The Church of God looks to you, as strong columns on whom she leans, both because of your office and because you have expert knowledge of this area—she looks to you, I repeat, to root out this heresy from the places where it rejoices to have found concealment, both by preaching and, if neessary, by force of arms with the help of the laity. But since conversion is better than extermination Christian charity should be extended to them. They should be offered both authority and reason, and compelled to alter their views by authority if they are Christians, and by reason if they are men. If they care to heed it, this letter which I have written to you against their errors may be of some value to them. If they read it carefully they may be able to recover their senses, which they have lost so completely, unless they want to be perverse and obstinate. If the heretics are beyond sense, and prefer folly to wisdom, damnation to salvation, and death to life, the letter may bring comfort to the secret thoughts of some Catholics, by clearing from their minds lapses of faith unknown to men, or arming them against those whose tongues, as the psalmist has it, are a sharp sword. This last point, indeed, is my chief reason for writing, for even if my work cannot move the heretics it may serve some other purpose for the Church of God. As you know it has been the practice of the Church in the past not to pass over in silence the many different heresies which have sought to disturb its faith so often, but to purge the blasphemies of all heretics by reason and sound authority, for its own protection and the perpetual instruction of us all. Though I am one of the least of the body of Christ and of the members of his Church, I have written this in the belief that it may help the heretics, if that is possible, and put Catholics into whose hands it falls on their guard against this wicked teaching and others like it.

Five of the seeds of heretical dogma which Peter de Bruys sowed and nurtured for nearly twenty years have produced especially poisonous crops. I have particularly concentrated on them so that both word and spirit can seize firmly upon the points where there is greatest injury to the faith, and show their danger the better. Since this is a long work, and you will be too preoccupied with the business of the Church to be able to read it for long at a time, I shall explain briefly what it discusses, and show which errors the arguments of my long letter are directed against.

The first proposition of the heretics is that children who have not reached the age of understanding cannot be saved by Christian baptism, and that the faith of others is of no value to them because they cannot use it. This is because according to them, one is saved in baptism only by one's own faith, and not anybody else's, because the Lord said, 'He that believeth and is baptized shall be saved, but he that believeth not shall be condemned.'

Their second tenet is that there should be no churches or temples in any kind of building, and that those which already exist should be pulled down. Christians do not need holy places in which to pray, because when God is called he hears, whether in a tavern or a church, in the street or in a temple, before an altar or in a stable, and he listens to those who deserve it.

Thirdly, they hold that holy crosses should be broken and burnt, because the instrument on which Christ was so horribly tortured and so cruelly killed is not worthy of adoration, veneration, or any kind of supplication. In revenge for his torment and death it ought to be dishonoured and insulted, hacked by swords and burnt by fire.

Fourthly, they deny the truth that the body and blood of Christ is offered daily and continuously in church through the sacrament, which they say is nothing at all, and should not be offered to God.

Fifthly, they deride offerings by the faithful of sacrifices, prayers, alms, and other things for the dead, and say that nothing can help the dead in any way.

As far as God has given me power I have answered these five propositions in my letter, and shown how the impiety of the wicked can be altered or confuted, and the faith of the pious strengthened.

Since the death of Peter de Bruys, when the zeal of the faithful at St Gilles avenged the flames of the holy cross which he had set alight by burning him with it—since this irreligious man, dispatched by flames to the flames, made his journey to eternity—his heir in wickedness, Henry, with I don't know who else, has not only amended his diabolical teaching, but altered it considerably. Recently indeed I have read in a book which is said to stem from him, not only these five propositions but several others which he has added. One's soul burns to attack them, and to obliterate his devilish words with divine sayings, but I am not yet quite certain that he believes or preaches these things, and I shall delay my reply until I am fully informed when they were said, and in what context. If I am fortunate enough to obtain surer knowledge as a result of your skilful investigation I shall write what I can to empty, with new arguments, the last filthy dregs from the cup of death which these wretched men are passing on to companions in misery, and which has now been emptied of part of its contents. Meanwhile, if it please you, I offer you this letter, in the hope that it may be of use to its readers for you to pass on to those who need it, wherever or whenever necessary, so that, as I say, it may be able to correct the heretics against whom it is written, and make Catholics, for whom it is written, more cautious of them and their kind. If anyone wishes to copy it he should not omit to add as a preface this shorter letter which indicates briefly why the longer one was written, and what it contains.

18 Eon de l'étoile: Sigebert of Gembloux

Eon de l'étoile is discussed by Cohn, *Pursuit of the Millenium*, pp. 44–6, the sources for him by Russell, *Dissent and Reform*, pp. 288–9, n. 23, and the possible significance of his name, *ibid.*, pp. 120–21, 289 n. 24, and Runciman, *The Medieval Manichee*, pp. 120–121. It may however be doubted how much weight should be placed on variations in nomenclature in the twelfth century. The continuation of the chronicle of Sigebert of Gembloux, *MGH, SS* VI, 389, 390, is the earliest independent account.

I was interested to be told by a group of psychiatrists to whom I read the passage immediately below and the account of Eon's appearance at the Council of Rheims that they describe a textbook case of paranoid schizophrenia.

1146 The heresy of the Eonites was active in Britanny. Their leader was a man of twisted mind named Eon, and though he was a fool who could hardly recognize the letters of the alphabet he blasphemously discussed and argued about holy books. Although he was not in holy orders and was unfitted to be so, he celebrated mass with wicked impertinence, deceiving and undermining his ruined followers. He ordained bishops and archbishops from among his adherents, and did many other evil things which were contrary to the divine law. In the end, filled with the spirit of the devil, he fell into such madness that he said and made people believe that he was the Son of God, claiming that it was to him that priests in church referred when they finished the canon of the mass with the words '*Per eundem Dominum nostrum*'. It is best to cover in silence the wicked and appalling things which these heretics called Eonites, that is followers of Eon, did in secret, lest they give rise to horror, or even spread the heresy among weak readers.

1148 Pope Eugenius [III] called a general synod at Rheims where much was discussed and decided about the state of the Church. Among other things he decided that the decrees of his predecessor Pope Innocent [II] should continue to be upheld, but whatever the false Pope Pierleoni had ordered or decreed should be regarded as null and void, proclaiming this judgement: 'We reject and declare invalid the ordinances made by the son of Pierleoni and by other schismatics and heretics.'

The heretic Eon of whom we have spoken was taken to this assembly, and brought before the pope by a Catholic bishop from Britanny. There he was questioned about his perverse heresy in the hearing of everybody and convicted. At the insistence of the bishop who had brought him, he was not deprived of life or limb, but the pope ordered him to be held in custody, where he died not long after.

19 Eon de l'étoile: William of Newburgh

William of Newburgh's account of Eon (*Historia rerum Anglicarum*, ed. R. Howlett, *RS*, pp. 60–4) must, since it was written some fifty years after the event, be treated with caution. It does, however, contain information which does not appear in other extant sources, and William's general reliability lends weight to his claim to have spoken to former disciples of Eon.

At about this time [1148] Pope Eugenius [III], who had been called from the monastic life to rule the Apostolic See, visited France to inspect the state of the Church there, and called a general council at Rheims. While he was in session, with a great assembly of bishops and nobles, a pestilential man was brought to him whose spirit was possessed by the devil. He had seduced so many people with his cunning tricks that he was followed by a terrifying number of disciples as he wandered about through various regions, and had greatly endangered churches and monasteries. After he had raged unchecked for a long time wisdom conquered wickedness, and he was captured by the archbishop of Rheims and brought before the council.

He was a Breton, named Eudo de l'étoile, an illiterate idiot. He was so demented by the manipulation of demons that because his name was Eun in French he believed that the words of ecclesiastical exorcisms, 'through him [eum] who will come to judge the quick and the dead and the world by fire' referred to him. Stupid enough not to be able to tell the difference between *Eun* and *eum*, but to be so incredibly blockheaded as to think himself the ruler of the living and the dead! His diabolic wiles gave him such power to capture the souls of the simple that a deluded multitude flocked to him like flies caught in a spider's web, and everyone of them followed him as though he were the Lord of Lords. Sometimes he travelled through different provinces at amazing speed; sometimes he rested with his followers in desert and uncharted places, and then, at the instigation of the devil, burst out unexpectedly to harass churches and monasteries.

Many of his friends and relations—for he was not low-born—approached him, hoping to rebuke him with the daring of familiarity or cautiously to discover how he had organized his band. He seemed to surround himself with magnificence, with the trappings and the haughtiness of royalty; his followers were anxious and active for his well-being, and seemed to live at the peak of happiness, expensively dressed and sumptuously fed. Consequently many who came to rebuke him were corrupted by his spurious glory. Remarkable things were done by demons, who fed that multitude in the desert though not with true and solid food, but with food made of air. We have heard from certain people who used to belong to his band, and since his death have wandered around the world doing penance, that they always had bread, meat, fish and more delicate foods to hand as often as they wanted it. It was evident that these meals were not solid, but made of air and served invisibly by the spirits of the air so that souls could be captured more readily by feeding them, because however satisfying the meal had been, it was followed by the emptying of the stomach by belching so that hunger returned again and the meal had to be repeated. Anyone who happened to meet the band, and taste even a little of their food had his mind turned by his participation in their devilish meal, and immediately joined the wicked multitude: it was extremely foolhardy to accept anything from them.

The story is told of a certain knight, a relation of his, who approached this plague-carrier and urged him in simple terms to abjure his evil sect so that he could be restored to his family through the communion of Christian grace. Eudo, cunningly keeping him waiting, showed him a great array of fantastic things, hoping that he would be made captive by the tempting allure of what he saw. 'You are my kinsman,' he said. 'Take whatever you like, as much as you want.' Being a sensible man, when he saw that his warning was having no effect he got up and left. But his squire saw among these pernicious things a remarkably beautiful hawk, and desired it greatly. He asked for it, received it and followed his lord joyfully, but when the lord saw it he said to him, 'Throw that thing away. It is not a bird but a demon in disguise.' The truth of his words was soon proved. The stupid squire ignored his advice, and as soon as he complained that the hawk had scratched his hand badly with its talons, it carried him up by the hand into the sky, and he was never seen again.

Since, as I have said, this plague-bearer had done so much damage, being manipulated by Satan, great men often sent out armies to find him and pursue him, in vain, for they did not find him. Yet when he had been used for the work of the demons, and the higher powers could not allow him to do more damage, or suspend the judgement of God any longer, he was captured easily by the archbishop of Rheims, and the crazy crowd that followed him was dispersed. His most faithful disciples and most prominent associates were taken prisoner with him.

When he stood before the council and was asked by the supreme pontiff who he was, he replied, 'I am Eun, who will come to judge the quick and the dead and the world by fire.' In his hand he held an oddly shaped stick, whose upper part was forked. Asked why he carried this he said, 'This is a most wonderful thing. When the stick is held as you see it now, with two points towards heaven, God possesses two parts of the world, leaving the third part to me. But if I hold the stick so that the two points which are now on top point towards the ground, and the lower part, which has only one point, towards the sky, I keep two parts of the world for myself and relinquish one to God.'

At this the whole council burst out laughing, and mocked the man who was so obviously touched in his senses. It was ordered by decree of the council that he should be imprisoned, so that the plague of his heresy should not break out again, but he survived only for a short time. His followers, whom he had decorated with names like 'Wisdom', 'Knowledge', 'Judgement' and so on, absolutely refused to accept any sound doctrine. They obstinately preferred to glory in their false names, and the one who was called 'Judgement' even fruitlessly threatened his gaolers with a sentence of terrible vengeance. They were consigned to prison, and then to the flames, since they preferred to burn rather than correct their lives. I have heard an old man who was there at the time say that the one who was called 'Judgement' cried repeatedly as he was lead to his death, 'Earth, open up', as though the earth would open up at this command, as it did for Dathan and Abiron, and devour his enemies. Such is the power of heresy once it is lodged in the heart.

20 Arnold of Brescia: John of Salisbury

It is arguable that Arnold of Brescia should not appear in this collection, for the only allegation of doctrinal error against him is the assertion of Otto of Freising, who wrote after his execution and shows signs of being anxious to justify it, that he 'held unreasonable views with regard to the sacrament of the altar and infant baptism.' (*Deeds of Frederick Barbarossa*, trans. C. C. Mierow, pp. 142–4, and in Wakefield and Evans, pp. 147–8.) But even if he were not indisputably guilty of failure to acknowledge the authority of the Roman pontiff he would deserve his place for having demonstrated more dramatically than any of his contemporaries what the political implications of religious revolt might be. John of Salisbury's description of him, from the *Historia Pontificalis* (ed. and trans. Marjorie Chibnall, pp. 59–60, 62–5) is the best narrative account. To it may be added that, according to Walter Map, he was born into the minor nobility of Brescia; that St Bernard's letters 195 and 196 (trans. Scott James, *The Letters of St Bernard*, pp. 329–32) show him enjoying protection in Swabia and Bohemia after his expulsion from Paris; and that Otto of Freising describes his execution in 1155 by the prefect of the city of Rome (in effect a papal functionary) to whom he had been handed over by Barbarossa: 'After his corpse had been reduced to ashes in the fire, it was scattered on the Tiber, lest his body be held in veneration by the mad populace.' The best modern discussion of Arnold is by R. L. Poole, introducing his edition of the *Historia Pontificalis*, pp. lviii–lxx, and of the Roman revolution and its background P. Partner, *The Lands of St Peter*, especially pp. 179–202; for the position of the emperors see K. Hampe, *Germany under the Salian and Hohenstaufen Emperors*, p. 147 ff., and P. Munz, *Frederick Barbarossa*, pp. 59 ff., 79 ff. There is a biography, *Arnold of Brescia* by G. W. Greenaway, and he is the hero of one of Gibbon's finest passages, *Decline and Fall* cap. lxix.

April 1149 The lord pope had been forced to leave Rome by the turbulence of the citizens, who had inflicted many outrages on him and his followers. For that greatest and most ancient of offices, the prefecture, authorized by the Church to give justice within a radius of a hundred miles, and enjoying executive power, had been reduced to an empty name. Instead the senators, created by the populace on its own authority, usurped all powers of jurisdiction and administration throughout the city. Appropriating the regalian rights of the Holy See for their republic, they used them to support the public burdens. As patricius they chose Jordan, a prominent members of the Leonis family; and undermined the pope's position by destroying the palatine fortress of Cencius Frangipani, whose family had always come to the assistance of the Church. They would undertake to restore the regalia only on condition that the Church should pay the senators' salaries and, if it wished to receive any emoluments, should bear the burdens of the city. The pope meanwhile had betaken himself to Tusculum, where, mustering his forces, he ordered an attack on Rome, and gave Cardinal Guy, nicknamed the Maiden, command over the army. Auxiliaries were received from the lands of the king of Sicily, but the fighting was unsuccessful. The Church merely incurred the heaviest expenses to little or no purpose. . . .

Negotiations for peace were proceeding between the pope and the Romans, and numerous legations sped to and fro between the two parties. But there were many obstacles in the way of peace, the greatest of all being the refusal of the Romans to expel Arnold of Brescia, who was said to have bound himself by oath to uphold the honour of the city and Roman republic. The Romans in their turn promised him aid and counsel against all men, and explicitly against the lord pope; for the Roman Church had excommunicated him and ordered him to be shunned as a heretic. This man was a priest by office, a canon regular by profession, and one who had mortified his flesh with fasting and coarse raiment: of keen intelligence, persevering in his study of the scriptures, eloquent in speech, and a vehement preacher against the vanities of the world. Nevertheless he was reputed to be factious and a leader of schism, who, wherever he lived, prevented the citizens from being at peace with the clergy. He had been abbot of Brescia, and when the bishop was absent on a short visit to Rome had so swayed the minds of the citizens that they would scarcely open their gates to the bishop on his return. For this he was deposed by Pope Innocent and expelled from Italy; crossing the Alps into France he became a disciple of Peter Abailard, and together with Master Hyacinth, who is now a cardinal, zealously fostered his cause against the abbot of Clairvaux. After Master Peter had set out for Cluny, he remained at Paris on the Mont Sainte Geneviève, expounding the scriptures to scholars at the church of St Hilary where Peter had been lodged. But he had no listeners except poor students who publicly begged their bread from door to door to support themselves and their master. He said things that were entirely consistent with the law accepted by Christian people, but not at all with the life they led. To the bishops he was merciless on account of their avarice and filthy lucre; most of all because of stains on their personal lives, and their striving to build the Church of God in blood. He denounced the abbot, whose name is renowned above all others for his many virtues, as a seeker after vainglory, envious of all who won distinction in learning or religion unless they were his own disciples. In consequence the abbot prevailed on the most Christian king to expel him from the Frankish kingdom; from there he returned to Italy after Pope Innocent's death and, after promising reparation and obedience to the Roman Church, was received at Viterbo by Pope Eugenius. Penance was imposed on him, which he claimed would be performed in fasts, vigils and prayers in the holy places of the city; and again he took a solemn oath to show obedience. Whilst dwelling in Rome under pretext of penance he won the city to his side, and preaching all the more

67

freely because the lord pope was occupied in Gaul he built up a faction known as the heretical sect of the Lombards. He had disciples who imitated his austerities and won favour with the populace through outward decency and austerity of life, but found their chief supporters amongst pious women. He himself was frequently heard on the Capitol and in public gatherings. He had already publicly denounced the cardinals, saying that their college, by its pride, avarice, hypocrisy and manifold shame was not the Church of God, but a place of business and den of thieves, which took the place of the scribes and Pharisees amongst Christian peoples. The pope himself was not what he professed to be—an apostolic man and shepherd of souls—but a man of blood who maintained his authority by fire and sword, a tormentor of churches and oppressor of the innocent, who did nothing in the world save gratify his lust and empty other men's coffers to fill his own. He was, he said, so far from apostolic that he imitated neither the life nor the doctrine of the apostles, wherefore neither obedience nor reverence was due to him: and in any case, no man could be admitted who wished to impose a yoke of servitude on Rome, the seat of empire, fountain of liberty and mistress of the world.

21 Arnold of Brescia: the Romans seek imperial intervention

Between 1147 and 1155 the citizens of Rome appealed to Conrad III and Frederick I to join them against the pope on several occasions. Whether, as has often been suspected, Arnold of Brescia himself was the author of the two letters that follow (the suggestion in the second case being that 'Wezel' was a pseudonym connected in some way with his period of exile in Swabia) cannot be established, but it is agreed that he was influential in Roman affairs at this time, that the letters reflect his opinions, and that they are written in a style more cogent and more original than the others.

The names of the three men whom Wezel suggests as emissaries at the end of his letter strengthen the suspicion that if he was not Arnold himself he was closely connected with him. Count Ulrich of Lenzburg who was imperial prefect at Zurich, came of a family which had been prominent in support of Henry IV against the claims of Gregory VII, and had been an influential counsellor of Conrad III; and Rudolf of Ravensburg and Eberhard of Bodmen seem to have been important landowners in the neighbourhood of Constance, where St Bernard tells us that Arnold had found support among 'the rich and powerful'. For the Donation of Constantine see Partner, *The Lands of St Peter* pp. 20n., 23–4.

The first letter was written in 1149, while Conrad III was returning from the second crusade, and the second to Frederick I in September 1152, after he had been elected as Conrad's successor but before he had been crowned, in the hope of persuading him to accept the imperial coronation from the Roman senate rather than from the pope. Both emperors replied in terms which made it clear that their disputes with the papacy would not encourage them to countenance popular rebellion, and after Frederick had been crowned by Hadrian IV, on 18 June 1155, he repressed the Romans in the bloodiest fashion, and arranged for Arnold's execution. The letters are in the correspondence of Wibald of Stavelot, ed. P. Jaffé, *Bibliotheca Rerum Germanicarum* I, pp. 335–6, 539–43.

[*A Roman senator to Conrad III*, 1149]

To the most illustrious and magnificent Conrad, lord of the whole world, king of the Romans by the grace of God, ever triumphant Augustus, 'surpassed, nor even approached by none', a faithful senator and the king's most faithful servant, though a petty underling in the train of such a lord.

That the royal majesty may be strong and sure I have devoted myself assiduously in the senate and wherever else I could to the exaltation of your imperial sway, and may therefore write to you confidently, albeit boldly, 'accept the counsel though you despise the servant.' If then a servant may offer his royal master good advice, come to Rome without delay, interpose yourself between the pope and the people, and sustain the Senate and people in your own defence. With the Romans you will be able to take the castle St Angelo, and hold it so that nobody in future will be ordained pope except at your will and command. Thus it was at the time of St Gregory, who would not become pope without the consent of the Emperor Maurice, and so it remained until the time of Gregory VII. And thus, I maintain, it ought to be, so that priests cannot make war and murder in the world. It is not permitted to them to bear the sword or the cup, but to preach, to affirm their preaching by good works, and not to wage war and cause strife in the world.

[*Wezel to Frederick I*]

To the most noble lord Frederick, Wezel wishes the greatest happiness in soul and body.

It gives me great joy that your race has chosen you to be its ruler. But I deeply regret that you have followed the advice of priests and monks who confuse human and divine law, and failed to consult, as you should have done, the holy city, mistress of the world, maker and mother of all emperors. You have not sought her confirmation, as a son should from his mother, though every emperor has reigned by virtue of it and none without it. If you still mean to be her son and servant you have not written to say so. Father Isaac wanted to confer his blessing upon Esau, but Jacob's mother sent for him, and gave him the advice which (though Jacob feared that it would not work) got him the blessing, and the dominion, while Esau was still out hunting—to the chagrin of the latter. So, if I may get to the point, you should listen carefully to what I have to say.

Your nomination, like those of your predecessors, has come from the blind— that is from the Julianists, heretics, apostate clerks and false monks, who betray their orders and injure both the Church of God and the civil power by exercising temporal dominion in defiance of the Gospels, of the apostles and the canons, in contravention of both human and divine law. St Peter, whose vicar they falsely claim to be, showed us what they are when he said, 'Flying the concupiscence of that which is in the world, minister in your faith, virtue: and in virtue, knowledge: and in knowledge, abstinence: and in abstinence, patience: and in patience, godliness: and in godliness, love of brotherhood: and in love of brotherhood, charity.' Let this suffice you. Those who have ignored it are blind, groping in the dark, like those whom the same apostle called

> lying teachers who shall bring in sects of perdition and deny the Lord who brought them: bringing upon themselves swift destruction. And through covetousness shall they with feigned words make merchandise of you. Whose judgement now of a long time lingereth not: and their perdition slumbereth not. Receiving the rewards of their injustice, counting for a pleasure the delights of a day: stains and spots, sporting themselves in excess, rioting in their feasts with you: having eyes full of adultery and of sin that ceaseth not: alluring unstable souls: having their heart exercised with covetousness: children of malediction. And many shall follow their riotousness, through whom the way of truth shall be evil spoken of. These are fountains without water and clouds tossed with whirlwinds, to whom the mist of darkness is reserved.

Can such men say with Peter, 'Behold we have left all things and have followed thee', or 'Silver and gold I have none, but what I have I give thee'? How then shall they hear from the Lord, 'You are the light of the world, the salt of the earth'? Though indeed what follows fits them well, 'If the salt lose its savour, wherewith shall it be salted. It is good for nothing any more but to be cast out and to be trodden on by men'—or by pigs.

St John said, 'He that saith he abideth in him ought himself also to walk even as he walked,' and, 'He who saith that he knoweth him and keepeth not his commandments is a liar: and the truth is not in him.' Our Lord said to Peter, and to the vicars of Peter, 'As the Father hath sent me, I also send you.' But he showed in what manner he himself had been sent by his Father when he said, 'If I do not the works of my Father, believe me not.' If Christ who committed no sin was not to be believed without good works how are they to be believed who not only do evil, but do it publicly? Hence it is said, 'How can you speak truth if you are evil?' Not only do they not speak the truth, they do not believe, for the Lord said, 'How can you believe who receive glory from one another: and the glory which is from God alone, you do not seek? So faith also, if it have not works, is dead in itself.' How can those who not only hanker after every kind of wealth, but also hold up wealth, which has deposed the son of God, as the saviour of the world and the deliverer of peace to the world, who have destroyed their false doctrine by riotous living— how can they hear the very first commandment of the Gospels, 'Blessed are the poor in spirit', when they are poor neither in spirit nor in fact? St Jerome said, 'Avoid like the plague the priest who is a business man, the rich man who has been poor, the proud man who has been humble.' How can they, weighed down with worldly business, fulfil the first of all the decrees of the Roman pontiffs, set out by St Clement in his letters, but promulgated by St Peter, which falls upon their deaf ears? When Peter ordained Clement he enjoined him, among other things, in these words:

> Conduct yourself irreproachably . . . [a lengthy passage from the Pseudo-Isidorian Decretals, in which St Peter instructs his successor to avoid entanglement in all worldly affairs, concluding] . . . Therefore you are called for this alone, to teach the word of God unceasingly.

The lie, the heretical fable which holds that Constantine simoniacally granted imperial property to Silvester I is seen through in Rome so universally that the hirelings and whores confute the most learned in argument upon it, and the so-called Apostolic and his cardinals dare not show their faces in the city for shame. For St Miltiades, the predecessor of St Silvester, asserted in his decretals that Constantine had been baptized already with these words: 'When the Church had survived among the storms of the world it came about that the principal Romans accepted the faith of Christ and the sacrament of baptism, and among them that most religious of men, Constantine, was the first to adopt the true faith.' History testifies that he was a Christian before he entered the city as emperor.

Listen, then, to what I say. Esau did not stay at home, but went hunting, ignoring the wishes and advice of his mother, so that when the blind man called he missed what had been promised him. Jacob obeyed his mother, covered his bare neck and hands with a cover of domestic discipline, and by divine will filched what the blind man had promised the hunter. That the emperor is not just a hunter, but ought to be skilled in law is attested by the Emperor Justinian in the very first of his laws when he says, 'The imperial majesty must be not only adorned by arms, but armed with laws, so that he may govern well at all times, in war and in peace.' A little later he shows how the Roman emperor should govern and make laws by saying, 'What pleases the prince has the force of law', which implies that he reserved to himself, with the people, all his authority and power. But since the empire and every dignity of the state pertains to the Romans, and not the Romans to the emperor, what law prevents the senate and people from making an emperor?

Do not hesitate therefore to send to Rome Count Rudolf of Ravensburg, Count Ulrich of Lenzburg, and Eberhard of Bodmen, who are skilled in the laws which govern the empire, with powers to negotiate. Hurry, before anything happens to damage your interests.

III A Period of Transition

THE division between this section and the last is to some extent arbitrary. Anticlericalism in its various aspects continued to be widely and coherently expressed after the middle of the twelfth century. About 1150, for example, a priest named Albero of Mercke, who lived near Cologne, was found guilty of professing seven heresies all of which related to the efficacy of sacraments administered by corrupt priests. He commanded some popular following, and seems to have been in the tradition of Henry of Lausanne. Thirty years later the same tradition retained enough attraction in the Languedoc to assure the popular appeal and rapid growth of the Waldensian movement, even after the great missionary success of the Cathars, but it no longer held a monopoly, or near monopoly, of western dissent.

Most of the documents which follow contain clear evidence that the Cathar penetration of the West had begun, probably stimulated by increased persecution in the Byzantine Empire as well as by growing commercial and military contacts between East and West. To establish the presence of the new religion in western Europe it is no longer, in this period, necessary to rely, with the proponents of Bogomil influence upon the heretics of the eleventh century, on general similarities of doctrine, real or alleged, or on the rejection of the sacraments of a corrupt Church. On the contrary, a comparison of the first systematic statement we have of Cathar beliefs, that of Eckbert of Schönau, with the opinions of Henry of Lausanne shows at once not only what they had in common but also how many and how important were their differences. Twenty years earlier a similar divergence was noted, though less fully and less clearly, by Eversin of Steinfeld between the two groups of heretics whom he describes; he also observed that one of them claimed direct affiliation to heretics in Greece, and had an organization of their own not unlike that which was described, a century later, by Rainier Sacchoni and Anselm of Alessandria.

If the fact of eastern influence on western heresy in these decades is clear, its details are not, and nobody has yet succeeded in producing a synthesis that commands agreement. One important example will illustrate the difficulties. Rainier Sacchoni and Anselm of Alessandria make it clear that among the Cathars there was serious dispute about the nature of the evil principle. Most of them, mitigated dualists, held that he was the creation of the good, a son or archangel who had gone into rebellion and set up his own material kingdom, but some, absolute dualists, believed that he also was eternal and un-created. When did this distinction appear in the West, and whence did it come? It used to be thought that it was familiar to Eckbert of Schönau (29), but R. Manselli ('Eckberto di Schönau', in *Arte e Storia*) has argued that Eck-bert's knowledge of absolute dualism came from his reading St Augustine, and that he had direct acquaintance only with mitigated dualists. Again, it has been held that absolute dualism was brought to the West by the *Publicani*. The reader of what follows may wonder why, for there is no evidence in the western sources that they held any such doctrine. But their name has suggested that they were emissaries of the Paulician church, originally an Armenian sect whose devotees were settled in the Balkans by the Emperors Constantine V in the middle of the eighth century, and John I and Basil II towards the end of the tenth. The Paulicans were believed to be absolute dualists, and hence, it was conjectured, to have infected with that doctrine some of the followers of Bogomil, who preached in mid-tenth century Bulgaria. Another allegedly absolute dualist influence has been found in the Messalian heretics who were influential at the same time in Byzantine monastic circles. This, broadly, is the argument of D. Obolensky, *The Bogomils*, much the best account of the movement. But in recent years both the nature of Paulician beliefs and their place in the evolution of eastern heresies have become intensely controversial yet again: see in particular N. Garsoian, 'Byzantine Heresy: a reinterpretation', (*Dumbarton Oaks Papers*, 1971), and P. Lemerle, 'L'histoire des Pauliciens d'Asie mineure' (*Travaux et Mémoires*, 1973), whose notes, with Obolensky's, will provide a guide to the enormous literature on these complex problems.

If it is not clear how many different sects are described in extracts that follow, or what their origins were, they leave little room for doubt that organized missionary work was afoot, though even here it is necessary to remember the possibility, discussed by A. Borst, 'Le transmission d l'hérésie au moyen âge', *Hérésies et sociétés* pp. 273–80, that the heretics may have travelled as much to avoid persecution as to spread their faith. Among mis-sionaries who do not appear in these documents were the first man to be described as a Cathar, Jonas of Cambrai, who was convicted of heresy (though its nature is not recorded) at Cologne between 1151 and 1156, in Trier after 1152, and at Liège between 1145 and 1164, and again between 1164 and 1167, (P. Bonenfant in *Le Moyen Age*, 1963), and those who were active around Besançon a little later according to Caesarius of Heisterbach, (*Dialogus Miraculorum*, II, XVIII, trans. Bland, I, 338). C. Thouzellier worked out the main course of the spread of Catharism in Europe in 'Hérésie et croisade', *RHE* (1954), and offers a general schema of the evolution of heretical move-ments—'tradition et resurgence'—in *Hérésies et sociétés*, pp. 105–20.

The broadening basis of heresy also began at this time to evoke a more systematic response from the Church. St Bernard's mission of 1145 was the first of a long series of Cistercian journeys undertaken at papal request which

73

eventually led to the foundation of the Dominican Order. The question of whether the assistance of the secular power should be summoned to deal with heresy—a policy enthusiastically advocated by the secular powers themselves —began to be anxiously discussed. Procedures for the identification of heretics and action against them became more formal, more elaborate and more severe, and though lynch law was still common the Church was being forced to work out its position and define its responsibilities: all this is excellently discussed by H. Maisonneuve, *Etudes sur les origines de l'inquisition* pp. 93–149.

22 Eversin of Steinfeld

The incident to which Eversin refers in this famous letter, *PL* 182, col. 676–80, seems to be that described in the *Annales Brunwilarenses* (*MGH SS* XVI, 727) s.a. 1143: 'A charge was brought against some heretics at Cologne in the church of St Peter, in the presence of Archbishop Arnold. Many were caught and bound, and purged themselves by the ordeal of water; others, bewildered by their own wickedness, took flight. Three were burned at Bonn, by authority of Count Otto, preferring to die rather than return to the holy Catholic faith.' St Bernard answered the letter with his sixty-fifth and sixty-sixth sermons on the Song of Songs (translated by S. J. Eales, *Works of St Bernard*, IV pp. 393–409, and no. 65 by Wakefield and Evans, pp. 32–8).

To his reverend lord and father, Abbot Bernard of Clairvaux, Eversin humble minister of Steinfeld,

I rejoice in your eloquence as though I have found great treasure. You remind us so forcefully of the goodness and sweetness of God in all your speech and writings, and especially on the song of the groom and his bride, of Christ and the Church, that we can truthfully say, with that same groom, 'thou hast kept the good wine until now'. He has appointed you to be our butler for this precious wine; do not cease to pour it, do not even pause, for you will not be able to empty the jug. Weakness will not excuse you, holy father: in this task piety is more important than bodily strength. Nor can you plead that you are busy, for I could propose nothing more necessary than this to our common work.

You can give us drink from so many jugs. You have poured enough from the first, and it has made us wise and strong against the teaching and charges of the scribes and pharisees; from the second against the arguments and missiles of the gentiles; from the third, against the subtle deceptions of heretics; from the fourth, against false Christians; from the fifth against the heretics who will come at the end of time, as the Holy Spirit manifestly said through the apostle, 'in the latest times some shall depart from the faith, giving heed to spirits of error and doctrines of devils, speaking lies in hypocrisy and having their conscience seared, forbidding to marry, to abstain from meats which God hath created to be received with thanksgiving.' Let the faithful drink from your sixth jug for strength against him who will surely be revealed in that revolt from the faith as 'the man of sin, the son of perdition who opposeth and is lifted up above all that is called God, or that is worshipped . . . whose coming is according to the second coming of Satan, in all power and signs and lying wonders and in all seduction of iniquity.' After that, when the sons of men have been intoxicated by the richness of the Lord God and the torrent of his love, the seventh draught will not be necessary.

Good father, you have poured enough for us all for our correction, edification and elevation when we are setting out, while we are on the journey, and when we have completed it, from your fourth jug, enough to avail until the end of time against the indifference and wickedness of false brethren. Now is the time for you to draw from your fifth jug, and let fly against the new heretics who are rising on every side from the depths of the abyss, in almost every church, as though their leader is released and the day of the Lord is at hand. There is a verse in the wedding song of the love of Christ and the Church which you must deal with, as you yourself have reminded me, 'Catch us the little foxes that destroy the vines', which is appropriate to this problem, and calls for your fifth jug. Therefore, father, I appeal to you to distinguish all the elements of their heresy which come to your notice, and produce arguments and authorities from our own faith to destroy them.

A group of heretics was found recently in these parts, near Cologne, some of whom readily returned to the Church. Two of them, however, one who was called their bishop, with his companion, defied us at a meeting of clerks and laymen, at which the archbishop and some great nobles were present, and defended their heresy with quotations from Christ and the apostles. When they saw that they were making no headway they asked for a day to be fixed on which they might bring forward men from among their followers who were expert in their faith. They promised that if they saw their masters refuted in argument they would be willing to rejoin the Church, though otherwise they would rather die than abandon their views. After this they were urged for three days to come to their senses, and refused, and then were seized by the people, who were moved by great enthusiasm, (though we were against it), put to the stake, and burnt. The amazing thing was that they entered and endured the torment of the flames not merely courageously, but joyfully. I wish I were with you, holy father, to hear you explain how such great fortitude comes to these tools of the devil in their heresy as is seldom found among the truly religious in the faith of Christ.

This is their heresy. They claim that they are the true Church, because the heritage of Christ survives in them alone. They are the true followers of the apostolic life, because they do not seek the things of this world, houses or land or any other sort of property, just as Christ did not seek them, and did not allow his disciples to possess them.

They said to us, 'You join house to house and field to field, and seek the

75

things of this world. Those who are thought most perfect among you, monks and canons regular, possess things not individually, but in common: nevertheless they do possess all of these things.' Of themselves they said:

We are the poor of Christ, wandering men; fleeing from city to city like sheep in the midst of wolves we suffer persecution with the apostles and martyrs. We lead a holy life, fasting, abstaining, working and praying by day and night, seeking in these things the necessities of life. We live thus because we are not of this world; you are lovers of the world, at peace with the world because you are wordly. False apostles have corrupted the word of Christ for their own ends, and have led you and your fathers astray. We and our fathers, the successors of the apostles, have remained in the grace of Christ, and will remain so until the end of the world. To distinguish between you and us, Christ said, 'By their fruits you shall know them.' Our fruits are the following in the footsteps of Christ.

In their diet they prohibit all milk and anything which is made from it, and anything which is produced by procreation. This is what they told us about their way of life. They wear veils at mass, but openly confessed to us that when they eat daily after the manner of Christ and the apostles they consecrate their food and drink as the body and blood of Christ, by reciting the Lord's Prayer, to be nourished with the body and limbs of Christ. They told us that they do not believe in the truth of the sacraments, which are only shadowy human tradition. They claimed that they baptize, and had been baptized, not merely in water but in the fire and the spirit, adducing the evidence of John the Baptist who, after baptizing in water, said of Christ, 'He shall baptize you in the Holy Ghost and in fire', and 'I baptize in water, but there hath stood a greater in the midst of you whom you know not', as though he would baptize by some other medium than water. They tried to argue that such baptism should be performed by the laying-on of hands, by referring to Luke's description of Paul's baptism, in the Acts of the Apostles, which at Christ's command he received from Ananias, where there is no mention of water, but only of the laying-on of hands. They take whatever references to the laying-on of hands are found in the Acts of the Apostles or the Epistles of Paul as references to baptism. Anyone who is baptized among them in this way is called *electus*, and has power to baptize others who are worthy of it, and to consecrate the body and blood of Christ at his table. But first he must be received by the laying-on of hands from among those whom they call *auditores* into the *credentes*; he may then be present at their prayers until he has proved himself, when they make him an *electus*. They care nothing for our baptism. They condemn marriage, but I could not discover the reason for this from them, either because they dared not tell it, or (more likely) because they did not know it.

There are other heretics in our area who are always quarrelling with these people. Indeed it was through their perpetual wrangling and discord that we discovered them. They hold that the body of Christ is not made on the altar, because none of the priests of the Church has been consecrated. They say that the apostolic dignity has been corrupted by involvement in secular affairs, and the throne of St Peter by failing to fight for God as Peter did, has deprived itself of the power of consecration which was given to Peter. Since the Church no longer has that power, the archbishops who live in a worldly manner within the Church, cannot receive it and cannot consecrate others. They cite in support of their argument the words of Christ, 'The scribes and Pharisees have sitten on the chair of Moses; whatsoever they shall say to you observe and do', as though the power of speaking and preaching was conferred by this and nothing else. Thus they empty the church of priests, and condemn the sacraments, except for baptism; even that must be for adults, and they say that it is conferred by Christ and not by the minister of the sacraments. On the baptism of children they take their view from the words of the evangelist, 'He that believeth and is baptized shall be saved.' They hold that all marriage is fornication, unless it is between two virgins, both the man and the woman, citing the words of the Lord when he replied to the pharisees, 'What God hath joined together let no man put asunder,' as though God joins such people in the manner of the first men, because the Lord said to the same opponents against their argument for divorce, 'From the beginning it was not so,' and, in the same place, 'He that shall marry her that is put away committeth adultery,' and, in the apostle, 'Marriage honourable in all, and the bed undefiled'.

They do not believe in the intercession of saints, and hold that fasts and other penances which are undertaken because of sin are unnecessary, because whenever the sinner repents all his sins will be forgiven. They call all observances of the Church which are not laid down by Christ or by the apostles after him superstitions. They will not admit the existence of the fires of purgatory, because when the soul leaves the body it passes at once either to eternal rest or eternal punishment, according to the words of Solomon, 'If the tree falls to the south or to the north, in what place soever it shall fall there shall it be.' Consequently they condemn the prayers and offerings of the faithful for the dead.

I appeal to you, holy father, to awaken your vigilance against this many-headed evil, and direct your pen against these beasts of prey. Do not reply that the Tower of David to which we flee is already adequately provided with bulwarks, that a thousand shields hang from its walls, and that it is furnished with every weapon for the valiant. We want those weapons to be collected together by your labour, on behalf of us simpler and slower people, so that they will be the fitter to track down these monsters, and the more effective in resisting them. You should know that the heretics who returned to the Church told us that they have a great multitude of adherents all over the world, including many of our own clerks and monks. Those who were burnt told us while they were defending themselves that their heresy had been hidden until now ever since the time of the martyrs, and persisted in Greece and other lands, and these are the heretics who call themselves apostles and have their own pope. The other lot deny our pope, but at least do not claim to have another one instead. These apostles of Satan have women among them who are—so they say—chaste, widows or virgins, or their wives, both among the *credentes* and among the *electi*, alleging that they follow the apostles who permitted them to have women among them.

Farewell in the Lord.

23 Heretics at Liège, 1145

Although this letter, from *PL* 179, col. 937–8 is addressed only to Pope L., there is little doubt that it belongs to the pontificate of Lucius II, (March 1144–February 1145); it is most unlikely that by the time of Lucius III (1181–5) the canons would have thought the heresy they describe such a novelty, or, on the other hand, that such heretics would have been found at all as early as the reign of Leo IX (1048–54?): for other arguments against that possibility see H. Silvestre, *RHE* LVIII, (1963), 979–80. That the letter is written by the canons of Liège rather than the bishop suggests that it belongs to the beginning of 1145 when Bishop Adalbero was in Rome, appealing to the pope in a quarrel with his clergy.

Liège was regularly the scene of heretical episodes: a decade before this, in 1135, an unspecified number of heretics was found there who, 'while appearing to observe the Catholic faith and lead a holy life, denied legitimate matrimony, held that women ought to be shared in common, forbade infant baptism and maintained that the prayers of the living are of no use to the souls of the dead. When they could not deny these heresies the people wanted to stone them, but they were frightened and took flight during the night. Three of them were captured and imprisoned, of whom one was burned at the stake, while the other two made a confession of faith and returned to the Church.' (*Annales Rodenses*, *MGH SS* XVI, 711).

To L., supreme pontiff, the church of Liège. . . .

We believe it manifest that the divine ordinance has placed the Roman See at the head of the Catholic Church to watch over its members, and to be a refuge for those who are threatened with destruction. Therefore, we draw your attention to some newly discovered plots of old enemies, since you are charged with care over every Church, so that your vigilance may confound the efforts of those who lead the souls of the simple into heresy under the guise of religion, and so that the Church of God, which we hear has been wounded in many places, may recover its strength and the integrity of the faith.

A heresy which is so varied in its manifestations that it cannot be described properly by any one name has been spreading to several areas from Montwimers, a village in France. Some of its adherents who were found among us were convicted and confessed. An angry crowd seized them, and wanted to burn them, but by God's mercy we were able to save almost all of them from immediate death, hoping that they might be converted. One of them was the man whom we have sent to your holiness with his request for absolution.

This heresy has distinct ranks among its adherents; there are *auditores*, who are being initiated into the heresy, and *creditores* whose conversion is complete, and they have their ordinary Christians, their priests and their bishops, just as we do. Its appalling blasphemies are these: that there is no remission of sin in baptism, the sacrament of the body and blood of Christ is meaningless, nothing is conferred by a bishop in ordination, nobody receives the Holy Spirit except through the merit of good works performed, marriage leads to damnation, the Church is Catholic only in its own opinion, and all oath-taking is criminal. The followers of this sect pretend to take our sacraments to disguise their wickedness. The man Haimeric whom we are sending to you for your judgement was one of their *auditores* until quite recently. He now wants to recompense God and the Church, and keep the vow which he made to the apostles when his life was in danger, that if he could be saved through their virtue and their prayers he would devoutly visit their shrines and give thanks for his safety. We have placed the other heretics in various religious houses to await whatever corresction you decide upon.

You should also know that according to those whom we have caught all the cities of Gaul and our own land have been seriously infected with this poison. Take care therefore that the germ does not spread even further: have it cauterised with proper diligence, and cured.

24 Périgueux, c. 1160

It used to be thought that this letter, from *PL* 181, col. 1721, described followers of Henry of Lausanne, and was written before St Bernard's mission of 1145. There is no evidence for either proposition, but there is a description of the same heretics evidently based on this letter, in the *Annals of Margam*, ed. H. R. Luard, *Annales Monastici* (London *RS*, 1864) I, 15, s.a. 1163.

I, Heribert the monk, wish all Christians to know that they should beware of false prophets who are trying to pervert Christianity. A large number of heretics has appeared in the region of Périgueux, claiming to lead the apostolic life. They will not eat meat, or drink wine, unless it be a little on every third day, they genuflect a hundred times a day, and they will not take money. Their sect is unusually perverse. Instead of 'Glory be to the Father', they say 'For thine is the kingdom', and 'Thou shalt rule the created universe for ever and ever, Amen.' They say that there ought to be no alms, because there ought to be no possessions. They hold the mass worthless, and say that it should not be regarded as a communion, but as a piece of bread. If one of them does attend mass, in order to conceal his heresy, he does not say the canon and does not receive communion, but spits out the host behind the altar or into the mass-book. They do not adore the cross, or the face of the Lord, but interfere with those who do adore, saying before the face of the Lord, 'Oh how wretched they are who adore you,' and repeating the psalm, 'In the likeness of the people'. Many have joined this sect, including nobles who have relinquished their property, as well as clerks, priests, monks and nuns. Nobody is so stupid that if he joins them he will not become literate within eight days, so that he can be re-converted neither by argument nor by example. They cannot be imprisoned; if they are taken no chains will hold them because the devil sets them free, with the result that they actually hope and desire to discover those who will torture them, and hand them over for execution. They make signs among themselves. Even if they are bound in iron chains and shackles and put in a wine-butt turned upside-down on top of them, and watched by the strongest guards, they will not be found the next day unless they choose to be, and the empty butt will be turned up again full of the wine which had been emptied from it. They do many other amazing things. Their leader's name is Pons.

25 The Publicani: at Arras 1162-3

In 1153 Eugenius III wrote to the clergy and people of Arras in support of their bishop's condemnation of a heresy which was spreading in the diocese, but whose nature is not specified (Mansi, XXI, col. 689-90). In 1157 a council at Rheims attacked 'the most wicked sect of the Manichees, who hide among the poor and under the veil of religion labour to undermine the faith of the simple, spread by the wretched weavers who move from place to place, and often change their names, accompanied by women sunk in sin,' and prescribed imprisonment, branding and exile for them and their followers (*ibid.*, col. 843). The council is discussed and the implications of their correspondence, which followed the discovery of such a group at Arras in 1162 are examined by Maisonneuve, pp. 108-18. The letters are from Bouquet, XV, 790, 792, 799.

The pope's anxiety to restrain the archbishop of Rheims was hindered by the fact that he was at this time in exile and dependent on Louis VII for support against Frederick Barbarossa (Fliche and Martin, 9.2, 69 et seq.).

Alexander . . . to Henry, Archbishop of Rheims. . . .

We have received the heretical citizens of whom you wrote to us with appropriate severity, and displayed towards them the harsh demeanour which it befits us to extend to such people. You should remember, however, that it is wise to be cautious, and less wrong to acquit sinners who ought to be condemned than to visit the wrath of the Church upon the innocent, better for churchmen to be less severe than they might than to be, or to seem, excessively harsh in discipline: as the scriptures say, 'Be not over just', for 'he that violently bloweth his nose bringeth out blood.' We are anxious to defer to you in this, as in all things, dear son, and to do you honour so far as our duty to God allows, and, God willing, will write again to tell you what we have decided, with the advice of our brothers, ought to be done.

Tours, 23 December 1162.

To Alexander . . . Louis, king of the Franks. . . .

My brother Henry, archbishop of Rheims, recently visited Flanders, where he discovered some wicked men, followers of a particularly vicious heresy, for they had fallen into the errors of the Manichees. They are called *Populicani* in the vernacular, and some of their observances make them appear more virtuous than they really are: if by any mischance they were to prosper they would do great damage to the faith, especially in the areas where their iniquities have spread, and they have become deeply rooted. If the archbishop had been prepared to ignore their wickedness and tolerate their depravity he might have had the large sum of money, six hundred marks of silver, that they offered him. Since he would give them no mercy they have appealed to you. Let your holiness deal carefully with this poisonous and pernicious sect, and realize that such a pest should be rooted out, not allowed to flourish. We pray that for the honour of the Christian faith you will follow the advice of our dear brother the archbishop and allow these people who have risen against God to be destroyed. Severity against them will be welcome to every lover of piety in that country. If you decide otherwise you will open many mouths against your blasphemy and that of the Holy Roman Church, and their murmur will not be easily stilled.

Alexander . . . to Louis. . . .

We received your highness's letter about those who are charged with heresy in Flanders, with due attention, and having studied it carefully think it right to inform your excellency that when some of them presented themselves before us with many letters and asserted that they were quite free of any taint of heresy, we wished to send them, with a letter from us, to judgement by our venerable brother, Archbishop Henry of Rheims. They did not want to go to him, and two of them returned, without the letter, and insisted on remaining with us: they would not return on any account, and preferred to be judged by our own verdict. Since we are always anxious to have your advice on all things and to follow it so far as God and righteousness permit, we refused to give them a hearing until we were properly furnished with the advice of yourself, the archbishop, and other men of religion. It is, as we say, our constant desire and intention to receive the advice of your highness and vigilantly to seek your honour and exaltation, to hear you sympathetically, and to honour you in all things, as the dearest son, and after God, the foremost defender of the Church.

Tours, 11 January 1163.

Alexander . . . to Henry, archbishop of Rheims. . . .

Since we are aware of your sincere and wholehearted devotion to the Roman Church and particularly to our own person we embrace you as our dear brother, and as an important officer of the Church and strive to do you honour and serve your convenience. We have been trying to get rid of the citizens of Arras, G . . ., J . . ., and R . . ., and the woman R . . ., who have been following our court for so long seeking judgement on their case. We must be especially careful neither to let the guilty go free nor to condemn the innocent and are also anxious to respect your wishes. Therefore we think it necessary to prolong this case so that we may benefit fully from the advice of you and your church, and of our brothers the bishops of France. Meanwhile we are sending these people home, on condition that when we send for them again they must come before us and accept our verdict and that of the Church without demur, and observe it exactly. Consequently we must ask you to make inquiries about them from people who will know about their manner of life and their beliefs, and report to us so that with God's help and the advice of you and your church and our fellow bishops we can reach a conclusion based on sound information. In the meanwhile it would be improper for these people to suffer any loss or danger to their persons or property, and we instruct you to make it clear to their fellow citizens that they must not harm or threaten them or their property in any way.

Dol, 7 July, 1163.

26 The Publicani: in England, c. 1163

This is the only appearance of heresy recorded in England during the eleventh and twelfth centuries. (William of Newburgh, II, XIII, ed. R. Howlett, *Chronicles of the Reigns of Stephen* etc., 131-4, also translated by Douglas and Greenaway, *English Historical Documents*, II 329-30.) It is accompanied by the first case of legislation against heresy by the secular power. Germanus' missions to England in 426 and 429 are described by Constantine of Lyons in Hoare, *The Western Fathers*, pp. 295-302, 306-8.

At this time some heretics came to England who were believed to belong to the sect commonly known as *Publicani*, who undoubtedly originated in Germany from an unknown founder and who have spread the poison of their wickedness through many lands. Indeed so many are said to have been infected by this plague throughout France, Spain, Italy and Germany, that they seem, as the prophet says, to have 'multiplied beyond number'. Wherever the leaders of the Church and secular princes treat them with too much laxity in their provinces these treacherous foxes emerge from their holes, adopt a specious appearance of piety to deceive the simple and take advantage of their liberty to ravage the vineyard of the Lord of Hosts more effectively. But when the fire of God kindles the zeal of the faithful against them they slink back into their holes and do less harm, though even then they continue to spread their poison secretly. Foolish and unsophisticated men whose powers of reason are limited become so thoroughly imbued with this disease once they have contracted it that they are stubborn towards all discipline, and it is very rare for any of them to return to the faith after they have been discovered and dragged from their hiding-place.

England has always remained free from these and other heretical infections, while so many heresies have been springing up so fast in so many other parts of the world. It is true that when this island was called Britain, after the Britons who lived here, it sent the future heresiarch Pelagius to the East, and in the course of time readmitted his heresy to the country; and the Church of Gaul with pious foresight twice sent St Germanus here to extinguish it. But after the Britons had been expelled from the island and the Angles had taken over so that it was no longer called Britain, but England, the germ of heretical infection never broke out here, nor was it introduced from anywhere else, to be spread and propagated, until the time of Henry II. Then, with the help of God, the pest which had crept in was so thoroughly crushed that it will be afraid to enter this island again.

Rather more than thirty people, both men and women, concealing their heresy, came here as though in peace to propagate their errors under the leadership of one Gerard whom they all regarded as their teacher and master. Among them he alone had some degree of learning; the others were simple and illiterate people, quite uncultivated peasants, Germans by race and language. Although they spent some time in England they succeeded in adding to their number only one woman, whom, it is said, they ensnared with magic incantations, and bewitched with certain wiles. They could not hide for long, for they were tracked down by men curious to know to what foreign sect they belonged, and were arrested, detained, and held in public custody.

The king was unwilling either to release or to punish them without discussion, and ordered an episcopal synod to meet at Oxford, where they were solemnly examined about their religion. The one who seemed to be literate undertook to defend them all, and speaking on their behalf said that they were Christians, and respected the apostolic teaching. Questioned in the proper order on the articles of faith they answered correctly on the nature of Christ, but of the remedies with which he condescends to alleviate human infirmity, that is the sacraments, they spoke falsely. They attacked holy baptism, communion and matrimony, and wickedly dared to belittle the Catholic unity which is fostered by these divine aids. When they were confronted with evidence drawn from the holy scriptures they replied that they believed what they had been taught, and did not want to argue about their faith. When they were urged to repent and join the body of the Church they rejected this sound advice. When they were faced with threats in the pious hope that they might repent through fear, they laughed and abused the words of the Lord, 'Blessed are they which are persecuted for righteousness sake, for theirs is the kingdom of Heaven.' To prevent the germ of heresy from spreading more widely the bishops had them publicly denounced as heretics, and handed them over to the king to be subjected to fleshly discipline. He commanded the mark of their heretical infamy to be branded on their foreheads, and ordered them to be driven out with rods and expelled from the city in view of the people, strictly forbidding anybody to give them hospitality or any comfort.

When sentence was pronounced they were led rejoicing to this greatest of punishments by their leader, who walked briskly before them chanting, 'Blessed are ye when men shall revile you', so greatly had they been deceived by this seductive spirit who had abused their minds. The woman whom they had converted in England left them in fear of punishment, confessed her errors, and was reconciled to the Church. Then the detestable brotherhood were branded on their foreheads and subjected to proper severity, their leader receiving the ignominy of a double branding, on the forehead and on the chin, as a badge of his pre-eminence. Then their clothes were publicly cut off as far as their belts, and they were driven from the city with ringing blows into the intolerable cold, for it was winter. Nobody showed the slightest mercy towards them, and they died in misery. This pious and inflexible severity not only purged the kingdom of England of the infection which had broken out then, but made certain, by striking the heretics with terror, that it would not happen again.

The Assize of Clarendon, 1166

Stubbs, *Select Charters*, p. 173: and Douglas and Greenaway, p. 410.

Ch. 21 Further, the lord king forbids anyone in the whole of England to receive in his land, or within his jurisdiction, or in a house under him, any of the sect of heretics who were excommunicated and branded at Oxford. If anyone receives them he shall be at the mercy of the lord king, and the house in which they have lived shall be carried outside the village and burnt. And each sheriff is to swear that he will observe this, and make all his officers, and the stewards of the barons, and all the knights and free-holders of the county swear it.

27 The Publicani: at Vézelay, 1167

From Hugh of Poitiers, *Historia Viziliacensis monasterii*, Bouquet, XII, 343–4. Vézelay had a history of conflict between the town and the abbey in the early twelfth century which culminated in a communal revolt in 1152 and its suppression in 1155 (Petit-Dutaillis, *Les communes françaises*, p. 127).

It appears that Abbot William sought the opinion of Herbert of Bosham, the companion of Becket, on how to deal with these heretics, and was advised to hand them over to the secular power for punishment after determining their guilt (*PL*, 190, col. 1462–3). Herbert refers to them as *Deonae*.

At this time certain heretics, called *Deonarii* or *Poplicani* were arrested in Vézelay. When they were questioned they tried to cover up their filthy and heretical sect by rambling and long-winded replies. The abbot ordered them to be separated from each other and imprisoned until they could be refuted by bishops or other eminent people who might happen to come our way. They were held for two months or more, during which time they were often brought out and questioned, sometimes with threats and sometimes with coaxing, about the Catholic faith. Finally, when this had been tried in vain for a long time, they were brought before the archbishops of Lyons and Narbonne, the bishop of Nevers, and many other abbots and learned men, and were charged with recognizing only the existence of God, and denying almost all the sacraments of the Catholic Church, including the baptism of children, the eucharist, the image of the living cross, the sprinkling of holy water, the building of churches, the efficacy of tithes and offerings, the cohabitation of husband and wife, the monastic order, and all the functions of clerks and priests.

At the approach of Easter two of them heard that it had been decided that they should die at the stake, and pretending that they believed in the true Catholic Church, demanded the ordeal by water. During the Easter procession they were brought into the middle of a great crowd, which filled the whole cloister, before Guichard, archbishop of Lyons, Bernard, bishop of Nevers, Master Walter, bishop of Laon, and William, abbot of Vézelay. Questioned item by item on the faith they said that they believed in the Catholic Church. Asked about their dreadful error about the sacrament, they said that they had not known anything about the sacraments of the Church except the afore-mentioned heresy. Asked whether they now truly believed as they said they did, and would prove that they no longer subscribed to the error of the sect by undergoing the ordeal of water, they replied that they would willingly do so, without any other judgement. At this the whole Church exclaimed with one voice. 'Thanks be to God!' Then the abbot said to all who were present, 'Brothers, what should be done with those who persist in their obstinacy?' Everybody replied, 'Let them be burnt. Let them be burnt.'

On the following day the two who seemed to have recanted were brought to the ordeal by water. One of them was judged by everybody to be saved by the water, (though there were some who afterwards cast doubt on the verdict), but when the other had been immersed he was unanimously condemned. At the instance of many, including the priests, and by his own request, he was brought out from prison, and submitted to the judgement of the water again, but when he was thrown in for the second time the water once more refused to receive him. Since he had been twice condemned everybody sentenced him to the stake, but the abbot, giving consideration to his condition, ordered him to be publicly flogged, and banished from the town. The others, seven in number, were burnt at the stake in the valley of Ecouan.

28 The Publicani: at Rheims, 1176-80

Most of this famous passage from Ralph of Coggeshall's *Chronicon Anglicanum* (ed. J. Stevenson, *RS* 1875, pp. 121-5) has also been translated by G. G. Coulton, *Life in the Middle Ages*, I, pp. 29-32 (2nd ed., Cambridge 1928).

In the time of King Louis of France, the father of King Philip, when the errors of heretics who are vulgarly called *Publicani* were creeping through the provinces of France, an old woman who had been infected by this plague was involved in a curious affair in the city of Rheims. William, the archbishop of Rheims, and uncle of King Philip, was riding outside the city one day with his clerks when one of the clerks, Master Gervase of Tilbury, saw a girl working alone in a vineyard. Moved by the lewd curiosity of a young man, as I heard from him myself after he had become a canon, he went over to her. He greeted her, and asked politely where she came from, and who her parents were, and what she was doing there alone, and then, when he had eyed her beauty for a while, spoke gallantly to her of the delights of love-making. She replied, with a simple gesture and in grave tones, avoiding the young man's eyes, 'God preserve me, young man, from ever becoming your mistress, or anyone else's, for if I lost my virginity and my body was once corrupted, there is no doubt that nothing could save me from eternal damnation.' When he heard this Master Gervase realized at once that she belonged to the blasphemous sect of *Publicani*, who were being searched out and destroyed all over France, especially by Count Philip of Flanders, who punished them unmercifully with righteous cruelty. Some of them had already come over to England, where they were detained at Oxford, and by order of Henry II disfigured by being branded on the forehead with a white-hot iron, and banished from the realm.

While Gervase was arguing with the girl and refuting her answer the archbishop intervened with his clerks. When he heard what the dispute was about he ordered the girl to be arrested and brought back to the city. There he spoke to her before his clergy, and put forward many authorities and reasoned arguments to confute her heresy. She replied that she herself was not well enough instructed to be able to answer such telling objections, but admitted that she had an instructress in the city who would have no difficulty in disproving the bishop's arguments. When she had revealed the woman's name, and where she lived, she was immediately sought out by the archbishop's servants and brought before him. Then she was bombarded by the archbishop and his clerks with questions and citations of the holy scriptures to convince her of the greatness of her errors, but she perverted all the authorities which they brought forward with such subtle interpretations that it was obvious to everybody that the spirit of all error spoke through her mouth. She replied so easily, and had such a clear memory of the incidents and texts advanced against her, both from the Old and the New Testament, that she must have had great knowledge of the whole Bible, and had plenty of practice in this kind of debate: she mixed truth with falsehood, and distorted the true explanation of our faith with evil intelligence.

When the obstinate minds of both women refused to be moved from their errors either by threats or by coaxing, by argument or by scriptural authority, they were locked in a prison cell until next day. Then they were brought back to the archbishop's hall, and there, before the archbishop and all his clerks, and in the presence of noblemen, publicly presented with many reasons for renouncing their errors. They absolutely rejected this salutary warning, and clung immovably to the error which they had conceived, so it was decided by common council to consign them to the flames. But when the fire had been lit in the city, and they should have been dragged by the archbishop's servants to the punishment which had been allotted to them, the wicked mistress of error called out, 'Madmen! Unjust judges! Do you think that you can burn me on your fire? I neither respect your judgement nor fear the fire which you have prepared.' So saying she took a ball of thread from her breast, and threw it through the great window, keeping one end of the thread in her hand, and calling loudly, in everybody's hearing, 'Catch!' At this she was raised from the ground in front of everyone, and flew through the window after the ball. We believe that she was taken away by the same evil spirits who once lifted Simon Magus into the air, and none of the onlookers could ever discover what became of the old witch, or whither she was taken.

The girl, who had not yet achieved such madness in the sect, remained behind. No reason, no promise of wealth, could persuade her to give up her obstinacy, and she was burned. Many admired the way in which she let forth no sighs, no tears, no wailing, and bore the torment of the flames firmly and eagerly, like the martyrs of Christ who (for such a different reason) were once slain by the pagans for the sake of the Christian religion.

The members of this abominable sect will choose death rather than renounce their errors, but there is nothing in common between their stubbornness and the constancy of Christ's martyrs, for contempt of death is the result of piety in the one case, and mere obstinacy in the other. They hold that children should not be baptized until they are old enough to understand it; that we should not pray for the dead, or seek the intercession of the saints; they advocate virginity, and condemn marriage as a cover for sin. They abhor milk and everything made from it, and all food that is the result of procreation. They do not believe in the fire of purgatory, but think that the soul leaves the body immediately after death, either for eternal peace or for damnation. They do not accept the Holy Bible, except for the Gospels and the letters of the apostles. They are uneducated people, and can, therefore, neither be convinced by reason, nor corrected by authority, nor moved by persuasion. They would rather die than abjure their evil sect.

Some of those who have investigated the secrets of their sect say that they believe that God does not concern himself with human affairs, and exercises no power or influence over the created world, but that there is an apostate angel, whom they call Luzabel who presides over the whole material creation, by whose will all earthly things are disposed. They say that the body is made by the devil, and makes the soul, and puts it into the body, so that there is always an unremitting battle between body and soul. Some people also say that they have underground hideouts in which they make wicked sacrifices to Lucifer at certain times, and perform sacrilegious ceremonies.

29 Eckbert of Schönau: sermon against the Cathars

Eckbert's thirteen sermons against the Cathars (*PL*, 195, col. 11–102) must have been written between the burnings at Cologne, in August 1163, to which he refers in the first sermon, and 1167, when Archbishop Rainhald of Cologne, to whom the prefatory letter is addressed, died, and Eckbert himself became abbot of Schönau: R. Manselli, 'Ecberto di Schönau', the closest study of the *Sermons*, concludes that they were composed in 1163. The information on which Eckbert draws was evidently collected over a long period of time, and a period of considerable development among heretical groups in the Rhineland (for which see Thouzellier, *RHE*, 1954). One interpretation of Eckbert's evidence in the light of this may be found in Russell, pp. 220–24.

The burning at Cologne in 1163 is described in the *Chronica Regia Coloniensis* (*MGH Script.*, 18, 114):

'Some heretics of the sect called Cathars came to Cologne from Flanders, and stayed secretly in a barn near the city. But when they did not go to church on Sunday they were found out by their neighbours. They were brought before the church court and thoroughly examined about their sect. When they would not be corrected by sound arguments and stubbornly maintained their position they were expelled from the Church and handed over to the lay court. On 5 August four men and a girl were taken outside the city and burned. The girl would have been saved by the sympathy of the people if she had been frightened by the fate of her companions and accepted better advice, but she tore herself from the grasp of those who were holding her, threw herself into the fire and was killed.' [Other references are collected and discussed by Mais-onneuve, pp. 111–12.]

Throughout the thirteen sermons Eckbert cites his knowledge of Cathar teaching and practice, but most of it is summed up in the prefatory letter (col. 11–14) and the first sermon (col. 13–21) translated here. He goes on, in his second sermon to attack the secrecy and exclusiveness of Catharism, contrasting it with the openness and universality of Catholicism. He calls them wretched halfwits, (*rustici viles*: in its context the phrase cannot refer to the social status of the Cathars) for arguing that the pearls which ought not to be cast before swine are the secrets of religion. The third and fourth sermons trace the rise of the Catholic Church, and attack the use of the text that 'faith without works is dead' as a justification for writing off the Catholic clergy of his day. The remaining ten sermons rebut the ten heretical opinions which he has listed in sermon one, keeping his promise to do it by means of scriptural exegesis.

Prefatory letter

To Rainhald, illustrious lord archbishop of Cologne, Eckbert, monk of Schönau.

It is common nowadays for heretics of a certain kind, whose errors have be-come notorious, to be found in your diocese. They are generally called Cathars, and are extremely dangerous to the Catholic faith, which they crawl through cunningly, undermining and corrupting it like grubs. They are equipped with passages from holy scripture, which—they think—support their views, and know how to use them to defend their lies and to attack Catholic truth, though they are ignorant of the true meaning which lurks in the divine words and cannot be grasped by the unskilful. I have written this work to describe their errors; to note the scriptural authorities with which they support their errors and show how these authorities should properly be understood; to defend the parts of our faith which they attack, and to point out, with divine assistance, with what scriptural authority our faith can be defended against such attacks, so that anyone who reads and remembers them will more readily be able to argue with these heretics if he happens to encounter them among the populace, as often happens. They are very fluent, and always have their case against us ready to hand. It is shameful if educated people like us find ourselves dumb and speechless before them.

When I was a canon at Bonn my friend Bertolf and I often used to argue with these people, and listen carefully to their opinions and arguments, and we also learned much from those who had left their groups, and escaped the snares of the devil. At the suggestion of my abbot, Hilduin, I have collected what I learnt of their beliefs in this way, and the arguments against them, in these sermons, and I pass them on to your highness for old acquaintance's sake If any of these heretics happen to be examined before you, you will be provided with the means of stopping their evil mouths, and of strengthening the wavering souls of gullible men who have been deceived by their dreadful words, and think they tell the truth. I ask you, if you think the composition of this book reasonable and see a way in which it may be of use to the Christian religion, to make it available as a reproach to this evil people for all time.

Sermon 1

Against what heresies the discourse is directed

The maiden church received a precious pearl as a wedding gift from her bride Jesus Christ—the Catholic faith. In modern times, alas, it suffers the attacks of many who labour to destroy it. In recent years, it seems to me, the dangers which our Saviour prophesied in the Gospels when he spoke of the signs which would foreshadow the Day of Judgement have begun to appear. According to St Matthew he said to his disciples, among other things, 'Then if any man shall say to you, here is Christ, or there: do not believe him. For there shall arise false Christs, and false prophets and shall shew great signs and wonders, insomuch as to deceive (if possible) even the elect. Behold I have told it to you. Behold he is in the desert: go ye not out. Behold he is in the closet: believe it not.'

If anyone has appeared who is mad enough to say that he is Christ I have yet to hear of him. But I have seen many of the false prophets who claim that Christ is in the closet. They are the hidden men, perverted and perverting, who have lain concealed through the ages. They have secretly corrupted the Christian faith of many foolish and simple men, so that they have multiplied in every land and the Church is now greatly endangered by the foul poison which flows against it on every side. Their message crawls like the crab, runs far and wide like infectious leprosy, infecting the limbs of Christ as it goes. Among us in Germany they are called *Cathars*, in Flanders *Piphles*, and in France *Tisserands*, because of their connection with weaving. As the Lord foretold they say that Christ is in closets, for they claim that the true faith of Christ and the true worship of Christ are to be found only in their meetings, which they hold in cellars, in weavers huts, and such underground hideouts. They say that they live the apostolic life, but they oppose the sacred faith and sound doctrine which has been handed down to us through the holy apostles from our Lord and Saviour himself. They are the people of whom Paul said in his Epistle to Timothy, 'Now the spirit manifestly saith that in the last times some shall depart from the faith, giving heed to spirits of error and doctrines of devils, speaking lies in hypocrisy, forbidding to marry, to abstain from meats, which God hath created to be received with thanksgiving by the faithful.'

The first heresy: marriage   There are indeed some among them to whom these words refer, who denounce and condemn marriage, and promise eternal damnation to those who remain in the married life until their death. Others approve of marriage between those of their number who come together as virgins, but say that they cannot be saved unless they separate before the end of their lives. Hence they forbid marriage.

The second heresy: avoiding meat Those who have become full members of their sect avoid all meat. This is not for the same reason as monks and other followers of the spiritual life abstain from it: they say that meat must be avoided because all flesh is born of coition, and therefore they think it unclean.

The third heresy: the creation of flesh That is the reason they give in public. Privately they have an even worse one, that all flesh is made by the devil, and must therefore not be eaten even in the direct necessity.

The fourth heresy: the baptism of children They hold various opinions about baptism. They maintain that baptism can be of no value to the children who are baptized, because they cannot seek baptism of their own volition, and cannot make any profession of faith.

The fifth heresy: baptism with water Another of the things which they say commonly, though secretly, is that no baptism with water can lead to salvation. Those who join their sect are rebaptized in a secret way, which they call baptism by fire and the Holy Spirit.

The sixth heresy: the souls of the dead They believe that at the hour of death the souls of the dead pass either to eternal happiness or to eternal damnation. They reject the view of the Church Universal that there are punishments in purgatory, in which the souls of certain of the elect are searched for the sins of which they were not fully cleansed by adequate penance in this life. Therefore they think it wasteful and vain to pray or give alms, or celebrate masses for the dead, and deride the tolling of bells which we carry on in our churches for the pious purpose of moving the living to pray for the dead and remember their own approaching end.

The seventh heresy: contempt for the mass They scorn and hold pointless masses celebrated in churches. They will go to mass and even receive the eucharist with the people among whom they live, to prevent their infidelity from becoming known. They say that the whole order of priests in the Roman Church, and in all churches of the Catholic faith, will be damned unless they become true priests in their own sect.

The eighth heresy: the body and blood of the Lord They believe that the body and blood of Christ cannot be made by our consecration, or received by us through communion. They say that they alone make the body of Christ, at their own tables. These words are deceptive: they do not mean the true body of Christ, whom we believe was born of a virgin and suffered on a cross; they call their own flesh and body 'of the Lord', and say that they have made the body of the Lord when they nourish their own bodies at ordinary meals.

I will not leave unmentioned what I have heard from a certain reliable man, who recognized their perfidy and the wickedness of some of their secrets, and left the sect.

The ninth heresy: the humanity of the Saviour He tells me that they are also in error about our Saviour, believing that he was not truly born of the Virgin, and did not truly have human flesh, but a kind of simulated flesh; that he did not rise from the dead, but simulated death and resurrection. Hence when Christians are celebrating Easter they either celebrate it carelessly if they are among their own people, or find excuses for leaving those among whom they live to avoid being compelled to worship with them. They have another festival instead, that of the death of the heresiarch Mani, whose heresy they undoubtedly follow, which Augustine in his *Contra Manichaeos* called *Bema*. My informant says that those to whom he had belonged called it *Malilosa*, and celebrated it in autumn.

In addition to these I have discovered a new and hitherto unheard of madness of theirs, which was clearly admitted by some of them when they were examined by a clerk in the city of Cologne, when they were burnt by the fervent zeal of the people.

The tenth heresy: human souls They say that human souls are apostate spirits which were expelled from heaven at the creation of the world; in human bodies they can come to deserve salvation through good works, but only if they belong to this sect.

For a long time now they have whispered these things abroad, going round the homes of gullible people. I hear that many unfortunate souls have been led off captive in the chains of their evil murmurings in recent times. They will cross sea and desert, so I am told, to win a Cathar, and stain all religious life with impious slander, saying that nobody can be saved without joining them. Therefore all who are zealous for the Lord must watch out carefully, and have their wits versed in the holy scriptures to capture these evil little foxes who are destroying the vineyards of the Lord of Sabaoth. Their errors are so many that no one has the strength to rehearse them all. I have laid out the ones which seem to me to be most dangerous, and arranged them in order; with God's help I propose to speak against those ones especially.

The origins of the Cathar sect

It should be known, and not kept from the ears of the common people, that this sect with which we are concerned undoubtedly owes its origin to the heresiarch Mani, whose teaching was poisonous and accursed, rooted in an evil people. They have added much to the teachings of their master which is not to be found among his heresies, and they are divided among themselves, for some of them assert what others deny.

Manichaeus, if I may speak of him for a moment, was born in Persia. He was called Mani at first, but his disciples later called him Manichaeus to prevent him from being thought mad, for his name, Mani, derived from mania, which means madness. For all that he was mad. He said he was the Holy Spirit, and had been sent to the world by Christ, as he has promised when he ascended to the throne of Heaven. Therefore he called himself an apostle of Christ, because he had been sent by him. Hence his disciples boasted that Christ's promise of the Holy Spirit was fulfilled in their master. In imitation of Christ who chose twelve apostles from the disciples, he also chose twelve of his followers as apostles. This number is retained by his followers to this day: they choose twelve of their elect, who are called masters, and the thirteenth is their leader. They have seventy-two bishops, who are ordained by the masters, and priests and deacons, who are ordained by the bishops, and these people are known among them as the 'elect'. People who seem suitable are sent out from the whole body to sustain and strengthen their heresy where it already exists, and to plant it where it does not.

I will now show that the teaching of Manichaeus and his followers is fundamentally opposed to the Christian faith.

We believe and confess that there is one God who made heaven and earth, and all that is in them, and this is the root of our faith. They teach that there were two creators, one good and one evil: God and the prince of darkness—I am not sure how accurately we could call him the devil. They are said to have had two quite opposite natures from the beginning of time, one good and the other evil, and they created the universe. The souls of men and all the other living animals and the quality which gives life to trees, plants and seeds, owed their beginning to God, and were created from his good nature—or rather they hold that each of such things is a part of God. Everything of flesh which lives on the earth, whether man or animal, originates from the prince of darkness, the devil, and is founded in his evil nature; this is why, as I have said, they avoid eating meat.

The message which these children of the devil have concocted for the damnation of all those who believe them and turn their minds away from the pure truth of the holy scriptures is alien to every human feeling: it must be spurned.

Among the errors of Manichaeus and his disciples this is clear: they say that the son of God never took on human flesh from the Virgin, but had an imitation of the human body; that he never suffered, or died, or was resurrected, but deceived human perceptions in all these things, so that though what is said about his humanity appeared to men to be true, there was no truth in any of it. Two magi, Zaroc and Arphaxat taught this in Persia before Manichaeus, and as I have already said, it has been firmly established about those who are called Cathars today. They are derived from certain disciples of Manichaeus, who were once called Catharists. Manichaeus the founder of the heresy, had many followers, who remained within a single sect while he lived. When he died, they disagreed among themselves, and split into three groups, called Mattharians, Catharists and Manicheans. All of them followed their own masters, but all have the name Manichean in common because the heresy of all of them originated from Mani. Those who were called Catharists were thought more wicked than the others, because of certain secret obscenities which they practised among themselves. Those about whom I am preaching these sermons undoubtedly follow their life and teachings. But I plan to explain why they were first called *Catharistae*, which means purified, elsewhere, in case the beginning of my book should become revolting if I recite all their depravities at once.

I have collected, and summarized briefly, what St Augustine wrote about the Manicheans in three of his books, the *Contra Manichaeos*, the *De moribus Manichaeorum* and the *De haeresibus*. I shall bind this summary at the end of my book so that my readers can understand the heresy properly from the beginning, and see why it is the foulest of all heresies. They may find that some of the things which they say themselves smack of Manicheism, and that St Augustine has discovered their secret thoughts. It is well known how before his baptism he was himself a member of the Manichean sect for a time, and afterwards described and refuted their errors and secrets in the books which I have named.

30 The 'Council' at Lombers, 1165

This account of the so-called 'Council' of Lombers, between Albi and Castres, is from Mansi, XXII, col. 157–68. The long refutations of each tenet professed by the heretics are omitted. They may be found, carefully abridged, in Roger of Hoveden, *Chronica*, ed. W. Stubbs, II, 105–7, and translated by H. T. Riley, *Annals of Roger of Hoveden* I, 423–47.

In the year of the Lord 1165 this final judgement was pronounced upon the arguments, assertions, and attacks on the Catholic faith which were pressed by certain men who caused themselves to be known as '*boni homines*', and who were supported by the men of Lombers. Judgement was delivered by William, bishop of Albi, after judges had been chosen and presented by each side. William was assisted by Goselin, bishop of Lodeve, and by the abbots of Castres, Ardorel, and Candeil, as well as Arnold de Beno, and other good men, both clerks and laymen were present, including Pons, archbishop of Narbonne, Adalbert, bishop of Nîmes, Gerard, bishop of Toulouse, William, bishop of Agde, Abbot Raymond of St Pons, Abbot Peter of Cendras, the abbot of Fontfroide, the abbot of Gaillac, the provost of Toulouse, the provost of Albi, the archdeacons of Narbonne and Agde, the prior of St Mary at Montpellier, the prior of Celleneuve, Master Blanc, and Hugh de Vereires; among the laity were [Viscount Raymond] Trencavel [of Béziers], the wife of Count Raymond of Toulouse, Sicard, Vicomte of Lavaur, Isarn of Dourgne, and most of the people of Albi and Lombers, and of various other townships.

At the request of the bishop of Albi and his assessors the bishop of Lodeve questioned the men who called themselves '*boni homines*' on several points.

First, he asked whether they accepted the laws of Moses, the Prophets, the Psalms, the Old Testament and the doctors of the New Testament. They answered in front of everybody that they did not accept the law of Moses, the Prophets, the Psalms, or the Old Testament, but only the Gospels, the letters of St Paul, the seven canonical Epistles, the Acts of the Apostles and the Apocalypse.

Second, he asked them to expound their faith. They said that they would not do so unless they were compelled to.

Third, he asked them about baptism of infants, and whether they are saved by it. They said that they would not talk about this, but were prepared to discuss the Gospels and Epistles.

Fourth, he asked them about the body and blood of the Lord: where it should be consecrated and by whom, who should receive it, and whether it is any better or more surely consecrated by a good man than a bad. They replied that anyone who took it worthily was saved, and anyone who took it unworthily thereby procured his damnation, and that it might be consecrated by any good man, whether clerk or layman. They would say no more, for they should not be forced to answer questions about their faith.

Fifth, he asked them what they thought about matrimony, and whether a man and woman could be saved who had been joined in the flesh. To this they would only reply that men and women are joined because of lust and fornication, as Paul said.

Sixth, he asked them about penance, and whether it could bring one to salvation at the moment of death; whether fatally wounded soldiers can be saved if they repent at the moment of death; whether one ought to confess one's sins to the priests and ministers of the Church, or to any layman, and to whom James referred when he said, 'Confess therefore your sins to one another.' They replied that it is sufficient for the sick to confess to whom they please, but that they would rather not comment on the soldiers, because James referred only to the sick. He also asked them whether it is enough to be contrite in heart and to confess, or whether after penance has been prescribed it is necessary to make amends by fasting, almsgiving, mortification and bewailing one's sins if the opportunity is available. They replied that James only said that they should confess to be saved; they did not aspire to be better than the apostle, or to superimpose anything of their own as the bishops do.

They also said a good deal that they were not asked about, such as that Jesus in the Gospel and James in his Epistle forbade the swearing of any oath whatever. They claimed that Paul laid down what sort of men ought to be ordained as bishops and priests, and that any who were not ordained according to Paul's instructions are not bishops and priests, but ravening wolves, hypocrites and seducers, men who want to be bowed to in the streets, to have the most prominent seats, to sit at the top of the table at banquets; who want to be called 'Rabbi' and 'master' contrary to the precept of Christ, to wear albs and white robes, and gold and bejewelled rings on their fingers, which Jesus, their master, did not command. Such men are not, they added, bishops or priests, or, if they are, then only the kind of priest who betrayed Jesus; they are evil, not good teachers but mercenaries, and should not be obeyed.

Against these allegations Archbishop Pons of Narbonne, Bishop Adalbert of Nîmes, Abbot Peter of Cendras and the abbot of Fontfroide cited many authorities from the New Testament. When these texts had been presented, because these people would not recognize any other authority, and the arguments heard, the bishop of Lodeve pronounced his final judgement of the law and of the New Testament, at the request of the bishop of Albi and the assessors above mentioned, in front of everybody.

[Goselin condemns the arguments of the *boni homines* on each point. He concludes:]

'These people stand not in the position of judges, but as accused. . . . They do not judge, they are judged. Moreover they have not been granted the right to preach in the Church. They are the heretics foretold by Paul when he said, "Evil men and seducers shall grow worse and worse: erring and driving into error. . . . There shall be a time when they will not endure sound doctrine, and will turn away their hearing from truth, but will be turned into fables", and, "From which things some, going astray, are turned unto vain babbling: desiring to be teachers of the law: understanding neither the things they say, nor whereof they affirm." It is the duty of the prelates of the Church to correct and punish their disobedience in front of everybody. Hence Paul, "Them that sin, reprove before all: that the rest also may have fear", and, to the bishops, "Having in readiness to revenge all disobedience", and "That he may be able to convince the gainsayers", and "speak and extort and rebuke with all authority." Again, "I have delivered such a one to Satan for the destruction of the flesh, that the spirit may be in the day of our Lord", and "I have judged him that hath so done", and "If anyone preach to you a gospel besides that which you have received, let him be anathema." '

The heretics replied that it was not they who were heretical, but the bishop who had pronounced judgement upon them. He was their enemy, a ravening wolf, a hypocrite and a foe of God, and his judgement was dishonest. They would not answer questions about their faith because they were on their guard against him as Jesus had warned them to be: 'Beware of false prophets, who come to you in the clothing of sheep, but inwardly they are ravening wolves.' He was persecuting them under false pretences. They were ready to show from the Gospels and Epistles that he and the other bishops were not good shepherds, but mercenaries.

The bishop said that his verdict had been lawfully pronounced, and that he was ready to prove in the court of the Catholic pope, Alexander, of King Louis of France, of Count Raymond of Toulouse, of his wife who was present, or of [Viscount Raymond] Trencavel, also present, that he had judged rightly, and they were manifest and notorious heretics.

Seeing that they were convicted and put to confusion the heretics turned to the crowd and spoke: 'Listen to us, good people. We will now confess the faith we hold, for your sakes and the love we bear you.'

The bishop interjected, 'Are you saying that you will do this for the sake of the people, though not for the sake of God?'

They continued, 'We believe in one true and living God, three in one, Father, Son and Holy Spirit; the son of God took on flesh, was baptized in the Jordan, fasted in the desert and preached our salvation; he suffered, died and was buried, descended into hell, was resurrected on the third day and ascended into Heaven; he sent the Holy Spirit to his disciples at Pentecost, and will come on the Day of Judgement to judge the living and the dead, and all who will rise again. We know that we should confess with our lips what we believe in our hearts. We believe that he shall not be saved who does not eat the body of Christ, which cannot be consecrated except in Church, nor by any but a priest, be he either good or bad, for it is done no better by the good than by the bad. We believe that no man can be saved except through baptism, and that infants are saved through baptism. We believe that a man and a woman may be saved if they are joined in the flesh; that every man must accept penance both in word and in his heart, from a priest, and be baptized in Church.' They added that they would accept anything else that could be shown them on the authority of the Gospels and the Epistles.

The bishop asked them whether they would swear that they held and believed this faith, and whether there was anything else that they had believed and preached which ought to be more fully confessed. They said that they would not take any sort of oath, for it was contrary to the Gospels and the Epistles. The Catholics present adduced arguments against this from the New Testament. When the bishop had heard the case he stood up and said: 'I,

Goselin, bishop of Lodeve, at the instance and command of the bishop of Albi and his assessors, give judgement that these heretics are wrong about swearing, and ought to take an oath if they want to be redeemed. Where faith is tested it should be guaranteed by oath. Since they have a bad reputation, and are well known as heretics, they must prove their innocence. In returning to the Church they must support their declaration of faith with an oath, as the Catholic Church maintains and holds proper, so that the infirm within the Church are not corrupted, and the diseased sheep does not infect the whole flock. This is contrary neither to the Gospel, nor to the Epistle of St James because. . . .'

When the heretics saw that they had been proved wrong on this point they said that the bishop of Albi had made an agreement with them that he would not force them to take an oath. The bishop of Albi denied this.

The bishop of Albi now rose and said, 'I applaud and confirm the verdict which Bishop Goselin of Lodeve has pronounced, and which has been given on my instructions. I warn the knights of Lombers that they must not give the heretics any support, on pain of losing the fine which they have placed in my hands.'

I, abbot of Castres, and chosen judge, approve this verdict and it has my consent. [Followed by all the others, including the laymen, named at the beginning of the report.]

IV The Triumph of Catharism

THE increasing determination of the papacy to control evangelical preaching, direct the religious life of the laity and eliminate heresy did not succeed in damming the currents of religious enthusiasm. On the contrary, the late twelfth and early thirteenth centuries saw still more diverse manifestations of lay piety, which flickered uncertainly on the boundaries of orthodoxy. Which side of it they found themselves on depended almost as much on the strategy adopted by the popes as on the content of their beliefs. The concern of this section is not with the general spiritual climate, or the evolution of ecclesiastical discipline, but with the establishment and convictions of Cathar communities in the Languedoc and northern Italy, but that theme cannot be wholly separated from the exuberant and shifting background represented here by Valdès and Lambert le Bègue, both, in their ways, heirs of a pre-Cathar dissenting tradition. This religious climate is excellently discussed by J. H. Mundy, *Europe in the High Middle Ages*, especially at pp. 283–316 and 515–61, and R. W. Southern, *Western Society and the Church*, pp. 272–318, while Brenda M. Bolton provides useful discussions of 'Innocent III's treatment of the Humiliati', 'Papal attitudes to deviants, 1159–1216', and '*Mulieres Sanctae*' in *Studies in Church History*, vols. 8, 9 and 10 respectively.

In 1167, according to the *Acta concilii Caramanensis*, an emissary from the dualist church at Constantinople summoned a meeting at St Félix de Caraman, some forty kilometres south-west of Toulouse. It was attended by a large number of the heretics of the Languedoc and by representatives of the churches of Italy and France. They agreed to set up a commission to delineate the boundaries of their churches of Toulouse and Carcassone, 'so that there would be harmony between them and neither would infringe the jurisdiction of the other', and the commissioners later recommended that the boundaries should coincide with those of the Catholic dioceses. Bishops were chosen and received the *consolamentum*, the central sacrament of Catharism, from Nicetas, as did Robert d'Espernon and Mark, bishops respectively of France and Lombardy.

The authenticity and the significance of this document, which purports to be a copy of the early thirteenth century 'from the ancient charter made at the instance' of the boundary commissioners themselves, have been seriously doubted for the past century. In 1946 Father Dondaine seemed not only to dispose of the objections which had been raised against its authenticity, but to provide a clear and compelling explanation of its meaning (*Miscellanea Giovanni Mercati*, V, 324–55). The dualist churches of the Balkans were divided on a fundamental point of doctrine. Some, the radical or Dragovitsan branch, held that the two principles of good and evil were independent and eternal. The moderate, or monarchist dualists, on the other hand, maintained that the evil principle was the creation of the good and had gone into rebellion against him. The distinction is that which was noted by Rainier Sacchoni and others between the Cathar churches of Desenzano and Concorezzo. This difference was one not only of doctrine but of organization. The first Cathars who appeared in western Europe, the argument runs, were moderate dualists, and Nicetas was a missionary from the Dragovitsans whose purpose was to convert them to radical dualism and to bring them into affiliation with his church; hence the need for the *consolamentum*, normally administered only once in a lifetime, to be repeated. Thus the *Acta concilii Caramanensis* recorded the crucial incident in an organized effort by the Dragovitsan Church to take over western Catharism. That such a take-over did take place, at about this time and under the direction of Nicetas, was confirmed by the *De heresi catharorum* and the *De hereticis* of Anselm of Alessandria which Dondaine published in 1949 and 1950. Hence, paradoxically, the new and apparently decisive onslaught on the authenticity of the *Acta* by Y. Dossat, 'Remarques sur un prétendu evêque cathare (1955–6) and 'A propos du concile cathare', (1969) is not of great importance: as he says it 'makes no appreciable difference to our perspective' of Cathar development in the West, though Moore, 'Nicétas, émissaire de Dragovitch: a-t-il traversé les Alpes?' (1973) argues that it does point to a direct connection between the appearance of absolute dualism in Toulouse and the communal struggles there in 1175–6.

The problems associated with the history and doctrines of western Catharism—its relationship with eastern dualism, with earlier movements in the West and with the Waldensians, with the social tensions and social development of the Languedoc and Lombardy at the end of the twelfth century, and with the life and organization of the Cathars themselves, are legion. Though it has been corrected at many points by more recent work, Runciman's *The Medieval Manichee*, pp. 123–70, is a good introduction for English readers, and there is a very fine, though severely Catholic, description of the Languedoc on the eve of the Albigensian crusade in the early chapters of M. H. Vicaire, *St Dominic*. W. L. Wakefield, *Heresy, Crusade and Inquisition* discusses heresy and its background well, though briefly, and has an up to date bibliography; it is also the best short account of the Albigensian crusade and the setting up of the Dominican inquisition in Toulouse. E. Delaruelle, 'Le Catharisme vers 1200: une enquête' (1960) provides a useful survey of the problems raised by the Cathars and their history, and the annual volumes of *Cahiers de Fanjeaux* (since 1966) record progress towards their solution, especially vol. 3, *Cathares en Languedoc*, which has contributions by most of the leading scholars in the field.

The views of those who would claim Catharism as a Christian and courtly philosophy of the Languedoc are most persuasively presented in the writings of R. Nelli (e.g. *Le phenomène cathare* (1964)), but C. Thouzellier and H. Rousseau indicate the weaknesses of this approach with ruthless cogency in *Annales* (1969), 128–41.

The relevant chapters of Fliche et Martin, *Histoire de l'église*, 9.2 and 10, by Foreville, Fliche and Thouzellier, provide a full background to this section. C. Thouzellier's classic analysis of the doctrinal controversies of *Catharisme et valdéisme en Languedoc* contains succinct comments on most of the questions connected with them, as well as very rich bibliographical notes, and three important studies are printed for the first time in her collected papers, *Hérésie et hérétiques*.

31 Lambert le Bègue: The sufferings of his friends

The career of Lambert le Bègue is discussed by Russell, *Dissent and Reform*, pp. 90–6, and E. W. McDonnell, *The Béguines and Beghards*, pp. 71 ff. The assertion of Gilles d'Orval in the thirteenth century that the Béguines were so called from his nickname, (which meant 'stammerer') is unfounded, and there is nothing to suggest that he was connected with any institution that resembled a béguinage, although the patterns of private piety and religious education which he reveals among his admirers are those from which the Béguine movement emerged in the Low Countries in the last decades of the twelfth century: on its origins see in addition to McDonnell the review by A. Mens in *Le Moyen Age* (1958).

Lambert is unique among those who found themselves censured by ecclesiastical authority in this period in that his defence survives, while there is no other contemporary account of the case against him. He was ordained priest in the diocese of Liège shortly after 1160 by Bishop Henry (d.1164), and ordered to refrain from preaching by Henry's successor Alexander at a diocesan synod in 1166. He incurred the still severer displeasure of the next bishop, Rudolf of Zahringen (1167–91), an imperial prince and notorious simoniac in consequence of whose condemnation Lambert was imprisoned in 1175. Three letters of his, of which the last and longest is translated below as **33**, and two from his supporters, were addressed to the Antipope Calixtus III, who reigned at Rome from 1168 until he was deposed after Frederick I reached agreement with Alexander III at the Peace of Venice in 1177. Lambert's appeal was successful, and he died in Liège in 1177.

The letter which follows is translated from P. Fredericq, *Corpus documentorum inquisitionis haereticae pravitatis Neerlandicae* II, 12–13.

Our hope and our salvation are in God, in whom is all hope and all salvation, and we seek the solace of pious consolation in the anguish of our tribulations. We are anxious to show your holiness and the Church Universal the storms of trouble and agony which have been inflicted upon us, to our unsought and undeserved injury. A certain priest named Lambert, a man of good repute and religious demeanour, has been living in Liège in the manner that befits a priest. He has tried strenuously to reform both clerks and people who have deserted the worship of God and separated themselves from him in their unworthy preoccupations. But because evil behaviour follows from evil dispositions, the clerks not only assailed him with slanderous words, but also strove to secure his immediate condemnation by false petitions and accusations. Inspired by the spirit of falsehood they approached the bishop and said that Lambert was a heretic who had wandered from the faith, and that the bishop should summon him before a general council where he would be convicted and condemned as a heretic. The bishop fixed a day for the council, and immediately suspended Lambert from his benefice and duties in his absence, without any opportunity to defend himself, as though he were a common criminal. He answered the summons, and when he was examined on the faith and the articles of faith they found nothing against him. Yet his enemies, such liars and so false in everything, persuaded the bishop to condemn this innocent man, whose morals contrasted so completely with their own, by ecclesiastical judgement, which Lambert resisted, relying on an appeal to the pope.

They summoned us also before the council, because we were seen to associate with him and to imitate his Christian teaching, but they did not find us at fault in any article of faith. They strove mightily to get us to condemn a man who merited no condemnation, and to denounce as heretical one whose teaching was sound in every point. Secure in our innocence, we asked to be allowed to seek the advice of more learned men, and, as though we were enemies, were refused what ought not to be denied even to enemies. At last, knowing what liars they were and how bitter was their hatred of us, we made this statement: 'We condemn and detest all heretical teaching.' They proclaimed that we had denounced Lambert. We did not wish either to lie or to violate our consciences. On these grounds they deprived us of our benefices and drove us from the diocese.

Reduced to exile and destitute of all help and advice we now beseech your holiness to be charitable towards our wretched condition. God is our witness that we have not invented a syllable of this.

32 Lambert le Bègue: A Bull of Calixtus III

Source: From Fredericq, *op. cit.*, pp. 13–14.

Calixtus, servant of the servants of God, to Rudolph, bishop of Liège, Henry the Provost, the archdeacons and cathedral chapter, and all the clergy of the diocese, greeting and apostolic benediction.

Provide, as prudent and discreet men, for the solicitous care of yourselves and your Church, and show yourselves zealous for the honour of the house of God, especially in those things which pertain to the security of the Catholic faith, and you will know that you are beloved and approved by us. But we are not only astonished but greatly troubled if it is true, as we have heard, that in contempt of the Apostolic See you have imprisoned and put in chains the priest named Lambert, who was slandered as a heretic, although he neither confessed nor was convicted but was willing to purge himself, and appealed for a judgement at the papal court. For one thing, while the benevolence of the Holy See permits judgement to others, it mercifully reserves the right of appeal to itself, so that it can help the oppressed and despoiled and rightly and canonically obstruct their assailants. It is decreed by divine will and prescription that the business of all churches, especially when it touches the Catholic faith, comes to us for final settlement, because the Roman Church was founded upon this rock by Christ, made the mother and head of all ranks, and the mistress of all ecclesiastical questions, so that what is bound on earth shall be bound in Heaven, and what is loosed on earth shall be loosed in Heaven. Therefore it astounds us the more that you have not trembled to imprison the aforesaid priest Lambert, and to bind him in chains, after he had appealed to us, and have not deferred as you ought to have done to the decision and dignity of the Holy See.

Wherefore we command you all, and firmly enjoin you by this apostolic letter, that as soon as you have read this letter you are to free the aforesaid Lambert from his chains and allow him to come to us and make a full answer to the charges against him. If anyone wishes to oppose him let him present himself before us also, either in person or through a messenger, with your letters, and if we discover anything culpable in Lambert we shall correct it as severely as propriety requires.

As for the priests Peter, Servatius, Wederic, Warner and Caesarius whom, as we hear, you have deprived of their office and benefices and expelled from their diocese, because they were closely attached to Lambert and would not denounce him as a heretic, since they knew that he had appealed to us, we solemnly command you to allow them without delay to perform their office and enjoy their benefices in peace until we have been able fully to establish what is the case against the aforesaid Lambert.

Given at St Flaviano, 2 September.

33 Lambert le Bègue: Lambert's final statement

The burden of Lambert's two earlier letters to Calixtus III, of which one was written while he was in prison and the other after his escape, is the same as this one, that his preaching was misrepresented and distorted by his enemies because his endeavours to procure reform threatened their own abuses. He had, for example, preached bitterly against 'the perverse and detestable practice which prevailed in the city and the towns around it of exacting payments, openly and irreverently, for baptizing children, bringing the sacraments to the sick and the last rites to the dying, and burying the dead.' (Fredericq, p. 20.) When he said that in some circumstances, such as that of martyrdom, salvation was possible without baptism by water he was accused of preaching that the sacraments were not necessary to salvation; false witnesses were produced against him and their evidence admitted without proper examination though he was ready to rebut it by the ordeal by fire (*ibid.*, pp. 10, 11).

Russell, *Dissent and Reform*, pp. 91–2, rightly warns against the assumption that Lambert's orthodoxy is any less probable because he appealed to the antipope rather than to Alexander III, on the ground that Calixtus' title was not questioned in an area such as Liège which still had a strong tradition of accepting imperial control over the papacy. In any case a verdict from Alexander III would hardly have cut much ice with Rudolph of Zahringen.

This letter is from Fredericq, pp. 26–32.

A great many things have been written to you, and said against me in your presence, which I could not answer point by point at the time. Like a jar with a narrow neck before a fast and heavy flow of water, I could catch little at the time, and a lot was spilt. Now that I have returned home I have been able to collect together some of what was allowed to pass, and am ready to answer every charge.

The first accusation, I gather, is that I was born of poor and humble parents. Now there is a rational and decent ground of attack! Wise men have often said that what is worthy to receive the faith is worthy of belief. Did not God the creator of the universe make every kind of man on the face of the earth out of one man? Did not David, Israel's greatest king, confess that he had been a shepherd when he said, 'He chose David for his servant, and took him from his flock of sheep'? What sensible man measures another by his parentage? Certainly not the philosophers of the gentiles. And the Lord himself, when he chose a virgin to be his mother, having no natural one, is not supposed or alleged carefully to have selected a queen or a king's daughter, or some other relation of the princes of this world, which refutes the propagators of this absurdity from the outset. He did the same when he chose his apostles. He did not call rich men to join him in his preaching, but the fishermen Peter and Andrew, and their cousins James and John, also fishermen. When the Jews foolishly reproached his birth as well as his teaching they said, 'Is not this the carpenter's son?', and 'Hath any one of the rulers believed in him, have the Pharisees?' By the grace of him who found it consistent with his dignity to be born in a stable I, his unworthy servant, had a smith for my father, and the reproaches which he bore for the nature of his parentage and of his teaching he has permitted me, though unworthy, to hear of mine. I am rebuked for being born of humble people and because my preaching is heard by weavers and tanners rather than princes, as though guilt resided not in sin, but in the arts necessary to mankind. I think the words of the psalmist are appropriate to my own case, 'The reproaches of them that reproached thee are fallen upon me.' I confess that the force of this prejudice might have overwhelmed me, if the Lord had not shown that he was with me by demonstrating it in his own life.

I hear they say that my parents were ignorant people. For that I shall always thank the Lord, that they never knew or spoke of lewdness and adultery, hatred and greed, murder and theft. As Job said, 'The simplicity of the just man is laughed to scorn. The lamp, despised in the thoughts of the rich, is ready for the time appointed.' Come then, vessel of grace and doctor of the gentiles to speak divine not human wisdom, and speak in consolation, 'There are not many wise according to the flesh, not many mighty, not many noble. But the foolish things of the world hath God chosen, that he may confound the wise; and the weak things of the world hath God chosen, that he may confound the strong; and the base things of the world hath God chosen, and the things that are contemptible hath God chosen: and things that are not, that he might bring to naught the things that are.' Certainly, leaving that aside, if I am worthy of any approval it is because I saw and heard my poor and humble mother turn aside the temptations which she thought served pride better than truth.

The next charge against me, I believe, is that I confessed to my bishop that I had taken up my rank as a priest unworthily, and asked him to deprive me of it, and that he did so. This story is partly true and partly false. I did confess to my bishop that I had not achieved that rank with complete propriety, but I did not ask him to degrade me and I was not degraded, and therefore steadfastly maintain that I was never restored or needed to be restored, as they allege, since I was never degraded. I cannot contain my surprise at their temerity in making this accusation, for I have celebrated mass a great many times in their own convent during the thirteen years since I made that confession. It is a yet stronger refutation of the canons of St Paul's, one of whom seems to have made this charge, that they gave me one of their churches where I worked for three years for the honour of God and the service of the Church. I painted it, made windows, filled in the holes in the walls, provided it with wax candles and everything else that was necessary to the conduct of services, and they moved me away from it not on the ground that I had been deprived of my office, but because I would not pay an increased rent. If a Daniel or such another were aroused by my injuries to seek a sign and overturn their deeds from their words and their words from their deeds his testimony would vindicate my innocence and leave their foulness without a hiding place. If they speak the truth when they claim that I gave up my priestly orders how did it come about that they allotted their own church to me as though I were a priest? And, since they did give me the church, how could what they say be true?

Another charge that they level is that because I preached a sermon at a general synod without being invited to do so, Bishop Alexander imposed silence upon me. That is obviously refuted by their own earlier accusation discussed above. If, as they say, I had been deprived of my office and had presumed to usurp it again how was silence imposed on me as though I were a priest when it ought rather to have been adjudged that I was revealed as an imposter who dared to preach without the necessary orders? A sensible and educated man will conclude that these contradictory accusations which clash head on with one another deserve, as the Lord said, to perish, and can hurt none but those who repeat them. As to the occasion to which they refer, I will not conceal it from you. At the council to which they refer, presided over by Bishop Alexander, I was anxious to secure the restoration of customs which had been soundly introduced some years before and served well for a time before they fell into neglect. I maintained that according to the rule and custom of Alexander's predecessor, Henry of blessed memory, the sons of priests ought not to be admitted to holy orders; that according to decrees promulgated at the Council of Rheims by Pope Eugenius III, priests and clerks ought not to have their clothes dyed in bright colours or slashed at front and rear; that in baptizing children no more than three should be brought to the font at a time, as the same council ordained; that omens and divinations should not be looked for in the celebration of the mass, as they are by some false priests. I readily confirm that I said all these things, not for the sake of preaching or putting forward my own opinions, but to secure the restoration of what had been undermined. When I saw that none of the points which I had raised with a view to obtaining decisions on them was being either accepted or discussed, I left the meeting freely with certain others; no sentence had been openly pronounced against me, nor any injury done to me.

The next accusation that they made was that I would like to have abolished pilgrimages across the sea and the custom of visiting the Holy Sepulchre. I have neither opposed nor tried to oppose this excellent custom, though I have advised forcibly, when I saw many attempt it frivolously and without proper preparation, that it should either be prosecuted diligently and soberly to the end, or some other good work undertaken instead. There have been too many who have accumulated their wealth from robbery and theft, from swindle, fraud and other kinds of wrongdoing, and have set out without intending to restore it fourfold, like Zacheus, or even once; too many who have injured their brother despite the commandment of their Lord, not once but frequently and seriously, and set off to offer gifts at his temple in Jerusalem without remembering the words of the scriptures, 'He that offereth sacrifice of the goods of the poor is as one that sacrificeth his son in the presence of his father', and 'The sacrifices of the wicked are abominable because they are offered of wickedness.' Such as these I have often urged to think again, lest their labour be wasted and they provoke still further the God whom they hoped to placate. Others have acquired worldly substance by honest labour, and seen their fathers in need, yet shut their hearts to them and set out for Jerusalem and other holy places with great expense. These too I have deliberately denounced, not to lead them into a trap but (what is better) to make them think, so that they would not sin and arouse the wrath of God not through failing to make offering, but through failing to distribute their wealth rightly. For God says, 'Deal thy bread to the hungry', and 'When thou shalt see one naked cover him', and Jesus said, 'Sell what thou hast and give to the poor', and at the Day of Judgement he will say, 'I was hungry and you gave me not to eat: I was thirsty and you gave me not to drink; I was a stranger and you took me not in: naked and you covered me not: sick and in prison and you did not visit me.' Why did this brother who accuses me, or any of his people, not come to me when I was imprisoned for making such assertions as these? Why does he not tremble because his habit is to ignore God's commands? For indeed I have heard that he went to Jerusalem, but never that he redeemed anybody from prison. Let them look to God for their salvation, lest the light which is in them be darkened while those who follow me in obscure paths see the light.

If my accuser cannot see this because of his pilgrim's staff I beg you, my lord pope, as the highest and only eye of the Church, to see it. I beg you and your colleagues and fathers, the lords cardinal to consider together carefully whether Paulinus of Nola and other saints laid down in their writings that prisoners should be redeemed, guests entertained, the hungry and thirsty refreshed, the naked clothed, the widow consoled and the flock protected, or that trips to holy places should be multiplied. Is there any region or province on earth that does not suffer an enormous variety of needs? Mankind suffers if priests attend to exercises on their own behalf instead of ministering to others. I prefer and hold worthier those who, like the Samaritan, do what they can for the poor, and think that their service should be approved, not reproved, for the love of charity is the best road to salvation.

As to the charge that I said that a man who wears the cross on his cloak looks in vain for God in Jerusalem because he was eaten yesterday—that is to say at Easter—it is a childish and groundless slander which I deem unworthy of a written response. I can dispel it with a few words, if anyone thinks it necessary, wherever and whenever they like.

The next accusation is that I have taught that it is not necessary to abstain on Sundays from work necessary to the support of human life, and that I forced some people to work in my own garden on the Lord's day. God is my witness that I neither said nor did any such thing. I will not conceal the origin of this calumny from your holiness. I used to strive always for the salvation of the simple, trying to reach them by example, by exhortation and by preaching to extirpate the vices of modern times and plant the seeds of virtue in their hearts. St Gregory said that we should give up worldly work on Sundays, and devote ourselves to every kind of spiritual employment, to repair on this day what had been neglected on others. Yet I saw that an infinite multitude of both sexes devoted the Lord's day not to restoring their negligence, but to multiplying their sins. They abstained from manual labour to watch mimes, plays and dancing girls, to take their holiday with drunkenness and gambling, to flock around armies of wicked women and eye them, or dance with them through the grounds of the churches and over the graves of their parents and relations singing obscene songs and indulging in lewd gestures. There was no argument that, like Phineos the son of Heli, they were not resting but mad. It was a minority that followed me in wearing the cloak of abstinence: most of them, far from observing the sabbath, revelled in their insanity. I pondered how best to admonish them, and recalled that by straining at a gnat one may swallow a camel: by abstaining from work on the sabbath day to devote themselves to these dissipations they might make the sabbath their enemy. I therefore pointed out that to engage in agricultural work and such things on Sunday is not sinful in itself, although it is better to observe it as a day of rest, while to desist from work in order to indulge in wickedness is to court damnation.

It is not true that I forced people to work in my garden on a Sunday, but I will not hide the basis of the accusation. I was building myself a house beside the church. When the walls were completed they did not sit firmly on the ground, and one Sunday, since they were unsafe, I amicably persuaded a few people who had gathered together for secular amusement to carry soil to the house to raise the foundations and make them support the walls properly. I approached them, made my request, and they agreed. It is ludicrous that since my accusers could find nothing better they bore this across the Alps to the Apostolic See, like a herd of oxen frightened by a single ant.

They also contend that my followers (*sectatores*) do not go to church, and do not take communion. Whether I have any followers in that sense, or have ever had any, I cannot say, but certainly I have never meant to. I know indeed that it is and always will be my duty to arouse my brethren to the prospect of damnation, and I would fear for my soul if I did not preach. As God said through Isaiah, 'Cursed be he that witholdeth his sword from blood', and through Peter, 'As every man hath received grace, ministering the same to one another: as good stewards of the manifold grace of God.' I devoted myself to preaching with all my strength, in the conviction that the gift given to me by the grace of Christ to be my vocation in this world ought not to be hidden away. I never asked anybody to follow me, but rather to follow him who died and rose again for them. I do not deny that there are those, poor clerks and many lay folk, who have seen my humble way of life, the meagreness of my diet, my contempt for glory and riches, my scrupulous attention to the conduct of worship and pastoral care, and—not very wisely I fear—have approached Christ through me, and come to observe his laws. And though I am accused of having followers they may be blessed through it, according to the apostle who speaks of 'followers of good works'.

How they conduct themselves now, or what state they are in, I do not know, since I was driven into exile and separated from them, but I can scarcely be ignorant of what their demeanour was when I did see them, or of how I left them. I saw them go frequently and regularly to church and pray with me with great devotion, conducting themselves most decently and reverently. They listened avidly to the word of God, and during the mass they witnessed the Lord's renewed suffering for them with sobs and sighs, so movingly that on a number of occasions when I myself stood by the altar with a stony heart I saw such striking evidence of their devotion and piety that divine love spoke to me, as it were, through them, and I felt my soul on fire. How can I describe with what contrition of heart, what outpourings of tears, what reverence and trembling, without any of the common jostling and clamour they would receive the body and blood of their Saviour? They would come forward as though in military order, the seriousness of their faces terrible to the wicked. When I saw their regularity and piety I felt that although my rank was greater my virtue was much less, and wanted to become like them, saying to myself, 'Let my soul die the death of the just, let my last hours be like theirs.' When they returned to their own homes they ate soberly and piously, and spent the rest of the day until Vespers—I am talking about Sundays—singing hymns, psalms and canticles, thinking over what they had heard in church, and encouraging each other to observe it. I saw that these women had realized the life and passion of the Blessed Virgin, Mother of Christ, and was anxious to assist them in their good work. I made a rhythmical translation of the Acts of the Apostles from Latin into the language that they knew, inserting exhortations at suitable places, for them to use on holy days so that they could exult in their purity in the midst of evil, and keep themselves free from the poisons of the world.

It is to this also that the charge against me refers, of opening the scriptures to the unworthy. They forget that the Lord promised the enjoyment of the kingdom of Heaven to all men, and that he did not eat the loaves, but handed them to his disciples to feed the multitude. Moreover, my accusers have a copy of the psalms translated into the vernacular by a certain Flemish master, with all its glosses and supporting authorities. Why do they not complain about that? Why do they not bring charges against him? Perhaps it is because a prophet is without honour in his own country, for that master is not a native of the country.

That is what these people, who are alleged not to have gone to church, were like when I left them. As I have said, I do not know how they are now. But I hear from some travellers that they are having to excuse, though not to do themselves, what Jeremiah condemned when he said that those who had lived in peace must take up their cloaks and tunics, and turn to war. Some of them, according to a message that has reached me, have been driven by their enemies to perjury, some imprisoned, or violently driven from their homes, and all the rest, except the richer or those who have succeeded in hiding themselves, exposed to contumely and persecution. I fear that we see the fulfilment of the Lord's prophecy, 'I will strike the shepherd, and the sheep of the flock shall be dispersed. He that hath ears to hear, let him hear.'

My detractors add that I have called it a lesser crime to trample the sacrament underfoot than to listen carelessly to the word of God. I have not. But I did point out that St Augustine called it as great a crime to listen to the word of God carelessly as carelessly to allow the sacraments to fall to the ground. If Augustine was right he should be heeded. If he was wrong he, not I, should be condemned.

I have rebutted these and other charges against me many times, partly in my letters of complaint to you, and partly in the book called the *Antigraphum Petri* which was long since submitted for your inspection. I need discuss them no further. To one charge which until now seems to have remained intact I will direct my weapons, and through his strength whose weakness is stronger than men I shall not so much destroy it as show that it is destroyed already by its own internal contradictions. It is—I have the sense of it, if not the words— that as a result of my reprehensible preaching the practice of celebrating masses for the dead on feast days every week, which had been common in those parts, has now almost come to an end. Let my friends and neighbours answer for me, and let my detractors decide which part they want of the charge which they have brought forward. Do they judge my teaching on this point sound or not? If sound why do they condemn it? If unsound why do they practise it? Do any of the people, as they charge, neglect to go to mass now, after being misled by me, who had been accustomed to attend the masses which I reduced? No. How then can priests, to whom alone it is conceded freely to celebrate mass, still maintain against their own decision what they charged me with teaching wrongly? If they seek to dispute this by quibbling, the vigour of their arguments against it will only serve to reveal the gaping maw of their avarice and greed.

It is plain, and has been from the outset, that my accusers fall into the trap which they had prepared for me. Deservedly so. They have repaid me evil for good, and hatred for love. Blessed be the Lord who delivers me not into the jaws of their trap, and snatches my soul from the snares of my hunters.

What sensible man will give credence to their assertions, when they are not even consistent in themselves? These cloudy accusations will not befog the eyes of wise men when even the simple can see at once what they are like and from what they arise.

If the See of Peter is founded on rock and not reeds let it now prepare a decree of canonical condemnation either against my detractors or against those who have taken up and disseminated their attacks.

That I have spoken the truth with the zeal of righteousness may not commend me to the clemency of your holiness, if someone else has shaken it with shafts of malice. For I know that the envy of a few among them (and not of the whole body of them), rather than knowledge of the truth, has driven them in ignorance to persecute me despite my innocence. 'But the chief priests persuaded the people that they should ask Barabbas,' says the Gospel. That was how a few people obtained the agreement of the ignorant multitude to the crime of crucifying our Lord. God is my witness that I neither want nor seek anything for myself but retreat from the company of other men, apart from those who refuse to believe the accusations against me. What shall I do when God comes to judgement? As I crawl like a worm on the face of the earth shall I dare to keep or seek a hundred pennies for myself when I have no prospect of rendering even one of the hundred thousand talents which righteousness will demand of my indigence? At the awful prospect of being weighed in such minutely accurate scales I have willingly renounced and always will renounce whatever sins have been detected in me either now or in the future. But I affirm and insist that I have sown the word of God fruitfully among his people, without avarice or self-seeking, and in conformity with Catholic doctrine.

34 The conversion of Valdès and its consequences

The origins of the Waldensian movement are obscure. That it began as a group of laymen dedicated to the struggle against Catharism is suggested by the confession of faith of Valdès which is edited by Dondaine, 'Aux origines du valdéisme' (1946), and translated by Wakefield and Evans, pp. 206–8; see also Maisonneuve, pp. 137–9; Dondaine, 'Durand de Huesca et la polémique anti-cathare' (1959), and Thouzellier, *Catharisme et valdéisme*, especially pp. 16–18, 27–79. Rousset, 'Recherches sur l'émotivité à l'époque romane' (1959), discusses similar, though orthodox, cases of religious conversion in the twelfth century in their relation to the social environment. This account is from the chronicle of Laon, *MGH SS* XXVI, 447–9.

At about this time, in 1173, there was a citizen of Lyons named Valdès, who had made a great deal of money by the evil means of usury. One Sunday he lingered by a crowd that had gathered round a *jongleur*, and was much struck by his words. He took him home with him, and listened carefully to his story of how St Alexis had died a holy death in his father's house. Next morning Valdès hastened to the schools of theology to seek advice about his soul. When he had been told of the many ways of coming to God he asked the master whether any of them was more sure and reliable than the rest. The master quoted to him the words of the Lord, 'If thou wilt be perfect go sell what thou hast and give to the poor and thou shalt have treasure in heaven. And come follow me.'

Valdès returned to his wife and gave her the choice between having all his movable wealth or his property in land and water, woods, meadows, fields, houses, rents, vineyards, mills and ovens. She was very upset at having to do this and chose the property. From his movable wealth he returned what he had acquired wrongly, conferred a large portion on his two daughters, whom he placed in the order of Fontevrault without his wife's knowledge, and gave a still larger amount to the poor. At this time a terrible famine was raging through Gaul and Germany. For three days a week, from Whitsun to St Peter-in-chains [27 May–1 August] Valdès generously distributed bread, soup and meat to anyone who came to him. On the Assumption of the Virgin [15 August] he scattered money among the poor in the streets saying, 'You cannot serve two masters, God and Mammon.' The people around thought that he had gone out of his senses. Then he stood up on a piece of high ground and said, 'Friends and fellow-citizens, I am not mad as you think. I have avenged myself on the enemies who enslaved me when I cared more for money than for God, and served the creature more faithfully than the creator. I know that many of you disapprove of my having acted so publicly. I have done so both for my own sake and for yours: for my sake, because anybody who sees me with money in future will be able to say that I am mad; for your sake, so that you may learn to place your hopes in God and not in wealth.'

Next day as he was coming out of church Valdès begged a certain citizen, formerly a friend of his, for God's sake to give him something to eat. The man took him home, and said, 'As long as I live I will provide you with the necessities of life.' When his wife heard this story she was very upset, and rushed distraught to complain to the archbishop that Valdès had begged his bread from someone other than herself. This moved everybody who was with the archbishop to tears. The archbishop requested the citizen to bring his guest before him. The wife seized her husband by his tattered clothes, and said, 'Is it not better, my man, for me to redeem my sins by giving you alms than a stranger?' After this, by the archbishop's command, he was not allowed to accept alms from anybody in the city except his wife.

1177 Valdès, the citizen of Lyons whom we have already mentioned, who had vowed to God that he would possess neither gold nor silver, and take no thought for the morrow, began to make converts to his opinions. Following his example they gave all they had to the poor, and willingly devoted themselves to poverty. Gradually, both in public and in private they began to inveigh against both their own sins and those of others.

1178 Pope Alexander III held a council at the Lateran palace. . . . The council condemned heresy and all those who fostered and defended heretics. The pope embraced Valdès, and applauded the vows of voluntary poverty which he had taken, but forbade him and his companions to assume the office of preaching except at the request of the priests. They obeyed this instruction for a time, but later they disobeyed, and affronted many, bringing ruin on themselves.

35 Legation in the Languedoc: Peter of St Chrysogonus

In 1178 a papal mission was dispatched to Toulouse at the request of Count Raymond V, with the support of Louis VII and Henry II, to attempt to convert the Cathars whose power in the region was growing rapidly. It was headed by a papal legate, Peter, Cardinal of St Chrysogonus, and included the archbishops of Bourges and Narbonne, the bishops of Bath and Poitiers, and Henry, abbot of Clairvaux. Peter's account of the enterprise is in *PL*, 199, col. 1119–24, and in two slightly different versions by Roger of Hoveden, *Gesta Henrici*, I, 202–6, and *Chronicle*, ed. Stubbs (RS 1867) II, 150–60. For the background to the mission, a discussion of how its methods foreshadowed those of the inquisition, and an account of the continued efforts against the heretics in this region for the next twenty years, see Maisonneuve, pp. 129–41, and Mundy, *Liberty and Political Power in Toulouse*, pp. 43–90.

Peter, by the grace of God cardinal-priest of St Chrysogonus, and legate of the Apostolic See, to all the children of Holy Mother Church who hold to the Catholic and apostolic faith, greetings in the Lord.

As the apostle tells us, 'there is one Lord and one faith' from whose simplicity none may stray without danger. On this foundation, to which there is no possible alternative, the apostles and their apostolic successors, inspired and instructed by the Holy Spirit, have laid sound doctrines as firmly and securely as if they were of stone, so that neither the force of the whistling winds nor the engines of the impious can shake it, however furious their assaults.

In these times certain false brethren, Raymond de Baimac and Bernard Raymond and other heresiarchs have transformed themselves into angels of light, now Satan's, preached against the Christian and apostolic faith, deceived many souls with their poisonous teaching, and dragged them with them to ruin. Yet now he who uncovers mystery, who gave his spirit to Daniel to confute the elders of Israel has seen souls destroyed by devilish wiles. He will not have their wickedness hidden any longer, or the purity of the Christian faith corrupted by their teaching, and for the greater glory of the faith his wonderful power has revealed in the sight and hearing of many the poisonous evil which formerly lay hidden.

The aforesaid Raymond and Bernard and others met our venerable brother Reginald, bishop of Bath, the vicomte of Touraine and Raymond de Neufchatel, who had come at our request to the land of Roger of Béziers to free our venerable brother the bishop of Albi. They claimed that they had been unjustly treated by the noble count of Toulouse and other barons, who had abjured them for ever, and offered to come before us to defend their faith if they could have safety in coming and going. Lest the souls of the simple who had been imbued with their filth should suffer any injury, and because if we refused them a hearing they might ascribe it to indifference on our part, the bishop and the vicomte agreed, on our behalf and on that of the count, that they could come before us in safety provided that they should be heard by ourself and our venerable brother the bishop of Poitiers, the legate of the Apostolic See, and other reliable men, before the whole people, and be approved by us if their faith were sound and healthy. After they had been examined by us, whatever the outcome, they could return safely to their homes, so that it would not appear that they had been led to a confession of the true faith through fear or violence, but after eight days if they had not returned to the true faith, they must be expelled according to the edict which had gone out from the lands of the princes who had abjured them.

We thought it wise to confirm the indulgence granted by the bishop and vicomte, even though, as we have said, an edict had already been issued by the count of Toulouse and other lords expelling the heretics from their lands. Then, with the bishop of Poitiers, the count of Toulouse, and about three hundred other clerks and laymen assembled with us in the church of St Etienne we urged them to expound their beliefs to us, to return to the Catholic faith, and by salutary confession to remove the infamy which they and the whole land had incurred through their damnable teaching. During the debate which followed this they produced in front of everybody a paper on which they had written the articles of their faith, and read it at length. When we noticed some words which seemed to be suspect, and might obscure their heresy unless they were more fully explained, we asked them to defend their faith in Latin, both because we did not know their language well enough, and because the Gospels and the Epistles from which they wanted to support their faith are written in Latin. It became clear that they dared not do this when one of them tried to speak in Latin, so badly that he could hardly string two words together. We were, therefore, forced by their ignorance, absurd though it was, to agree to discuss the sacraments of the Church in the vernacular.

They said that there were not two principles, and confessed clearly and firmly, in public before us and the others we have mentioned, that one supreme God created everything, both visible and invisible, and that this was proved by the scriptures, the evangelists and the apostles. They confessed that one of our priests, whether good or bad, just or unjust, even if they knew him to be an adulterer or an undoubted criminal, could confer the body and blood of Christ, and that through the strength of the holy word handed down by the Lord the bread and wine became the body and blood of Christ.

They agreed that children and adults baptized by our baptism are saved, and that none can be saved without it, and absolutely denied that they had any other baptism or laying on of hands such as had been charged against them. They affirmed without reserve that if a man and woman have been joined in a marriage which is not impeded by sin they may render their conjugal debt to one another, and that being married they are free from blame and may be saved, but will never be damned for that reason. They agreed that archbishops, bishops, priests, monks, canons, hermits, Templars, and Hospitallers can be saved. They said that it was right and proper that churches founded in honour of God and the saints should be visited devoutly and that priests and other ministers should be treated with honour and respect, and first fruits and tithes paid to them, and that they should be reverently and faithfully obeyed in all parochial matters. They added, among other praiseworthy sentiments, that alms ought to be given to the Church and to the poor, and to God himself. They said, according to our clear understanding, that they believed all this, although they were said to have denied it in the past.

After we had examined them, and they had made this spontaneous confession of faith, we went into the church of St Jacques. There an enormous crowd of people gathered, behaving as though they expected some great spectacle, and together with ourselves heard the confession of faith which had been written on the paper we mentioned above read out in the vernacular tongue. They were heard patiently, and without any interruption, and when they had finished speaking of their own free will, we asked them in the hearing of all the people, since their explanation of their beliefs seemed so praiseworthy and so Catholic, whether they believed in their hearts what they said with their lips, and whether as had often been alleged, they had ever preached anything to the contrary. They replied that they did believe it and had never preached anything against it. At this the count of Toulouse and many other clerks and laymen who had heard them preach otherwise, greatly astonished and burning with zeal for the Christian faith immediately convicted them as manifest liars. Some of those present steadfastly maintained that they had heard from some of the heretics that there are two gods, one good and one evil: the good god had created everything invisible, and everything that could not be changed or corrupted, while the evil one created the sky, the earth, man, and other visible things. Others said that they had heard them preach that the body of Christ could not be conferred through the ministry of priests who were unworthy or guilty of any crime. Many testified that they had heard them deny that a man and his wife could be saved if they slept together. Others firmly said to their face that they had heard from them that the baptism of children is ineffectual, and heard them proclaim other blasphemies against God, the Church and the Catholic faith so appalling that we would prefer not to specify them.

However righteous their previous confession, which had seemed to be enough for salvation if they had believed it in their hearts and spoken it in their heart of hearts, they were men of twisted minds and dishonest intentions. They did not want to relinquish their heresy when on the surface some authority or other seemed to support their slothful and foolish minds, on the pretext of the words which, according to the Gospel, the Lord said, 'Do not swear at all. Let your speech be: Yea, yea, and No, no.' They claimed that this meant that they ought not to swear, though the Lord himself is recorded as having sworn, for it is written, 'The Lord hath sworn' etc. and elsewhere, 'I have sworn by myself saith the Lord.' Again, the apostle says, 'an oath for confirmation is the end of all their controversy.' Those who read the holy scriptures will find many other passages like this which permit us, because of their fickleness, to swear to anyone whom we wish to persuade. But, like the fools they were, these men did not understand the scriptures, and fell into the trap which they themselves had laid. Although they held swearing to be a dreadful thing, forbidden by the Lord, they were convicted of swearing in their own statement of confession. When they said, 'in the truth which is God we believe this, and declare that it is our faith', they did not realize that to adduce the truth and word of God in support of their assertion was undoubtedly to swear, as the apostle said when he wrote, 'this we say unto you in the word of the Lord, and God is my witness', and similar things which anyone who reads and understands the holy scriptures can easily find.

When they had been convicted by many and sufficient witnesses, and there were many more who were ready to testify against them, we urged them strongly to lay aside their heresy and return to the unity of the faith, for it is not the custom of the Church to deny mercy to returning sinners. We warned them that since they had been excommunicated because of their perverted preaching and sect by the lord pope, by our venerable brothers the archbishops of Bourges and Narbonne and the bishop of Toulouse, and by ourself, they should come to us to be reconciled according to the form of the Church. But they had turned into the paths of wickedness, and their minds were hardened: they refused. Before the people, who applauded continually, and booed them vigorously, we lit candles, and with the bishop of Poitiers and the other clerics who had assisted us throughout declared them excommunicate, both them and their master the devil. Therefore, we urge everybody to avoid the aforesaid Raymond and Bernard and their associates, who have been excommunicated and handed over to Satan.

If they ever presume to preach to you anything other than what they confessed in our presence, as we have described, reject their preaching as false and contrary to the Catholic and apostolic faith, and drive them, as heretics and forerunners of Antichrist, far from your company and from your lands.

36 Legation in the Languedoc: Henry of Clairvaux

Henry's account of the mission is in *PL* 204, col. 235–40, and the *Gesta Henrici*, pp. 214–220. It has been translated by Riley from the slightly different version of Roger of Hoveden, I, 481–9. On Peter Maurand and his family, see Mundy, *Liberty and Political Power*, pp. 60–62, and on Henry of Clairvaux, Y. M. J. Congar, in *Studia Anselmiana*, (1958).

Listen, Oh heavens, to our lament! Let the earth feel the grief of our heart! Let Catholic Christians mourn the fate of Christ and the faithful people beware the afflictions of the faith. Let the people of the world, the sons of men, decry the blow to the salvation of man, the subversion of all the living be mourned by all the living. A new Philistine stands in our times before the ranks of Israel, the order of heretics, an army of apostates, irreverently reviling the troops of the living God, impiously presuming to blaspheme against the majesty of the Lord. David, why do you hesitate? Why do you tremble, man of faith? Take up your sling and stone, and smite the brow of the blasphemer: let the evil head which he holds so imprudently high be raised by your hands on the point of his sword. If the army of Christ should lose this battle, if Mother Church is in the least degree maltreated, we shall know that it is not merit that our cause lacks but supporters. We know too that victory will not be denied to our champion if he fights in the love of Christ. But as, according to the word of the Lord, 'The harvest is great but the labourers are few', the despoilers of your fields, good Jesus, insinuate themselves deceitfully in the guise of labourers, ready to pull up the unripe crop instead of harvesting what is ripe, to forestall your harvest with their own destruction.

Where then are the farmers whom you have set over the fruitful and pleasant field which flowers with your blood and is watered by its sprinkling? Let men rise and come to our aid, and make themselves our rampart against these savage beasts. Arise, husbands, and fathers; arise, princes of nations and leaders of peoples. Drive off these vile animals, or put to flight at least the little foxes. It would be better to capture them, but who is fit to do it? They have no regular paths, but follow winding routes, and their newest abominations are concealed in the labyrinth of their deceits. They slip from the hand like fawns, and like snakes escape more easily the more tightly they were grasped. But by the grace of God, though they cannot be captured they can be driven away, so when they make known the damage they were doing among us let them be confounded and perish. That this may be the easier I shall explain what I have seen and experienced myself, so that if it is not done in the future we shall have to blame their wickedness less than our defects and the carelessness of our own people.

Recently at the command of the lord pope, and at the request of the pious princes, Louis, king of the French and Henry, king of the English, I accompanied the venerable Peter, legate of the Apostolic See, and those wise men the bishop of Poitiers and the bishop of Bath, to Toulouse, which is an extremely populous city, said to be the mother of heresy and a fountainhead of error. We went to find out whether the troubles of the town were as great as the noise that was made about them. We found the city so diseased that from the soles of its feet to the top of its head that there was not a healthy piece in it.

We had not been told a third of the terrible ills that that noble city nourished in the bosom of its unbelief. The abomination of desolation had found a place in it, and the likeness of serpents of which the prophets speak has found a home in its alleys. Heretics ruled the people and lorded it over the clergy—it was a case of 'as with the people so with the priest'—so that the life of the shepherd was shaped for the ruin of his flock. When heretics spoke everyone applauded; if a Catholic spoke they would ask, 'Who is he?', finding it startling and wonderful that there should be among them one who dared do more than murmur the words of the true faith. The plague was so strong in the land that they had not only their bishops and priests, but their own evangelists as well, who twisted and ignored the truth of the Gospels, and made new Gospels for themselves, who seduced the people and preached to them new doctrines drawn from their own evil hearts.

I tell you no lie when I say that among them there was a certain old man, wealthy and well-connected, great even among the ten greatest men of the city, whom the devil had so blinded with sin that he said that he was St John the Evangelist, and held the word that was with God in the beginning of created things, as though there is another God. In that city he was the leader of the damned, the chief of the heretics. Though he was a layman and un-educated, and knew nothing, the waters of perdition flowed from him as though he were a fountain of diabolical wisdom. By night the shadowy owls flocked to him, and he sat among them like a king surrounded by his army, dressed in clothes which looked like a dalmatic, and became the teacher of the fools. The whole city was so full of his disciples and his teaching that no one was brave enough to dare to oppose it. Such was the licence of the heretics that as we entered the city they mocked us as we travelled through the streets, making signs with their fingers, and calling us imposters, hypocrites and here-tics. However, after a time, when we had rested for a few days, one of our number was appointed to preach the word, and to discuss the rule of the true faith before the crowd of infidels. When orthodoxy had been preached to the people the sinners were humiliated in Zion, and the hypocrites were so pos-sessed by fear that where they had formerly interrupted the speakers they now did not dare to appear before them. You could see and hear that the foxes had been turned into moles. Instead of running about in the open as they had done before they buried themselves in holes in the ground and underground cellars, so that they could gnaw and destroy from below the roots of the holy plants which they no longer dared to attack in the open. Lest the colour of the leopard should betray itself by the pattern of its spots they assumed evil and ingenious ways of speech, so that if they were tested in discussion they could put on a show of orthodoxy, and pretend that they believed as we did. From that day the lord legate and the rest of us who wanted to meet these wild beasts whose timidity and confusion had driven them, like loathsome reptiles, into the depths of the earth, devoted great effort and attention to having them compelled to appear in public so that we could examine them, and make them renounce in daylight the works of darkness. At the instruction of the legate the bishop and certain of the clergy, the consuls of the city and some other faithful men who had not been touched by any rumour of heresy were made to promise to give us in writing the names of everyone they knew who had been or might in the future become members or accomplices of the heresy, and to leave out nobody at all, for love or money.

After a few days a very large number of names had entered this catalogue, and among them was that of the great Peter Maurand whom they called St John the Evangelist, as we said before. We consulted together about him, and decided to begin our investigation with him, so that the rest of the heretics would be frightened when they saw the cunning of the false evangelist condemned by the simplicity of the true Gospel. The count of Toulouse, who supported us faithfully, sent messengers to order him to appear. Trusting in his riches and his relations he refused the first command, making a haughty and false excuse for delay. The next day, preferring persuasion to threats, the count gently urged Peter, through his friends and acquaintances to come, and after many difficulties, having to use threats as well as arguments, brought him before us.

One of our number began to admonish him, 'Some of your fellow-citizens accuse you, Peter, of having defied the rule of truth faith and fallen into the wickedness of the Arian heresy, and moreover of both being led by others and leading others yourself along the paths of error.'

Breathing deeply he replied, bare-faced liar, that he was not one of them. Asked to confirm this by oath he answered that the simple word of so eminent and respectable a man as himself ought to be believed. However, when we all insisted on having the oath he promised that he would swear it at once, for if he had obstinately persisted in refusing he might have been identified as a heretic on that very point, since such a refusal would be characteristic of that heresy. The relics of the saints were soon respectfully brought in and received with such solemn reverence and devotion that the faithful were moved to tears, while the heretics who were at the meeting found their hiding places preferable to such a sight.

During the chant which we sang with copious tears to invoke the grace of the Holy Spirit, manifest fear and paleness overcame Peter, and colour of face and courage of mind alike forsook him. When the Holy Ghost approached how could any spirit remain among its enemies? You could see him shaken as though by some paralytic disease, and deprived of speech and sense, though everyone said that he was so eloquent that he usually overcame all others in argument. Why go on? The wretched man swore to all those around him that he would truthfully explain his beliefs on every point of faith which we should put to him. Then an extraordinary thing happened, which gave great pleasure to the pious who were present. A book had been brought in, on which Peter had taken his oath, and when one of the clerks present sought a forecast of what would happen by seeing what passage he opened it at, this text from the scripture turned up: 'What have we to do with thee, Jesus, Son of God? Art thou come hither to torment us before the time?' Truly, Lord Jesus, they had nothing to do with you. Your father has taken them from the vine of truth, cut them off as unfruitful branches, and thrown them away to rot. But to us who are gathered in your name it gave great joy and the glory of your strength resounded in thanksgiving and praise. Peter was required, according to his oath, simply to tell us, without deceit, what he believed about the eucharist. In his heart he did not believe in justice and did not speak the confession which would have secured his safety. Instead, contrary to his own decision to lie about everything, he betrayed the truth of his own falsity: he said that he held, by a new doctrine, that the holy bread of eternal life consecrated by a priest in the word of the Lord does not become the body of the Lord.

At this everybody jumped up, swamping him, as it were, in the tears which were produced by his contempt for the sacraments of Christ and by Christian compassion for his wretched condition. No more was needed: they gave their answer to the count. Peter was adjudged a criminal and a heretic, and immediately, with the most solemn promises from his relations, put in custody. The story of what happened flew through the streets and squares of that great city. The mouths of the faithful were opened, O Christ, and Catholic lips unsealed in your praise. The glory of faith broke forth as though for the first time in that city, and the community which had been given up for lost breathed again in the hope of eternal salvation.

From that moment the word of God grew and multiplied and the face of the whole city grew brighter as it escaped from the darkness of error into the shining light of truth.

Meanwhile Peter came to his senses, and was moved to repentance by the Lord who looked down on him, for he realized that he deserved death both in this life and the next. He sent several mediators through whom he sought the opportunity of giving satisfaction to us, promising to be converted so that he could be freed from the fear of imminent death, and enjoy the benefits of a better life. He came, he was received, and standing naked in the sight of the assembled people, he cast off the corruption of his former wickedness. There before everybody he confessed his heresy; there he gave the hand of reality; there he renounced his error and swore by his right hand in front of them all, giving sureties to the count himself and many of the leaders among his fellow-citizens, that he would submit himself to the legate in everything, and fulfil his commands in every respect. At this the people were told to meet again on the following day at the church of St Sernin, solemnly to see and hear what form of penance Peter would be expected to perform.

As they had been told, everybody assembled again on the following day. The crowd was so large and so dense that the legate could hardly perform the mass without a crush in the space within the rails of the altar which had been left empty for that purpose. Before that enormous crowd Peter, now our man, was led naked and barefoot from the doorway of the church, being scourged by the bishop of Toulouse and the abbot of St Sernin until he prostrated himself at the feet of the lord legate on the steps of the altar. There, in face of the church, he abjured all heresy and pronounced a curse on all heretics and was reconciled with the sacraments of the Church. All his possessions were confiscated and taken from him, and the penance was laid on him that he should depart as an exile from his native land within forty days, and spend three years at Jerusalem in the service of the poor. In the meantime he was to go round every church in Toulouse on each Lord's day, naked and barefoot, with disciplinary scourges, to restore all the goods which he had taken from churches, to return all the interest which he had won by usury, to make amends for all the injuries that he had inflicted on the poor, and to rase to its foundations one of his castles which he had polluted with meetings of heretics. Good Lord, what tears of holy joy were poured forth then! How the people, joyous and devout, added their graces and praises to the song of the heavenly choir, when such a creature as this was brought forth from the caverns of iniquity, and this ravening wolf transformed into a sheep of Israel!

After he had been dealt with the lord legate sent for others to be examined, for a great number were known to him either through public suspicion or private accusation. I myself tearfully sought his permission to return home, since the business of our chapter now required my presence. Permission was granted, provided that I went through the diocese of Albi, to warn the lord of the land, Roger of Béziers, to release the bishop of Albi, whom he held in chains in the custody of the heretics, and to cleanse his whole territory according to the order of the lord legate, by driving out the heretics. With the bishop of Bath, whom I have mentioned before, I entered the damnable region, which is like a great cess-pit of evil, with all the scum of heresy flowing into it. Roger went off to the most remote and inaccessible part of his land, fleeing from a bad conscience and despairing of the merit of his case. He was an agent of evil, who hated the light of truth, and after retreating to the works of darkness could not bear our approach to talk to him. Nevertheless we reached a well-fortified stronghold of his, which the inhabitants simply and appropriately called 'the castle'. His wife lived there with a strong guard and a large household. Almost all the inhabitants of the castle were either heretics or their sympathizers, and the power of the Lord above prevented them from presuming to murmur against the faith which we preached. Although we were there in their lands, in their power since we were surrounded by heretics on every side, the word of the Lord which we showered on them in continual rebuke and exhortation, was not obstructed.

When we saw that nobody among them would dare to answer us, we declared Roger a traitor, a heretic and a perjurer for having violated the peace and the personal safety of the bishop, and in the name of Christ boldly condemned him to excommunication in public, before his wife and his knights, on behalf of the lord legate and the kings of France and England. It is clear from this that a fine door is open to Christian princes to avenge the wounds of Christ, and bring to the desert the garden of the Lord, and to the wilderness the sweetness of paradise. In case anyone thinks that nothing can be done against them, everyone should know that it was the general opinion in the city of Toulouse that if our visit had been three years later we would hardly have found anyone there who would call upon the name of Christ. In addition to all this the count of Toulouse has sworn to the assembled people of the city that henceforth he will neither show favour to heretics, for money or gift, nor support them any longer on his lands.

37 The Cathar heresy in Lombardy

The *De heresi catharorum*, ed. Dondaine (1949), pp. 305–11, with an important introduction, was composed between c. 1170 and c. 1200. It is the earliest account of Catharism in Italy, and was a source of others until recently better known, including the *Brevis summula* (ed. C. Douais, *La somme des autorités à l'usage des prédicateurs méridionaux au XIIIe siècle*, Paris 1896, pp. 114–43), and the *Adversus Catharos* of Moneta of Cremona, (ed. Th. Ricchini, Rome 1743, partly translated by Wakefield and Evans, pp. 308–29).

When the Cathar heresy first began to spread in Lombardy a bishop named Mark ruled the whole of Lombardy, Tuscany and the Marches. Mark derived his orders from the Church of Bulgaria. A man named Papa Nicetas came to Lombardy from the region of Constantinople and began to question the validity of Mark's Bulgarian orders. Mark and his subordinates, after some hesitation, gave up the Bulgarian orders, and accepted the orders of Dragovitsa from Nicetas, and he remained in that order with his co-religionists for some time.

Some time later a man called Petracius came from across the sea with some companions, and brought news about one Simon, a bishop of Dragovitsa from whom the orders which they had received from Nicetas had originated. According to Petracius, Simon had been found with a woman, and had committed other offences. By this time Mark was dead, and had been succeeded as bishop by a man called John the Jew, whom he had ordained. As a result of what Petracius said some people began to deny the validity of the ordination which had been handed down from Simon, and others did not, so that a dispute arose between them, and they divided into two parties. One party continued to follow John the Jew, while the other chose Peter of Florence as their bishop, and each party remained in this way for some years.

Some of the wiser men among them, however, regretted the division, and were anxious to return to unity. They decided to choose envoys from each side, and send them together to a bishop in France (*ultra montes*) agreeing that each side would accept whatever this bishop told them to do about their division without arguing. The bishop listened to the case on each side, and examined them carefully. His judgement was that the two Lombard bishops should meet, with their followers, and draw lots. On whichever of them the bishopric fell by lot the other was to be under him, and all of their followers, formerly divided, were to obey him. When the bishop had been elected in this way he was to go to Bulgaria to be ordained as bishop, and when he returned home after being ordained in Bulgaria, he was to administer the *consolamentum* again to all his followers by laying his hands upon them. The envoys accepted the judgement, and returned to Lombardy to announce it. When the time came for the judgement to be carried out, and the lots drawn, Peter of Florence, the bishop of one party, refused to accept the judgement and the drawing of lots, so his followers degraded him from the bishopric. Consequently, according to the judgement, the episcopacy fell to John the Jew, who was willing to accept the procedure, but some of the other party, enemies of his, spitefully refused to accept him.

After this some of the leaders went to John the Jew, and begged him to resign the bishopric, because he was unacceptable to so many. They said that if he did so it would make it possible for peace and harmony to reign among them; they in their party would choose someone in his place, and somebody in the other party would replace Peter of Florence, who had prevented the judgement from being implemented; lots would be drawn between these two, as the judgement required, and whichever of them was chosen would become, unconditionally, bishop for the whole body. John was moved by their arguments, and realized that he could not hold the office in peace and quiet, so, being anxious for the divided community to be re-united, he resigned. This was made known.

According to their agreement, the two parties met at Mosio, and there decided that each party should choose somebody acceptable to them from the other. From John the Jew's party the other party chose a man named Garattus, and from Peter of Florence's party the others chose John the Judge. The whole body was to obey ungrudgingly whichever of these two was chosen bishop by lot. The lot fell on Garattus, and the troublemakers were now pacified. They decided on a date by which they would find companions and expenses for Garattus to undertake the journey to Bulgaria, to receive the *consolamentum* and be ordained. When he returned the whole community would be given the *consolamentum* again, as the French bishop had ordered in his judgement. When they had decided this they all went home.

But before the date which had been fixed for his journey, Garattus was found guilty of having a woman: there were two witnesses. Because of this there were many who maintained that he was unworthy of his rank, and therefore they no longer considered themselves bound by their promise of obedience to him. The community which had once been divided into two parties was now dispersed into six. Before the date at which they had promised to give Garattus companions and expenses for his journey to Bulgaria some heretics from Desenzano formed a congregation, chose John Bellus as their bishop, and sent him to Dragovitsa to be ordained; the bishop of this sect is now Amizio. The community at Mantua and their followers chose Caloiannus to be their bishop, sent him to Sclavonia, and when he had been ordained he served as their bishop. In the same way a man called Nicholas was selected by the congregation at Vicenza, and sent to Sclavonia for ordination, to be their bishop when he returned. Two more bishops were ordained in Tuscany. Garattus was deserted by all these people, although they had promised obedience to him. He had forbidden these elections, in case they should undermine his authority over the whole community, but they ignored his orders, and disobeyed him from the outset.

After all these bishops had been ordained some heretics at Milan who did not approve of such actions wanted to recognize Garattus as bishop, according to their promise. Garattus saw that he had been deserted by the great majority, and would not accept; he said that John the Jew who had humbly resigned the bishopric in his desire to exchange unity for division, was far worthier of it. When John refused they sent a delegation to France to ask the advice of the bishop who had given the original judgement. When he heard of the divisions among them he was very upset, and sent John the Jew to Bulgaria to be ordained and to complete the implementation of his judgement, so that he could be bishop in Lombardy for everybody who was willing to accept him. This was done, and after his death he was succeeded by Joseph, and when Joseph died he was succeeded by Garattus. Garattus and his followers hold that the aforesaid bishops and their followers were bound by the promise which they had made to him in the first place, would be guilty unless they were released by him, and had accepted their ordination as bishops against the laws of God and reason. Because of this he will not receive any of these bishops in the communion of prayers or services, except Caloiannus whom he has recently absolved and made peace with.

This is the story of how Cathars, by far the worst of heretics, perverters and adulterators of Christian teaching, began in unity and became divided first into two parties, and then into six.

The beliefs of the first party of the heretics Marchisius of Soiano, the heretical bishop of Desenzano, and Amizio, his *filius major*, the bishops of one party of the Cathars, who have their orders from Dragovitsa, believe and preach that there are two gods or lords, without beginning or end, one good and the other evil. They saw that each of these has created angels, the good god good angels, and the evil god evil ones, and that the good god is almighty in Heaven, while the evil god controls the mechanisms of this world. Lucifer, they say, is the son of the evil god, referred to in St John's Gospel, 'you are of your father the devil' and 'he is a liar, and his father the devil': the liar, as they understand it, is obviously Lucifer. According to them Lucifer ascended into Heaven from this world, his kingdom, because he said, according to the prophet Isaiah, 'I will ascend above the height of the clouds, I will be like the most high.' He then transformed himself into an angel of light. The angels admired his handsomeness, and interceded for him with the Lord, and he was taken up and made steward of the angels. Hence in St Luke: 'There was a certain rich man who had a steward.' During his stewardship he led the angels astray, and there was a great battle in Heaven, and 'the dragon was thrown out, the serpent of old', with the angels whom he had led astray: it is described in the Apocalypse, 'and his tail drew the third part of the stars of heaven and cast them to the earth.'

The angels were composed of three elements—body, soul and spirit. Their bodies remained in Heaven, unoccupied, the 'dry bones' mentioned in Ezekiel, and so did their spirits, but their souls were taken to Lucifer, and put in bodies in this world. They say that Christ, the son of God, came to save these souls, as he said: 'The son of man came not to destroy souls but to save', and again, in Matthew, 'I was not sent but to the sheep that are lost of the house of Israel', and 'The son of man is come to save that which was lost, and to lead back the hundredth sheep which had strayed.' They hold that the psalm, 'O God, the heathens are come', refers to this battle, and that there are garments and crowns and seats in Heaven which they have lost and must recover, mentioned by the apostle: 'There is laid up for me a crown of justice which the Lord the just judge will render to me in that day.' The judgement has already been pronounced, because it is said, 'The prince of this world is already judged.' They say that human bodies are given life partly by evil spirits fallen from Heaven. The souls do penance in the bodies, and if they are not saved in one body they enter another body, and do penance in that. When penance is complete the soul is reunited with the body and spirit which remain in Heaven, according to the words of the apostle: 'And may the God of Peace himself sanctify you in all things; that your whole spirit and soul and body may be preserved shameless in our Lord Jesus Christ.'

The beliefs of the second party among the heretics Caloiannus, bishop of one group of the heretics, who had his orders from Sclavonia, and Garattus, bishop of the other lot of perverters of Christian doctrine, who has his orders from Bulgaria, agree in believing and preaching that there is one God, omnipotent and without beginning, who created the angels and the four elements, and that Lucifer and his associates sinned in Heaven. But they differ among themselves as to the origin of their sin.

Some of them say—but this is a great mystery—that there was a certain evil spirit which had four faces, one of a man, one of a bird, one of a fish and one of a beast, which had no beginning and lived in the chaos, but had no power of creation. They say that Lucifer, who had been virtuous until then, went down and saw the face of the evil spirit, worshipped it, and was led astray by its conversation and suggestion. He returned to Heaven, and there seduced others, and they were thrown out of Heaven, but they did not lose their natural talents. Lucifer and the evil spirit wanted to separate the elements, but could not. They obtained a good angel from God, as an assistant, and with God's agreement, using the strength and power of the good angel, they separated the elements. Lucifer, according to them, is the god who is said in Genesis to have created heaven and earth in six days. After that he shaped the form of Adam from mud of the earth, and choked the good angel into it, to provide life, as it says in the Gospel, 'Laying hold of him he throttled him, saying: "Pay what thou owest." ' Then he made Eve, so that through her he could make Adam sin. They also say that the fruit of the forbidden tree was fornication. According to some of them spirit is propagated by spirit, as flesh is by flesh, as the Gospel says, 'That which is born of the flesh is flesh, and that which is born of the spirit is the spirit.'

At this point there is disagreement among them. Some of them reject this view, and say that the spirits destined to be saved were created at the same time, and are fed into human bodies gradually, by the will of God. On the other hand those who maintain that spirit is propagated by spirit believe that the whole of this world comprises these evil spirits, that is, both those which are to be saved, and those which are to be damned. The former, who say that the spirits destined to be saved were created at the same time, claim that the spirits which fell are embodied, and will not be saved, and therefore progress from one body to another, and will do so until the end of time; thus on the Day of Judgement there will be some good and some evil spirits, and the good ones will take their places, while the evil will be eternally damned. Here they differ among themselves; some say that some of the spirits which fell will be saved, because they did not fall of their own will, but sinned, as it were, under compulsion, and that those which sinned deliberately will be damned. And they say that other spirits have been created by almighty God, to take the places of those which will not be saved.

All Cathars believe that everything in Genesis—the flood, the deliverance of Noah, God's words to Abraham, and the destruction of Sodom and Gomorrah—is the work of the devil, who is referred to as God. The same 'God' led the people out of Egypt, gave them the law in the desert, led them into the Promised Land, and sent them prophets. Through these prophets he made them offer him the blood of animals, so that he could be worshipped like God. If any of these prophets happened to predict anything about Christ they did so by the power of the Holy Spirit, as it were, under compulsion, and unconsciously they say that God did all this not himself, but through the devil, as through an agent. Hence they argue that the devil made all this, with the knowledge and power bestowed on him by God at the creation, to rule it without end, by God's full permission and intention, so that the fruits of salvation might be gathered by penance in this world.

The members of the Sclavonian sect believe that Jesus Christ the Son of God, John the Baptist and Mary were three angels, who seemed to be flesh. They say that Christ did not really become flesh, did not eat or drink, was not crucified, did not die, and was not buried, and that everything that he did as though he were human was done not in reality but in appearance. Some of the Bulgarian heretics believe that Mary was a real woman, and that the son of God assumed true flesh, really ate, and was crucified in the flesh, but did not ascend in the flesh: he discarded the flesh in the Ascension.

They say that John the Baptist was sent by the devil with baptism of water to obstruct the preaching of Christ. When he pointed to Christ with his finger, or predicted his coming he did it not in himself, but as a vehicle of the Holy Spirit, as though he spoke unknowingly, under compulsion: he was like a speaking-tube, as Caiaphas prophesied, though he did not know it. Few Cathars disagree with this; even the Bulgarians believe it.

They all condemn marriage, and deny the resurrection of the visible flesh. All say that baptism of water has never led to salvation, even the baptism of water administered by the apostles.

Garattus, who was ordained by the Bulgarians is still bishop of the Concorezzans: Nazarius is his *filius major* and Gerald of Brescia his *filius minor*. Caloiannus is bishop of Mantua, and was ordained by the Sclavonians. His *filius major* is Orto of Bagnolo, who is now bishop, and his *filius minor* Aldricus de Gilinguellis of Milan. Marchisius of Soiano is bishop of the Dragovitsans, and Amizio his *filius major*. Nicholas of Vicenza is bishop of Sclavonia, Petrus Gallus his *filius major*, and Prandus his *filius minor*.

38 Orvieto: the martyrdom of Peter Parenzo, 1199

The dissemination of Catharism in Italy often accompanied and became involved with civil tension which had their origins in other causes: for another example, at Milan in 1176, see Wakefield and Evans, p. 151 (from *Acta Sanctorum*, 11 April 591) and for discussion Maisonneuve, pp. 148–9, 171–3, and Violante and Manselli in *Hérésies et Sociétés*, pp. 171–202. At Orvieto the opportunity for Cathar domination of the city was provided by the dispute between the city and Innocent III about jurisdiction over Acquapendente, which revolted against Orvieto in 1196: see D. Waley, *Medieval Orvieto*, pp. 12–15. Rustico was bishop of Orvieto 1168–76, and Richard 1178–1202. This extract is from the *Vita S. Petri Parentinii* (*Acta Sanctorum* May V, 86–9), by Master John, a resident of Orvieto who probably wrote c. 1200, immediately after the events which he describes.

A Florentine named Diotosalvo sowed the seeds of Manicheism in Orvieto, with the help of Gerard of Marzano, immediately after Hermanninus of Parma, in the time of Bishop Rustico. He was a son of evil, who like Satan transformed himself into an angel of light, for in dress and deportment he presented a deceitful appearance. He denied the sacrament of the body and blood of Christ, and the efficacy of Catholic baptism; he said that alms and prayers do not help the dead to attain absolution; that St Sylvester [pope, 314–35] and all his successors are suffering the tortures of the damned; that all visible things are the creation of the devil and subject to his power; that any good man has the same merits and prerogatives as St Peter, the chief of the apostles, while any evil man suffers the same punishment as the traitor Judas, and a number of other pernicious doctrines which may readily be found in the book *Contra haereticos.*

The good bishop of Orvieto, Richard, manifested his pastoral watchfulness by throwing the two heretics out of the city. They were followed by two women, Milita of Monte-Meato and Julieta of Florence, both daughters of iniquity. They adopted the semblance of religion, so that by appearing eager to hear the holy offices they seemed to be sheep though in reality they were wolves. The bishop was deceived by their religious disguise, and advised their admission into the confraternity of the clergy for regular prayers. Milita, like another Martha, feigned anxiety about the state of repair of the cathedral roof, while Julieta, like Mary, pretended to embrace the contemplative life. Many of the ladies of our city and their relations began to respect them as very holy women. So, as beloved enemies or highly virulent germs these snakes in the grass drew many men and women into the labyrinth of their heresy under the pretext of piety. The bishop realized that their religious aspect had deceived him. With the advice of the canons, the judges and other reliable men he resolved to fight in defence of the Church of Christ. He pursued the heretics with such vigour that some were hanged, some beheaded, and some burned. Others preferred exile to execution, and those who died in their heresy were buried in a stinking graveyard outside the church.

Some time after this a dispute arose over the town of Acquapendente between Pope Innocent III and the Orvietans, who claimed that it belonged to them. Orvieto was placed under interdict, and the pope kept the bishop at Rome for nearly nine months, to the great annoyance of the citizens. While the shepherd was away some of his sheep strayed and were devoured by wolves, for when they have no watchful guardian the people easily fall into sin. While the bishop was away a doctor of the Manichees named Peter the Lombard came from Viterbo and began to hold secret conclaves in Orvieto with other heretical leaders. Many of the people and nobles who heard them preaching were deceived by the sirens' song, abandoned the bark of St Peter, and began to steer into dangerous waters.

As their evil doctrines took root in the minds of their hearers the number of heretics increased so much that they began to preach against the Catholics in public, and to threaten that if they had to make war on them they would drive them from the city. The notion began to grow upon them of confiscating the goods of any Catholics who would not join their sect, and expel them or kill them, so that they could turn the city, with its impregnable fortifications, into a citadel for heretics from all over the world to hold against the Catholic Church. The Catholics, afraid that the tunic of Christ would be irreparably torn, met together under divine inspiration and sent some of their number to Rome to find a rector who would acquire the pope's favour for the Orvietans, make peace with the Romans, and extirpate the heresy from the city.

The messengers whom the Orvietans sent to Rome were delighted to accept Peter of Parenzo as their lord and rector. The pope recognized him, and ordered him, for the remission of his sins, to cleanse Orvieto of the fever of heresy. He promised him that if he died in the attempt he would be assured of eternal glory. Peter was young in years, but old in wisdom, constant, intelligent, eloquent and clear-headed, conscientious in public affairs and firm in the pursuit of justice, but firmer still in defence of the Catholic faith. He was so generous with alms that if he were riding through Rome with some friend he would find out from the governors of the hospitals how many paupers they had; then he would secretly give money to buy food for them, and come back alone at supper time to wait on the paupers as though he were their domestic servant. He had given up tithes from the Romans and Tuscans, and other improper customs and dues.

Peter Parenzo was called to be lord and rector of Orvieto in February 1199. He was received with joy and honour, with laurels and olive-branches, by all the citizens, high and low, and since he had come to bring peace to the oppressed his task received approval from the outset. He began by forbidding jousting at the Lent carnival, since at that time many murders had been committed under the cover of sport. The heretics, who always hate unity among Catholics, determined to obstruct this laudable plan. On the first day of Lent they started a brawl, pretending that it was a game. The whole city was fighting in the piazza, with swords and lances, stones were thrown from the towers and palaces around it and the peace was shattered. Peter Parenzo mounted a horse and broke up the fight by riding between the sides, exposing himself to the danger of death. By divine protection he passed through their ranks unharmed. So that punishment should be as justice required, since if those who had been fighting were not punished the price of crime would seem too low, he had the towers and palaces from which the skirmishing had been conducted razed to the ground so that everybody was punished in proportion to his wealth and without regard to persons. From the many who had fought, with great bloodshed, he exacted lawful recompense with severity. In doing this he afforded an occasion for the enmity and hatred of those who had been punished, for it would be difficult to balance the scales of justice and give equal weight to undeserved hostilities and unjust hatreds. Since he could not please everybody, and especially the wicked, he retained the friendship of good Catholics.

In his campaign to uproot the heretics from the meadow of the Church with the sickle of justice, he often used to confer with Bishop Richard in the cathedral, in the place where he is now buried. After consultation with many sound men he proclaimed publicly that anyone who returned to the Church (which does not deny its consolations to those who come back to it) before a stated day would be received with mercy and good will; anyone who refused to return before the day fixed would be liable to the penalties laid down by civil and canon law. The bishop, who burned against the wickedness of the Manichees, received the evidence of the heretics who returned to Catholic unity, and with pastoral solicitude passed it on to Peter Parenzo. He bound the remainder in iron fetters: some he sentenced to be publicly flogged, some were exiled from the city, and some fined, which was bitterly lamented by the greedy; he exacted large recognizances from others, and had the houses of many of them destroyed. Thus the rector of our city followed the royal road, inclining neither to the right nor to the left, and thus his maintenance of justice sowed the seed of his own persecution in the bosoms of those whom he punished according to the rigour of the law and rule of equity.

When this had been settled Peter went to Rome, to spend Easter with his family. He was anxious to present himself to Pope Innocent while he was there, and they met on the way from St Peter's to the Lateran, near the basilica of St Daniel.

'Peter, I want you to show that you are governing my city loyally.'

'I am ready to obey you, holy father.'

'How are you ruling the city? Have you carried out my orders against the heretics?'

'My lord, I have punished the heretics of Orvieto so severely that they are publicly threatening to kill me.'

'My son, you must fear God more than the threats of men. Pursue the heretics boldly. They may slay your body, but they can do no harm to your soul, for God retains his power over it.'

'What will become of me?'

'My son, by the authority of God, and of the apostles St Peter and St Paul I absolve you from all your sins if you die at the hands of the heretics.'

Peter bowed low, and accepted the promise with gratitude. Thus fortified he went home joyfully, declared his brothers his heirs, and quietly made his will, as though he foresaw his death. When his mother and his wife realized what he was doing they shed bitter tears.

While the rector was away from Orvieto the heretics whom he had punished so justly met and resolved to effect the recovery of their pledges and the revocation of the sentences. They found one of his servants, Ralph by name, and promised him a large sum of money to betray his master to them. Inflamed with avarice the traitor was eager for an opportunity to deliver his lord into the hands of his enemies. Meanwhile Peter said goodbye to his friends and relations, and set out for Orvieto on 1 May, to be received by the Orvietans next day with garlands, flowers and great joy. Far from giving up his persecution of the heretics, he bravely ignored their threats and warnings and visited them with the full penalties of the law. Divine providence had blessed the future martyr with such constancy that he often raised his hands to heaven, in public or in private, and swore to God, the Virgin and the prince of the apostles that if ever he died by the sword he would do so defending the Catholic faith against heretics, for he would be adorned with the glory of sanctity if he accepted the danger of death at their hands. Indeed he deserved to win his soul's desire, for he did not lie.

The traitor Ralph, another Judas—it is right to give him the name of the man whose crime he imitated—awaited an opportunity to betray him. On 20 May 1199, when Peter of Parenzo was dining with Henry of Rome, the judge, and other guests, the traitor accepted a chicken leg from the hand of the lord of Orvieto, and did not scruple to receive a cup from his fingers, the more boldly to carry out his crime. He was furthering his plan to deceive his lord, and had not forgotten that the heretics were lurking in ambush around the rector's palace, intending to enter his presence disguised as Catholics.

When Peter had taken his boots off and was about to go to bed the heretics knocked at the door of the palace and asked to see him. Then Ralph, with many others, seized him at the door of his palace, bound his throat so that he could not shout, gagged him and muffled his head in skins. They were going to take him to a lonely place outside the city, but Peter, already seeing himself as a martyr, begged them not to take him outside the city walls, because he had no boots on and could not walk far in his slippers. Ralph gave him his leggings to cover his feet. Then they began to argue among themselves, some wanting to take him into the forest, others to the castle of Rispampani, which was a stronghold of wicked men. They argued among themselves until the whole gang (*synagoga*) of them decided to take oaths of mutual loyalty, and then they marched him off to a hut.

When they arrived they surrounded him, like so many wolves around a harmless lamb, and demanded that he should return all the recognizances that he had taken from them, give up the lordship of the city, and make a sworn statement that he would pester their sect no longer, and, indeed, would favour them, as the price of his life. Peter, rocklike in his faith, said that he was willing to return their money and recognizances from his own chamber, but he would not give up the lordship of the city, and would not swear any oath or give any pledge not to molest their sect; he would rather submit to any torture than stray from the path of the Catholic faith by consenting to their heresy. He would not evade his orders, or ensnare himself in the web of perjury, for the government of Orvieto had been entrusted to him, on oath, for one year. The heretics threatened to kill him if he did not accept their demands, but neither threats nor terror could shake the rock of his faith.

They argued with him, roaring like lions, until one of them growled, 'Why are we wasting words on this scoundrel?' He raised his fist and struck Peter in the mouth, knocking out a tooth and leaving his face streaming with blood. Another, seized by the same fury, grabbed a millstone and hit Peter on the back of the head, so that he fell to the ground and got a mouthful of dust, which he received as a holy sacrament. The others imitated their cruelty and killed Peter with swords and knives. He was stabbed four more times. Others, lusting to satiate the vindictiveness of their evil souls, tore the hair from his head. They carried his body to a well which was overgrown with vegetation, intending to throw him into it so that nobody could find him, but they found that they could neither move the body nor open the well. The body remained immovable so they fled. They left it beside a nut tree which had formerly been sterile, but that year by God's will it produced two heavy crops in witness of the martyrdom.

Early next morning six monks on the way from Orvieto to the mill found the body of the lord and rector of Orvieto, far from home. They thought that it was the corpse of some murdered merchant, but the radiance of dawn drove the shadows away, and the death of the Lord Peter was revealed.

[The discovery caused great distress in Orvieto. In popular reaction against the heretics some were lynched, others were brought to trial, and some escaped from the city only to be overtaken by plague. A variety of miracles emanated from the corpse, which was buried in the Cathedral.]

39 Rainier Sacchoni: On the Cathars and Waldensians

Rainier Sacchoni was a native of Piacenza, one of the strongholds of dualism in Lombardy. It is not clear which Cathar church he belonged to, but he rose to eminence in it, and apparently became leader of a local community before he was converted to Catholicism in 1245. He became a Dominican and an inquisitor, and worked in collaboration with Peter the Martyr, who was assassinated on 6 April 1252; an attempt on Rainier's life was planned at the same time. Between 1254 and 1259 he was chief inquisitor in Lombardy, and we last hear of him in July 1262, when he was summoned to Viterbo by Urban IV to report on his work. Fuller accounts of Rainier and the Lombard inquisition may be found in Dondaine, *Le liber de duobus principiis*, pp. 57–63 and Lea, *History of the Inquisition* II, 191–231.

The treatise was written in 1250, not to refute or even to discuss heretical teachings, but to facilitate the work of the inquisition. Though opinions vary on the importance of the divisions among the Cathars which Rainier describes, and though his information is not always complete—he omits Razès, for instance, from his list of Cathar churches in France—his accuracy is undeniable. This translation is made from the edition of Dondaine, pp. 64–78. It should be remembered throughout that Rainier uses 'Cathar' in the strict sense, meaning *perfecti*, not their novices or followers.

In the name of the Lord Jesus Christ. Once there were many sects of heretics but they have now been almost destroyed. Two of importance, however, are still to be found, the Cathars, or Patarini, and the Leonistae, or Poor Men of Lyons. Their beliefs are presented in this work.

The different sects of Cathars   It must be realized that the first sect, the Cathars, are themselves divided into three main groups, or sects, those of Desenzano (the Albanenses), Concorezzo and Bagnolo, all in Lombardy. Other Cathars, in Tuscany, the Marches, or Provence, do not differ in their views from these three, or some of them.

All Cathars agree on certain general principles, though they may disagree over details, all of which we shall discuss. We begin with what they have in common.

BELIEFS COMMON TO ALL CATHARS

All Cathars believe that the devil made the world and everything in it, and that all the sacraments of the Church, both that of baptism by water, which is material, and the others, do not help us to salvation, and are not true sacraments of Christ and his Church but devilish frauds of a church of the wicked. We shall see later how many sacraments the heretics themselves have, and what they are like. All Cathars also believe that conjugal relations are always mortal sin, and that adultery or incest will not be punished any more severely in the future life than legitimate conjugal relations, for which reason these offences are no more severely punished among them. Again, all Cathars deny that there will be a resurrection of the flesh. They hold that it is mortal sin to eat meat, eggs or cheese, even in urgent necessity, because they are the fruits of sexual union. The taking of oaths is not permitted on any account, and is also mortal sin. Secular powers sin mortally if they punish heretics or evil-doers. Nobody may be saved except through them. Baptized children will be no more lightly punished in eternity than thieves and murderers, though as we shall see the sect of the Albanenses seems to differ a little from the others on this point. They all deny purgatory.

CATHAR SACRAMENTS

The Cathars, who behave more like apes than men, have four sacraments, which are false, silly, unlawful and sacrilegious: the laying-on of hands, the blessing of bread, penance and ordination, and I will deal with them in that order.

The 'consolamentum'

They call the laying-on of hands the *consolamentum*, spiritual baptism, or baptism of the Holy Spirit. Without it according to them, mortal sin cannot be forgiven, and the Holy Spirit cannot be conferred on anyone: it is given only by them, through the *consolamentum*. On this the Albanenses differ somewhat from the others. They say that the hand contributes nothing (since according to them it was created by the devil, as we shall see), and it is only the Lord's Prayer said by whoever performs the ceremony that is effective. The other Cathars say that both the laying-on of hands and the Lord's Prayer are necessary and required. All Cathars agree that the *consolamentum* does not produce remission of sin if the performer of the ceremony is in a state of mortal sin. The *consolamentum* is performed by two people at least, not only by bishops and their assistants but also in emergency by Cathar women.

The breaking of bread

The Cathars' blessing of bread is a ceremony of breaking bread which they perform every day at both the morning and the evening meal. It is done in this way. When Cathar men and women meet at the table they all stand, and say a 'Pater Noster'. Then the foremost among them, either by rank or by seniority, takes a piece of bread, or more if the number present requires it, breaks it saying, 'The grace of our Lord Jesus Christ be with us all', and distributes it to everybody at the table, not only the Cathars, but their followers, even if they are thieves, adulterers or murderers. The sect of Desenzano say that the material bread is not blessed and cannot receive any blessing, because according to them it is the creation of the devil, and in this they differ from the others, who maintain that the bread is truly blessed. None of them believe that the bread becomes the body of Christ.

The false penance of the Cathars

Now we must examine the nature of penance among the Cathars. It will be shown that it is quite false and vain, deceitful and poisonous. For true confession three things are necessary: contrition in the heart, confession by the mouth, and expiation by works. I, brother Rainier, once a leading heretic and now by the grace of God a priest in the Dominican Order, albeit an unworthy one, say without any doubt, and bear witness before God, who knows that I tell the truth, that not one of those three things is to be found in the penance of the Cathars. The poison of heresy which they drink from the mouth of the serpent of old does not allow them to sorrow for their sins. This is a four-fold error: eternal glory is not diminished for the penitent by any sin, and the punishment of hell is no greater for those who do not repent; the fire of purgatory awaits nobody, and guilt and punishment are waived by God through the *consolamentum*. They all believe that the traitor Judas will not be punished any more heavily than a one-day-old child, and that all will be equal either in salvation or in damnation. The sect of Desenzano differs here, saying that each will be restored to his original state, and that in each kingdom, God's and the devil's, some will be greater than others, though not according to merit.

To this I must add that many who are infected with this heresy regret that they did not fulfil their lusts before they subscribed to the errors of the Cathars. This is the reason why many of their believers, both men and women, are not afraid to treat their sisters or brothers, daughters or sons, nieces or nephews or cousins as they would husband or wife. It may be, however, that some of them at least are repelled by horror and becoming shame.

It is quite clear that they do not repent of the sins which they committed before their profession of heresy. They never restore the fruits of their usury, theft or rapine to anybody, preferring to keep it, or rather to hand it over to sons and nephews who remain in the world. They hold that usury is not sinful.

I can say without hesitation that in the seventeen years in which I lived among them I never saw one of them pray secretly alone, away from the others, or cry, or beat himself and say, 'Lord, forgive me for my sin', or show any other sign of contrition. They never seek the help or protection of the angels or the Blessed Virgin, or the saints and never fortify themselves with the sign of the cross.

Cathar confession   Now let us consider the confession of the Cathars—what its nature is, how they perform it, and to whom. The confession takes this form: 'I am here, before God and you, to confess and accept the guilt of all my sins of every kind, and to be pardoned by God and by you.' This confession is made in public, when as many as a hundred or more male and female Cathars and their believers may be present. After making the confession each of them receives the *consolamentum* of which we have spoken. It is made especially to one of their bishops who holds a book containing the Gospels, or the whole New Testament, before his breast. When absolution is made he places the book on the head of the penitent, and the other Cathars, who are at his right hand, begin their prayers.

When one of them has committed a sin of the flesh or some other which they consider mortal after he has received the *consolamentum* he must confess this great sin individually and receive the *consolamentum* again privately from his bishop and at least one other.

Venial sins they confess in the following way. They bow to the ground before the bishop, who holds the book before him, and one, speaking for them all, cries in a loud voice, 'We come before God and you to confess our sins, for we have sinned greatly, in word, in deed, in thought and in imagination', and so on. From this it is clear that all Cathars die in their sins unshriven. They confess in this way every month, if it can be managed.

Now let us see whether Cathars do good works in atonement for the sins which they committed before they became heretics. Surprising though it may seem to the ignorant, I maintain that they do not. They often pray and fast, and abstain at all times from meat, eggs and cheese, which might seem to be in penance for sins, and of which they often boast foolishly. But they commit a three-fold error which means that these are not penances. First, they hold that guilt and error are wholly erased by the *consolamentum* and prayer, or, as we have seen, in the case of the sect of Desenzano, by prayer alone. Secondly, they say that God does not punish anybody either in purgatory, whose existence they deny altogether, or temporally in this world, which they hold to be the creation of the devil. This means that good works performed by Cathars have no connection either with penance or with the remission of sin. Thirdly, they believe that everyone ought to perform these works as though by divine command, a ten-year-old boy who never committed any mortal sin before he became a Cathar just as much as an old man who has sinned incessantly. Among them a Cathar would not be punished more severely for drinking some poison to kill himself than for avoiding death by eating a chicken on medical advice, or under some other necessity, and according to them he will not be punished more severely hereafter. We have already seen their views on marriage.

They give few or no alms, none to strangers, except perhaps to avoid scandal among their neighbours and earn their respect, and very little to their own poor. Once more the reason for this is threefold. First, they do not expect it to bring them any greater glory or remission of sins hereafter. Second, they are nearly all greedy and grasping. This is why the poor among them can hardly ever find anybody to shelter them in time of persecution, since they do not possess the necessities of life or anything which would enable them to restore to their protectors homes and chattels destroyed on their account, while rich Cathars have no such difficulty. Therefore they gather wealth if they can, and keep it.

Another point to remember about their prayer is that they think it absolutely necessary to pray when they eat or drink. They carry this so far that many of them when ill tell those who are looking after them not to place any food or drink in their mouths unless they can say at least a '*Pater Noster*'; in this sense it is true that many of them kill themselves in this way.

From all this it will be quite clear that they perform no penance, and have absolutely no repentance of their sins. They neither confess them nor make atonement for them, however much they injure themselves, and they will be most severely punished for their errors hereafter.

Now we must examine the fourth and last Cathar sacrament, ordination: how many orders they have, their names, the duties of each order, and how and by whom they are ordained. Finally we shall see how many Cathar churches there are, and where.

Cathar orders and their offices

There are four orders of Cathars. The first and highest is that of bishop; second, *filius major*; third, *filus minor*; and fourth and last, deacon. Those of them who have no orders are referred to simply as Christians.

The office of bishops It is the bishop's duty always to take precedence in whatever they do, whether in the *consolamentum*, the breaking of bread, or opening prayer. The *filius major* does the same in the absence of the bishop, and the *filius minor* in the absence of both the bishop and the *filius major*.

The two *filii* must also travel about, either separately or together to visit all the Cathars under their bishop, who are bound to obey them. The deacons perform the same duties in every respect for those who are set under them, in the absence of the bishop and the *filii*. It should be noticed that the bishops and *filii* have separate deacons in each city, and especially those where Cathars live.

The office of the deacon The duty of the deacons is to hear the monthly confession of venial sins, of which we have spoken already, from those in their charge, and to absolve them by enjoining upon them a fast of three days, or one hundred genuflections. This they call a service, or, I should say, a prescribed service.

How the bishop is ordained These orders are created by the bishop, or by the *filii* with the permission of the bishop. The ordination of a bishop used to be performed in this way. When a bishop dies his *filius minor* ordains the *filius major* as bishop, and he in turn ordains the *filius minor* as *filius major*. Then a new *filius minor* is chosen by all the prelates and their followers who are present at the meeting where the choice is made, and ordained by the bishop.

The procedure for ordaining the *filius minor* is universal among the Cathars. The ordination of the bishop, however, has been changed among the western Cathars, who say that by such a procedure the son seems to invest the father, which is wrong. They have a different procedure, which is that before his death the bishop ordains the *filius major* as bishop, and if either of them dies the *filius minor* is made *filius major* and bishop on the same day. This is why a Cathar church may have two bishops. Hence John of Lugio, who is one of those ordained in this way, always describes himself in his letters as 'John, by the grace of God *filius major* and ordained bishop, etc.'

Both of these forms of ordination are obviously wrong. On the one hand no human son appoints his own father, and on the other we read nowhere of any church having two bishops, any more than of a woman having two legitimate husbands.

The method of ordination All of these orders are conferred by the *consolamentum*. The privilege of bestowing the orders and of giving the Holy Spirit belongs only to the bishop or whoever is senior among them, who holds a copy of the New Testament above the head of whoever is receiving the *consolamentum*.

An important doubt among them All Cathars suffer from great doubt and danger to their souls. If one of their prelates, and especially a bishop, secretly commits any mortal sin, such as has often been found among them, all those to whom he has given the *consolamentum* have been deceived, and will be damned if they die in that state. In order to avoid this danger all Cathar churches, with one or two exceptions, receive the *consolamentum* for a second, or even a third time.

THE CATHAR CHURCHES

There are sixteen Cathar churches altogether. Blame not me, dear readers, for giving them the name of churches, but rather those who do so. They are: the church of the Albanenses, or Desenzano; the church of Concorezzo; the church of Bagnolo; the church of Vicenza, or the March; the church of Florence; the church of Spoleto; the church of France; the church of Toulouse; the church of Carcassonne; the church of Albi; the church of Sclavonia; the Latin church of Constantinople; the Greek church there; the church of Philadelphia, in Asia Minor; the church of Bulgaria; the church of Dragovitsa. All these stem originally from two.

Where they are The Albanenses are found in Verona and other Lombard cities; there are about five hundred of them, of both sexes.

The sect of Concorezzo is spread throughout Lombardy, and there are about fifteen hundred or more, of both sexes.

The Bagnolans are found in small numbers at Mantua, Brescia and Bergamo, in the Romagna and a few around Milan—about two hundred of them.

The church of the March has some members in Vicenza, but none in Verona —about one hundred in all.

Those of Tuscany and Spoleto have almost one hundred.

The church of France is found in Verona and Lombardy, and has about one hundred and fifty members.

The churches of Toulouse, Albi and Carcassonne, with what was once the church of Agen, but is now almost destroyed, comprise nearly two hundred.

The Latin church at Constantinople has about fifty, and the Greek church there, with those of Sclavonia, Philadelphia, Bulgaria and Dragovitsa, about five hundred altogether.

The reader may be sure that there are not more than about four thousand Cathars in the whole world, a calculation which they have often made themselves.

OPINIONS PECULIAR TO THE ALBANENSES

We have already shown what doctrines, sacraments and ministers all Cathars have in common. Now we must explain the variations between them beginning with the church of the Albanenses, or Desenzano, who err on more points than the others.

Note first that the Albanenses are divided into two parties which hold different and conflicting opinion. One is headed by Balasinanza, their bishop of Verona, whose followers consist mainly of old men, with only a few young. The head of the other party is John of Lugio, of Bergamo, their *filius major* and ordained bishop. His followers are mostly young, with a few old men, and his party is larger than the other.

The opinions of the Balasinanzans

The first party sticks to the old teachings, to which all Cathars and Albanenses subscribed between about 1200 and 1230, both those which were peculiar to the Albanenses and the universal teachings which we have described already —that there are two eternal principles, one good and one evil. They hold that the trinity of Father, Son and Holy Spirit is not one god, and the Father is greater than the Son and the Holy Spirit. They believe that each principle, or each god, created his own angels and his own world, and that this world, with everything in it was created, made and shaped by the evil God. They think that the devil went to Heaven with his angels, fought a battle against the Archangel Michael and the angels of the good god, and carried off a third of his subjects. Then he imprisoned them in human bodies and in animals, changing them from one body to another until they should all be led back to Heaven. Hence they call all these subjects of God as they see them, 'the People of God', 'Souls', 'Sheep of Israel', and many other such names.

They claim that the Son of God did not really assume human nature from the Blessed Virgin, who was an angel, but only the appearance of it. They say that he did not truly eat or drink, suffer or die, and was not buried or resurrected: all of this was only in appearance, for we read in Luke, 'being [as it was supposed] the son of Joseph'. They interpret all Christ's miracles in the same way.

They say that Abraham, Isaac, Jacob, Moses, and all the ancient fathers and also John the Baptist were enemies of God and servants of the devil. The devil is the author of the whole of the Old Testament, except for the books of Job, the Psalms, Solomon, Wisdom, Ecclesiastes, Isaiah, Jeremiah, Ezekiel, Daniel and twelve of the prophets, some of which they say were written in Heaven —that is, before the fall of Jerusalem, which they think was Heaven.

They teach that this world will never come to an end, that the Last Judgement has already been made, and will not be made again, and that hell, eternal fire and eternal punishment are in this world and nowhere else.

These doctrines were held by all Albanensians at the period I mentioned except some of the simple, to whom they were not revealed.

The opinions of John of Lugio

The opinions of John of Lugio and his followers are described below. It should be understood that John holds some of the views which we have already described, but has drastically altered others for the worse, and has invented some new heresies of his own, as we shall see.

The two principles John of Lugio, an Albanensian, holds that there are two principles, that is gods, or lords, one good and one evil, but his doctrine differs, as we shall see, from that of the Balasinanzans. He wholly denies the unity and trinity of God of the Catholic faith.

The names which he gives to the evil principle According to him the evil principle is referred to in the holy scriptures by many names—malice, wickedness, avarice, impiety, sin, pride, death, hell, calumny, vanity, injustice, damnation, confusion, corruption and fornication. He says that all these are gods or goddesses deriving their being from malice, which he asserts is their cause, and which is occasionally signified by these vices. He also says that the evil principle is referred to in the phrase of St James, 'an unquiet evil full of deadly poison', and in the day of which the Lord says in the Gospel, 'sufficient for the day is the evil thereof'. The apostle's words in II Corinthians mean the same thing, 'It is and it is not', and so is Mount Seir of which Ezekiel says, 'thou has been an everlasting enemy of the Lord.'

It is meant even by the stomach of which the apostle says, 'whose god is their belly'.

Again, he teaches that the idols of the peoples of which we read throughout the Old Testament are, naturally, evil gods, malign spirits, and that the gentiles made images of them to worship them more. Why go on? It would be tedious for me to write down all the fables about idols and vices that John has peddled to support his errors.

The opinions of John of Lugio on creation, and what creation is Now let us see what John of Lugio believes about the creator of all things visible and invisible: first what it is to create; second, whether creatures were made or created, from nothing; third, whether the creatures of the good god were created good, simply and purely with no sort of malice; and fourth, whether there is ever any free will.

To create, according to him, is to make something from other pre-existing material, which it always means, and not from nothing. He distinguishes three kinds of creation. First, there is creation from good of better, as Christ was created from the Father; hence Isaiah said, 'I, the Lord, have created him', and the apostle 'made a high priest for ever'. Second, he places the creation of good from evil as the apostle puts it, 'we are his workmanship, created in Christ Jesus', and as is said in Genesis, 'In the beginning God created heaven and earth'. Here, he says, 'In the beginning', refers to the Son, who said, 'I am the beginning, who also speak unto you'. Hence John argues clearly that God the Father did not create Heaven and earth from nothing, but from something else which was good, like those whom the apostle called 'created in Christ in good works'. The third kind of creation, he says, is to make bad into worse to support which he cites the section of Justinian's *Codex* 'on Heretics and Manichees' from 'All heresies prohibited by divine law and imperial con-stitutions' to 'and create ministers which they are not'. [Digest, I, 5.2.] He says that all creatures have been eternally good creatures when they are those of the good god, and evil when they are those of the evil god; the creators did not precede their creatures in eternity, and yet are their causes. The relation-ship between God and his creatures in eternity is like that between the radiance (or rays) of the sun and its rays; the radiance does not come before the rays which compose it in time, and yet is their cause, and their nature.

He also says that this world was made by the devil, or rather the father of the devil, and that it had no beginning and will have no end. He believes that the good god has another world, in which there are men and animals and other things like the visible and corruptible creatures of our world. In this other world there is marriage, fornication and adultery from which children are procreated; more wicked still, the people of the good god have married the daughters of the other race, that is the daughters of the devil, or devils, against his orders, and from this evil and forbidden union giants and other things have been born at various times.

Whether the good god made his creatures without malice   Now we should consider whether the good god made his creatures pure and without malice. We shall leave aside many of John's blasphemies, such as his contention that God is not omnipotent. He says that God wills all good things and can do them as far as it depends on him and his creatures, who necessarily obey him, but that the will and power of God are obstructed by his adversary. He argues that each god acts upon the other eternally, and that the cause of evil is that the evil god acts against the true god and against his son and all his works for ever. To support this he adduces many authorities, such as the words of the Lord to Satan in Job, 'Thou hast moved me against Job, that I should afflict him without cause', and where Job said to God, 'Thou are changed to be cruel to me.'

He argues that the devil is more powerful than the subjects of the good God. From this premise he concludes that the good god cannot make his creatures perfect, as he would like to. This happens to him and to his creatures through the resistance of the evil god, who has inserted a certain malice into them for ever, to enable them to sin. In support of this he cites Ecclesiastes, 'He that could have transgressed and hath not transgressed: and could do evil things, and hath not done them', which he applies, quite foolishly to Christ. Or, again, he cites Job, 'in his angels he found wickedness', and 'the stars are not pure' etc., and the beginning of Genesis, 'Now the serpent was more subtle than any of the beasts of the earth which the Lord God had made.' From this he infers that all animate things participate in subtlety, but the serpent more than any of them, which is why he committed the deception. To all this he adds that nothing has free will, not even God himself, since he cannot make his will effective against his enemy.

He also says that every creature of the good god has power to act for evil when deceived by error, which he calls the greatest god of evil, except Christ. In him the power of sinning, or the ability to do wrong, has been so oppressed by his great goodness that it has lost its efficacy: this is an extraordinary thing, peculiar to Christ. Therefore, he is worthy of praise, and the book of Wisdom says of him, 'Who is he and we will praise him?', while all other creatures of the good God are blameworthy. In support of this he cites the apostle, 'for the creature was made subject to vanity, not willingly', and 'we know that every creature groaneth.'

John holds that when God inflicts a penalty for the sins of his creatures he does evil, acting not as God but rather in the service of his adversary. He claims that when God said, 'I alone am and there is no other God', and 'See ye that I am God', he spoke twice because his enemy moved him, for, as Job says, the true god speaks in such a way once, and does not repeat himself. God, he would have it, has no foreknowledge of evil from the resources of his own knowledge, because evil does not flow from him: he discovers it through his enemy. He believes that the true god caused the flood, destroyed Pentapolis, and overthrew Jerusalem because of the sins of his people—in brief, that everything that the people of Israel suffered both in Judaea and in the Promised Land was visited on them by the true god, under the influence of his adversary, because of their sins. John says, and indeed believes, that all these things happened in the other world, the kingdom of the true god.

The souls of the people of God are transmitted from body to body, and in the end will all be freed from pain and guilt.

John accepts the whole Bible, but he thinks that it was written in another world, in which Adam and Eve were created. He believes that Noah, Abraham, Isaac and Jacob, and the other patriarchs, all the prophets and John the Baptist were good men and lived in another world. He grants that Christ was descended from the patriarchs, in the flesh truly assumed the flesh from the Blessed Virgin, truly suffered, was crucified, died and was buried, and rose again on the third day, but he thinks that all this happened in another world, not in this one. In this other world, he says, the whole human race incurred death for its sin. This sin was the origin and cause of all evil, as we have already seen.

When the bodies had been buried the souls, of course, descended into hell, that is into this world, and Christ descended into hell to help them. There will, John says, be a resurrection of the dead, when each of God's souls will receive its own body.

In this other world also, according to him, the true god gave the law of Moses to the people, and there the priests offered sacrifices and ceremonies for the sins of the people, as the law obliged them to do. It was in the same world that Christ performed true miracles, raising the dead, giving sight to the blind, and feeding a crowd of five thousand people, apart from the women and children, with five barley loaves.

Why go on? In the whole Bible whatever has been read as referring to this world John bends to mean some other one.

How John of Lugio wrote a book about his heresies This heresiarch, John of Lugio, has committed all these errors and blasphemies, and many others which it would be lengthy and tedious to relate, to a large book of ten quires, a copy of which I have and have read. I took these doctrines which I have cited from it. It is important to note that John and his allies do not dare to reveal their opinions to their *credentes*, in case the *credentes* should desert them because of the novelty of the teaching and the division which they cause among the Albanensian Cathars.

The Albanensian Cathars condemn the Cathars of Concorezzo, and *vice versa.*

ERRORS PECULIAR TO THE CATHAR CHURCH OF CONCOREZZO

These people believe only in one principle, but many of them fall into error on the matter of trinity and unity. They profess that God created angels and the four elements from nothing, but they err in believing that the devil, with God's permission, made all visible things, including this world. They say that the devil made the body of the first man and put into it an angel who had sinned in some way, and that all souls are inherited from that angel.

They reject the whole of the Old Testament, thinking that it was written by the devil, except for phrases which are used in the New Testament by Christ and the apostles like, 'Behold a virgin shall conceive', and so on. They condemn Moses, and many of them are dubious about Abraham, Isaac and Jacob and the other patriarchs, and especially the prophets. Many of them now think that John the Baptist was good, though once they all condemned him.

They say that Christ did not assume a human spirit, but nearly all of them hold that he did assume flesh from the Blessed Virgin.

The errors of Nazarius, their bishop Nazarius, once one of their bishops, and a very old man said before me and several others that the Blessed Virgin was an angel, and that Christ assumed not a human but an angelic nature, or heavenly body from her. He said that he had learnt this heresy from a Bulgarian bishop and *filius major* nearly sixty years ago.

It is important to remember that all Cathars who hold that Christ assumed a human body say that his body neither was nor should have been glorified. They think that on the day of his Ascension Christ left his body in the sky; he will put it on again on the Day of Judgement and after the Judgement has been given it will be melted into basic matter, like a rotting corpse. The souls of the Blessed Virgin and the apostles are not in glory, and will not be until the Day of Judgement: they are in the sky, in the same place as the body of Christ.

THE CATHARS OF BAGNOLO

Now we come to the church of Bagnolo. They agree with the Cathars of Concorezzo on nearly all these points, except that they say that souls were created by God before the world was made, and sinned even then. They believe, like Nazarius, that the Blessed Virgin was an angel, and that Christ did not assume human nature from her; he assumed a heavenly body, and did not truly suffer any pain in death.

THE CATHARS OF TOULOUSE, ALBI AND CARCASSONNE

Finally we must note that the Cathars of the churches of Toulouse, Albi and Carcassonne subscribe to the errors of Balasinanza and the old Albanenses, as do almost all the foreign Cathar churches which I have mentioned. No Cathar church agrees with the church of Concorezzo about everything. The church of France agrees with that of Bagnolo. Those of the March, Tuscany and Spoleto agree with the Bagnolans more than the Albanenses, but are gradually drawn towards the Albanenses.

All the Cathar churches accept one another, even though they hold different and contradictory doctrines, except the Albanenses and Concorezzans who, as I have said, damn one another in turn.

If Cathars of either sex do not confess to the aforesaid errors, either those peculiar to particular sects or the ones which they all hold in common, they are undoubtedly lying hypocrites, which is what you would expect of Cathars, as the apostle said when he made a clear prophecy about them—unless perhaps they are simpletons or novices, to many of whom their secrets are scarcely revealed.

THE HERESY OF THE 'LEONISTAE', OR POOR MEN OF LYONS

We have said enough of the heresy of the Cathars. Now let us turn to that of the *Leonistae*, or Poor Men of Lyons. They are divided into two parts, the

Poor Men from North of the Alps [*Pauperes Ultramontani*] and the Poor Men of Lombardy, the latter being descended from the former.

The first, the Poor Men from across the Alps, say that the New Testament prohibits all swearing as mortal sin. They also reject secular justice on the ground that kings, princes and potentates ought not to punish evil-doers. They say that an ordinary layman may consecrate the body of the Lord, and I believe that they apply this to women as well for they have never denied it to me. They allege that the Roman Church is not the Church of Jesus Christ.

The Poor Men of Lombardy The Poor Men of Lombardy agree with the others about swearing and secular justice. On the eucharist they are even worse, holding that it may be consecrated by any man who is not in mortal sin. They say that the Roman Church is a church of evil, the beast and harlot which are found in the Book of Revelations, and that it is no sin to eat meat during Lent or on Friday against the precept of the Church, if it is done without offence to others.

They also say that the Church of Christ remained in bishops and other prelates until St Silvester, and failed in him, until they themselves restored it, though they do say there have always been some who have feared God and been saved. They believe that children can be saved without baptism.

This work was faithfully compiled by Brother Rainier in AD 1250. Deo Gratias.

40 Anselm of Alessandria: on heretics

The treatise of Anselm of Alessandria, who was active as an inquisitor in Lombardy between 1267 and 1278–9, was written as a complement to the much better known *Summa* of Rainier Sacchoni, a copy of which appears to have been inserted in the original text. It is translated from the edition of Dondaine, 'La hiérarchie cathare en Italie', *AFP* 20 (1950), pp. 308–18. The notes which Anselm added after he had completed the main body of the treatise (*ibid.*, pp. 318–24) are omitted. Except for the information that Mark and his associates 'brought the heresy from Naples to Lombardy about 1174', they add only more details, largely repetitive, on the French and Lombard Waldensians, notes on inquisitorial procedure, and a list of the Cathar hierarchy in Italy at the time at which Anselm wrote. Dondaine's masterly introduction, (*ibid.*, pp. 234–305), which will remain the fundamental treatment of the origins of Catharism in western Europe, is supplemented by Thouzellier, 'Hérésie et croisade', *RHE* 1954.

The beginning of the heresies

A Persian named Mani once asked himself, 'If there is a God where does evil come from? And if there is no God, where does good come from?' From this he deduced the existence of two principles. He preached around Dragovitsa, Bulgaria, and Philadelphia, and his heresy prospered so much that they made three bishops, of Dragovitsa, Bulgaria and Philadelphia. Later the Greeks from Constantinople, three days journey from the border of Bulgaria, went there to trade. They made converts when they came home, and appointed a bishop who was called the bishop of the Greeks. Later the Franks went to Constantinople to conquer the land, and discovered this sect; they were converted, and set up a bishop who is called the bishop of the Latins. Later some Slavs came to Constantinople from Bosnia to trade, returned home, and preached the heresy, which spread widely. They established a bishop called the bishop of Sclavonia, or Bosnia. After this the Franks who had come to Constantinople returned to their own country, preached the heresy, made converts, and set up a bishopric of France. Because it was the Bulgars who had led the French astray in Constantinople, heretics are known as Bulgars all over France. The Provençals, who are neighbours of the French, were converted by them, and the heresy spread among them so much that they made four bishops, of Carcassonne, Albi, Toulouse and Agen.

A long time after this a French notary came to Lombardy, to the district of Concorezzo in the county of Milan. There he met Mark, a native of Colognio, nearby, and converted him. Mark in turn converted two of his friends, John the Jew and Joseph. Mark was a grave-digger, John a weaver, and Joseph a smith. One of them went to Milan, to the eastern or Corencian gate, and converted a friend of his called Aldricus de Bando. The converts had a meeting with the notary, who sent them to Roccavione, near Cuneo, where some French Cathars had settled. The bishop of the heretics was not there, but at Naples. They found him there, and stayed for a year. Then Mark was made a deacon by the imposition of hands, and the bishop sent him back to his native area of Concorezzo to preach. Through his preaching the heresy spread widely in Lombardy and later in Tuscany and the March of Treviso.

Some time later a man called Papa Nicetas, their bishop at Constantinople, came and said that there were so many of them that they ought to have a bishop. They chose Mark as bishop, and all the heretics of Lombardy, Tuscany and the March obeyed him, and Papa Nicetas confirmed him. A little later Mark heard that Papa Nicetas had made a bad end to his life, and decided that he had better make the journey abroad to be ordained as bishop by the bishop of Bulgaria. In Calabria, however, he met a Cathar deacon called Hilary who told him that there was no way in which he could cross the sea so he turned back again. When he was in the district of Argentea he was captured and imprisoned. Feeling ill, and on the point of death, he sent word to John the Jew and the other Cathars to choose a new bishop. All the Cathars of Lombardy chose John the Jew of Concorezzo. John the Jew went to Argentea, was confirmed bishop by Mark, and returned to Lombardy. A few days later Mark was released from prison, and set out for Lombardy, but he died before he reached John the Jew. The Lombard Cathars, including John himself, were worried because Papa Nicetas, who ordained Mark, who in turn, ordained John, had made a bad end. This came to the ears of one Nicholas of the March, who wanted to be bishop himself, and set about stirring up disagreement among the Cathars. He asked them, 'What do you believe about Mark? Do you believe that he made a good end, or not?' They replied, 'Yes, we believe that he made a good end.' 'John the Jew says that Mark made a bad end, and because of this he wants to go abroad to receive the *consolamentum* again.' Thus the heretics became divided into parties, which corresponded to five areas: those of Concorezzo kept John the Jew as bishop; those of Desenzano, in the diocese of Brescia, made Philip bishop, but soon afterwards he took up with two Cathar women, left the Cathars and returned to live in the world with the pair of them. This Philip is said to have subscribed to the opinion that neither man nor woman can sin with any part of the body beneath the waist, in which he has had many disciples. The Cathars of Mantua chose Caloiannus, and when he died shortly afterwards, Orto of Bagnolo, so they are called the Bagnolans. Those of the March chose Nicholas, who had sown the dissension among them, and those of Florence Peter of Florence, who was bishop there and for the whole of Tuscany.

A note on the four Cathar bishops of Lombardy

The Cathars have four bishops in Lombardy. The present bishop of Concorezzo is Mandennus; the first bishop they had for themselves was John the Jew, after him Garratus, which is why they are called *Garratenses*. After him there was Nazarius for almost forty years, then Gerard of Cambiato, and then Mandennus. The Albanenses began with Philip, who was succeeded by Balasinanza for almost forty years, then John of Lugio, and then their present Bishop Bonaventure of Verona. The Bagnolans began with Caloiannus, after whom they are called the *Caloianni*, and then Orto of Bagnola, after whom they are called Bagnolans; he was succeeded by Andreas, and then by Hamund of Casalialto, their present bishop.

The divisions among the Concorezzans

I believe that the so-called French heretics have Viventius of Verona as their bishop. [Cathar bishop of Toulouse before he went into exile.]

It should be noted that the Concorezzans are divided between the ancients and the moderns. Some of them accept the view of Nazarius, who was once their bishop, others those of Desiderius, once *filius major* in their sect: thus there was disagreement between the bishop and the *filius major*. Nazarius and his followers did not believe that Christ really ate material food, or that he truly died and was truly resurrected. He also denied that Christ performed physical miracles on human bodies. Desiderius and his followers believed that he did perform physical miracles. All Cathars agree that Christ did not descend into hell. Nazarius and his followers believe that the spirit which was in John the Baptist was the same as that in the prophet Elijah, and that it was an evil, diabolical spirit. Nazarius believes in a book which he calls the *secretum*; Desiderius and his disciples do not believe in the *secretum*, which they think evil. Nazarius says that Christ had no soul, only Godhead; Desiderius believes that he had a soul, though few agreed with him in this. Nazarius holds that Christ was not God, and was not one with the Father; Desiderius that Christ was God, and in essence one with the Father. Nazarius thinks that Christ brought his body down with him from Heaven, entered the Virgin through her ear and left again by the same route, and resumed the same body at the Ascension. Desiderius holds that Christ had a real body made of the flesh of Adam, and the Blessed Virgin had a real body composed of the flesh of Adam, and was a real woman: Christ truly died, and truly rose again in that body, but when he ascended to Heaven he left it in the terrestrial paradise, where the Blessed Virgin remains—for according to him she never died. He believes that the soul of John the Baptist also lives there, along with the souls of all good men who have died, which he supports with the text 'wheresoever the body shall be there shall the eagles be gathered together.' He says that they will remain there until the Day of Judgement. On the Day of Judgement Christ will resume his body, and in that body he will judge the good and the evil, and then he will lay it aside, and it will again become part of the primordial matter, just like the bodies of animals.

All the Concorezzans believe that the prophets sometimes spoke with their own voices, sometimes with the voice of the Holy Spirit, and sometimes with that of the evil spirit. They all say that the sixteen prophets were good men but when they spoke with the spirit they were always provided with what they said by the devil. When they spoke with the Holy Spirit it was because God had something inside them, by means of which they might sometimes speak for his purpose, as when Isaiah said, 'Behold a virgin shall conceive and bear a son', and other things which are in the New Testament. But the prince of the world, the devil, did not know this.

All the Concorezzans agree that the sixteen prophets, and the others from the Old Testament who are saved, rose again at the death of Christ, and are those of whom it is said, 'many bodies of the saints arose and coming out of the tombs after his resurrection . . . appeared to many'—and, they add, received the imposition of hands from Christ.

Nazarius believes that the devil made the sun from one part of the crown of Adam, and the moon from another part, and the moon and stars, and five other stars which are not in the firmament from the crown of Eve, as well as a seat where Satan sits in the sky, and from which he rules the whole world below him, except the good souls in it. He thinks that all the stars are made

from jewels. Desiderius accepts none of this. Nazarius also thinks that the sun
and the moon are animate beings, and that they make love every month:
dew and honey are the products of this lust, and therefore Nazarius will not
allow the eating of honey. Again, Nazarius and his followers, like the Bagnolans
and the Albanenses, interpret the scriptural references to matrimony wholly in
a spiritual sense, and believe that they were addressed to those who are within
the Church. Desiderius and his followers, on the other hand, take them to refer
to physical marriage, and to be addressed to those who belong to the Church
by faith, but not by vows, that is to the *credentes*.

One of the Albanensian leaders, Lanfrancinus of Vaure says, and this is the
Albanensian view, that not all the sheep, or souls, which descended or fell
from heaven are embodied: some of them are being purged in a misty ether,
without bodies, and are undergoing a worse punishment than those which
are in bodies, though they will be saved sooner. These are referred to in the
Gospel, 'And other sheep I have that are not of this fold'.

All that the Concorezzans should be asked is whether God made the body of
Adam, and shaped Eve from his rib, or whether he made your body or mine
himself, directly and not through an intermediary. If they say yes, the question
follows whether God the Father did this by his own word, or if the devil
received some other power or office from God, by virtue of which power or
office he did it.

No Cathar can conceal his heresy completely. When the Concorezzan
Cathar tries to dissimulate he says that God made Eve with the rib, and shaped
and formed your hand, but he means that this was only so *in posse*; be believes
that it was the devil who did it in fact. He means by *in posse* that the devil's
power was bestowed on him in the first instance by God, either from the
creation, or from the moment when, according to them the devil said to God
'Have patience with me and I will pay thee all', when God bestowed upon
him the power of making all things.

The views of the Bagnolans

These are three stands of opinion among the Bagnolans. Some agree with the
Concorezzans, some with the Albanenses, and some take an intermediate
position. These last believe in a single principle. They agree with the Concorezzans about the creation of the world and of man. On the question of the
sins of the angels in heaven they say that there were some who sinned by
voluntarily going with the serpent, and these will never return, and none of
them will be saved: they are the demons. Others were dragged off forcibly
by the serpent, and they alone among the sinners will be saved. The spirit of
Adam and Eve came from among those which were dragged off by force.
They say that other spirits were transferred from the spirits of Adam and

Eve to make up the deficiency left by the evil spirits which had sinned voluntarily, and that these spirits of Adam and Eve were put into bodies by the devil. The transmission of spirit from spirit is natural, like that of body from body, or plant from plant, but it is the work of the devil.

The Bagnolans believe, like the Concorezzans, that all punishments, and all rewards for the good, are equal. They do not believe that Christ was a real man, or that he had a real body: they hold that he brought it with him from Heaven. Nor do they believe that he really suffered or died or felt any pain, nor that he really rose again: this, they say, was only appearance. They believe that Christ is lesser than the Father.

All Cathars believe firmly and generally that the devil is responsible for rain and snow, for thunder and lightning, and for hurricanes.

No Cathar fasts on the vigil of any saint or apostle or of the Blessed Virgin, for they say that that whore, the Church of Rome, invented vigils to make money, and they do not observe any feast day, or Sunday, or take any holidays, except perhaps to avoid giving rise to scandal.

The imposition of hands among the Cathars

The imposition of hands, which the Cathars call baptism, or the *consolamentum*, should always be performed by a number of them, but if it is necessary it may be done by one man, or one Cathar woman, alone. The Concorezzans say that it is only effective if the recipient is actually touched by the hand, on the head and shoulders. Hence they say that if a Cathar puts his hand and arm through an aperture to give the *consolamentum* to a sick man lying in bed, who cannot move on his bed, and if the hand is held in such a way that it is as close to the patient as one's mouth is to one's nose, it is still no good, unless it touches. The Albanenses, on the other hand, can perform the *consolamentum* effectively without touching the recipient, if they cannot reach him, even if the distance between them is as far as the voice can carry. Therefore they can do it effectively even if there is a wall or a river in the way, so that we must be careful when we are holding suspects against Cathars approaching the sick, or even the house in which they are detained.

First the person who is to receive the *consolamentum* makes three genuflections before the officiating prelate and says, 'Benedicite, benedicite, benedicite: good Christians pray to God to lead me to a good end, and keep me from a bad end. I implore you by the mercy of God to do that good to me which God has done to you.'

The prelate replies, 'May the Lord bless you' three times, and then, 'We grant you the good which the Lord has given us freely, as God has given us his grace.' Then he explains what rules the initiate must observe in future. If he says that he is prepared to keep them all the prelate holds out a book to him, the New Testament or the Gospels. He takes it and holds it to his heart, closed, and the prelate says, 'you have received the book in which is written the divine law, which must never be separated from your heart.'

The initiate replies, 'Pray God grant me grace to keep it, for it is my will to keep it always.' Then he hands back the book, genuflects three times and says, 'Let us praise, Father, Son and Holy Spirit. To Holy Church and good Christians, I confess before you all the sins which I have committed since birth, which you must pray God to forgive me, as far as you have power to do from God and the Holy Church.' He rises, and the prelate says, 'May he who has power in Heaven and earth remit your sins as we do as far as we have the power from God and the Holy Church.' Then the prelate places the book on his head, and his hands on his shoulders, and all the professed Cathars present do the same. The prelate says, 'Lord forgive your servant all his sins, and receive him into your righteousness.' Then the prelate says seven 'Our Fathers' and all the others, including the initiate, do the same. Then the prelate says three times, 'Let us praise the Father, Son and Holy Ghost', and the others reply, 'He is worthy and just.' The prelate says an 'Our Father' and the others repeat it, as before. Again the prelate says, 'Let us praise Father, Son and Holy Ghost', and the others reply, 'He is worthy and just.' The prelate recites the Gospel of St John, 'In the beginning was the word', or St Matthew, 'Take up my yoke upon you.' When the Gospel has been read the prelate says, 'The grace of our Lord Jesus Christ be with you always' and they reply, 'Amen. Benedicite, spare us', 'Father Son and Holy Ghost remit all our sins', and repeat, 'Benedicite, spare us' to the prelate as before.

The prelate then removes the Gospel from the initiate's head, and he is placed among the Cathars, who say to him, 'Now you are one of us, in this world a sheep among wolves.' They then perform the 'Duplam'.

Penance among the Cathars

The Cathars observe four kinds of penance. For open and mortal sin the bishop enjoins upon them three days continuously of 'crossing over', when the sinner neither eats nor drinks anything for three days, and after that three periods of forty days on bread and water. All Cathars, incidentally, observe three periods of forty days fasting, but those to whom it is prescribed as penance for mortal sin must not allow their forty days to coincide with the forty days which everyone observes in common. They also lose their rank permanently, and may not perform the *consolamentum* except when it is absolutely necessary.

The second penance is for those who sin mortally, but in secret. They receive the *consolamentum* afresh, and twenty seven days of 'crossing over' when they neither eat nor drink—though not in succession. They do not lose their rank, but do lose the bishopric if they hold it, and cannot perform the *consolamentum* except in dire necessity.

Thirdly, there is the penance for those who long and desire to do something which is regarded as mortal sin, but do not do it. They are given twenty-seven days, not in succession, of 'crossing over', and must decide for themselves whether to receive the *consolamentum* afresh; they forfeit the bishopric, but not their rank.

Finally, for the ordinary daily sins which one confesses for all once a month, they do as Brother Rainier says (p. 135) and are given three days on bread and water, which are called 'days of service'.

On Cathar abstinence

There is a common rule of abstinence among them, according to which all Cathars, of every sect, fast for three days each week, on Monday, Wednesday and Friday. They tell people that they fast on bread and water, but this is not true, for they abstain from wine, oil, fish and shellfish, and eat all the other things that they usually eat on ordinary days.

All the Cathars observe three fasts of forty days. The first begins at the same time as our Lent, and lasts until Easter; the second is from the first Monday after Whitsun to St Peter's [1 August]; the third from the first Monday after Martinmas to Christmas. In the first there are two weeks which are especially strict, the first and the last, when they do not drink wine, or eat oil or vegetable. They do not eat fish or shellfish at all during the three fasts, unless they are seriously ill. In the second and third fasts they have only one strict week, the first in each.

Mealtimes

When the cook has prepared the meal he goes to the master and says, 'Let me know if it is pleasing to the Lord and to you.' The master replies, 'May the Lord let you know if it pleases him.' The cook genuflects low and replies, 'Benedicite', and the master replies, 'May the Lord bless you.' The cook does and says the same again and the master replies, 'May the Lord bless you.' The cook genuflects a third time and if he is a professed heretic says, 'Bless and have mercy upon us,' but if he is only a believer, 'Benedicite, Good Christians, pray to the Lord to lead me to a good end and spare me a bad end', to which he adds, 'Dinner is ready. When it pleases the Lord and you, go to eat it.'

The master replies, 'May Lord reward you,' and turning to the other Cathars, 'Let us eat.' Then he begins prayer with the words, 'Bless us and have mercy upon us', to which all reply, 'May Father, Son and Holy Ghost spare us and forgive our sins.' Then he says three times, 'Let us praise the Father, Son and Holy Ghost', the first time aloud, the second silently, and the third aloud, and all the Cathars reply, 'He is worthy and just', and recite thirteen 'Our Fathers'. After a fourteenth 'Our Father' the master says, 'Let us praise the Father, Son and Holy Ghost', as he did before. Everybody replies, 'He is worthy and just', and they all recite an 'Our Father'; the master says three more 'Our Fathers' and then, 'Let us praise Father, Son and Holy Ghost' and they reply as before. The master says, 'The grace of our Lord Jesus Christ be always with us', and they answer, 'Amen.' Finally the master says, 'Bless and have mercy upon us', and they answer, 'Father, Son and Holy Ghost' as before.

They worship in this way fifteen times a day.

At table When they are all seated round the table, upon which are bread and wine at least, or water if it is one of the times for it, they stand up again. The master takes a loaf and breaks it, but does not pass it round, and says, 'Bless and have mercy upon us.' They reply as above, and say an 'Our Father'. 'Let us worship Father, Son and Holy Ghost,' he says, and they reply as above. 'The grace of our Lord Jesus Christ be always with us. Amen.' Finally the master says, 'Bless and have mercy upon us' and gives some of the bread to everybody present, both believers and others. If any of the bread is left over it does not matter if it is given to the pigs.

How they behave in the houses of others

When a Cathar or a believer of one of the sects enters a strange Cathar household, especially if he does not know which of the people he meets there are Cathars, he says, 'Greetings. May we better ourselves here?' Or he may say, 'Is there a bent stick here?' If there is anyone present who is not of their faith, or of whom they are nervous, the master replies, 'Sit down' which indicates the presence of someone they distrust, if not, 'do as you please.' Then the new arrival says, 'Tell me, if it please God and you,' and the master replies, 'May God tell us if it pleases him.' The new arrival makes a deep genuflection and says, 'Benedicite.' He genuflects again saying, 'Bless and have mercy upon us', if he is a professed Cathar, and if he is only a believer, 'Bless and have mercy upon us. Good Christians pray to God to lead me to a good end and protect me from a bad one.' The master answers, 'The Lord bless us and keep us in his service', if he is a perfect, or if he is a believer, 'May the Lord lead you to a good end and save you from a bad one.' Then he stands up and performs what they call the 'caron', a kind of embrace which involves putting the head first to the right side and then to the left.

The differences between the French and the Lombard Waldensians

The difference between the Waldensians of France and Lombardy is that the French say that any man whether good or bad, whether priest or not, may perform the mass and confer the other sacraments, while the Lombards say that he can only do so if he is in a state of grace. The Lombards are in error about the sacraments, and do not baptize correctly. Again, the Lombards work. All of them, French and Lombard alike, despise the institutions of the Church; they believe that marriage between cousin and cousin is legitimate if there is no objection to it except in the rules of the church.

[The *summa* of Rainier Sacconi is inserted here.]

Neither French nor Lombards bow to the cross or the altar, because 'The idols of the gentiles are silver and gold, the works of the hands of men.' The French say that any good man may be a priest, and the church, the Lombards that there is no church unless at least two are gathered together. The French consider the Lombards damned, and *vice versa*.

The French will not work for themselves or anyone else for gain, and will not sell or own anything. They wear their clerical badges on their feet, sandals or shoes cut away at the top; they keep no money—though their companions keep it for them—have nothing for food from one day to another, and wear only one coat. The women are the same, except that they do not wear sandals. The Lombards also wear sandals.

The French say that the pope can no more forgive sin than anybody else, and that the Roman Church is a scarlet woman, not the Church of God. The Lombards say this too. They both deny that the Pope is Peter's vicar on earth.

They both believe in baptism of oil and water by the Roman Church, but not in its rules. They take no notice of fasts prescribed by the Church, and do not think it sinful to break a fast. Their women preach. They do not believe in the indulgences granted by the Roman Church. The French bless themselves and their food; the Lombards do not, though they make a sign with their hands over it. The French believe in the fathers of the Church when it suits them to do so, and say that St Silvester betrayed the Church by accepting possessions. Their bishop is William of Albi.

The reasons for the division between them were the question of work, and the contention of the Lombards that sinful priests could not perform the mass.

Good John of Piacenza was the leader of the Lombards at the time of this division, when the French excommunicated them.

I, brother A., have written this after discovering it from two women who had been Waldensians for a long time, members of the French sect, and were later converted and did penance in seclusion at Alba.

Introductory Reading[1]

THIS list and the references in the notes are intended only as a preliminary guide to what is immediately useful. A comprehensive list of publications since 1900, compiled by H. Grundmann, may be found in J. Le Goff, ed., *Hérésies et sociétés*, also published separately as *Bibliographie zur Ketzergeschichte des Mittelalters* (1900–66), and J. B. Russell, 'Some Interpretations of the Origins of Medieval Heresy' (1963) is useful for older work.

The general history of the period is well outlined by C. N. L. Brooke, *Europe in the Central Middle Ages*, and J. H. Mundy, *Europe in the High Middle Ages*, whose chapter on 'Heresy and Enthusiasm' is of very great interest, and there are modern accounts of the Church by D. Knowles and D. Obolensky, *The Christian Centuries*: II, *The Middle Ages*, and R. W. Southern, *Western Society and the Church in the Middle Ages*. The literature on cultural and intellectual history is immense: a good recent introduction is P. Wolff, *The Awakening of Europe*. R. W. Southern, *The Making of the Middle Ages*, is a classic, particularly good on orthodox religious attitudes.

In general I confine myself to works in English and French, but there are no adequate substitutes in either language for H. Grundmann, *Religiöse Bewegungen im Mittelalter*, A. Borst, *Die Katharer*, or R. Manselli, *Studi sulle eresie del secolo xii* and *L'eresia del male*. Sir Steven Runciman, *The Medieval Manichee*, is a clear exposition of the traditional view—already being undermined while the book was being written—that there was a single dualist tradition which stretched from the Manichees to the Albigensians; F. Niel *Albigeois et cathares* is vulnerable to the same criticism, but shows a remarkably sympathetic insight into Catharism. H. C. Lea's *History of the Inquisition in the Middle Ages* is a great book though now seriously dated, and similar views are presented by A. S. Turberville, *Medieval Heresy and the Inquisition*. J. Guiraud, *Histoire de l'inquisition au moyen âge* is rich, if erratic, and H. Maisonneuve, *Études sur les origines de l'inquisition* is indispensable. The general conclusions of J. B. Russell, *Dissent and Reform in the Early Middle Ages* have been severely and justly criticized, but many of his accounts of individual episodes are thorough and useful, and though the introductory chapters of N. Cohn, *The Pursuit of the Millenium*, are extremely selective and not wholly accurate they offer a fresh and important approach to the understanding of popular religious movements. The social and cultural implications of popular heresy are explored in a series of very fine papers presented at a colloquium at Royaumont in 1963, published with generous extracts from discussion in Le Goff, ed., *Hérésies et sociétés*. Its appearance and that of C. Thouzellier's brilliant study of the debates between *Catharisme et valdéisme en Languedoc* are important landmarks in the recent development of heretical studies; Mlle Thouzellier's *Hérésies et hérétiques* is a valuable collection of her shorter studies,

[1] Full bibliographical details when not given here may be found in the bibliography.

including some previously unpublished. The series of *Cahiers de Fanjeaux* (Toulouse, annually since 1966) is also useful. W. L. Wakefield and A. P. Evans, *Heresies of the High Middle Ages* is especially useful for its translations of Catharist writings, and has an excellent historical introduction and voluminous notes which provide a good guide to the secondary literature. The publication is expected soon of *The Concept of Heresy in the Middle Ages (Medievalia Lovanensia*, IV), and of M. D. Lambert, *Medieval Heresy*, which will be the standard account of the subject that we need so badly.

G. Widengren, *Mani and Manichaeism* is a good introduction to the beliefs and writings of the Manichees, though its treatment of their origins and early history is contentious: a different view is presented by P. R. L. Brown, 'The Diffusion of Manchaeism in the Roman Empire', with valuable references, reprinted in his *Religion and Society in the Age of St Augustine*. Brown's *Augustine of Hippo*, pp. 46–61, contains a brief but very illuminating exploration of the Manichean mentality, whose impact on Augustine had such great consequences for the future. The standard accounts of Bogomilism are D. Obolensky, *The Bogomils*, and H. C. Puech and A. Vaillant, *Le traité de Cosmas le prêtre*, and for its relations with the West H. C. Puech, 'Le catharisme médiévale et le bogo-milisme', in *Oriente ed Occidente* is particularly important.

Walter Wakefield, *Heresy, Crusade and Inquisition in Southern France*, is an admirable discussion especially of the last two of its three topics, and translates important material on the setting up of the inquisition in Toulouse which should be added to that in his earlier collection, and in chapter four above, pp. 113–54. A. P. Evans contributed a fine chapter on the Albigensian crusade to K. M. Setton and M. Baldwin (eds.) *A History of the Crusades*, II, (Philadelphia 1962), pp. 277–324.

Zoe Oldenbourg, *The Massacre at Montsegur* is a popular history of the Albigensian crusade which lacks the weight of P. Belperron, *La croisade contre les albigeois et la réunion du Languedoc à la France*, but has the opposite bias: neither supersedes A. Luchaire, *Innocent III: II, La croisade des Albigeois*. Mme Oldenbourg shows the same sympathy for Catharism in her two fine novels of the crusade, *Destiny of Fire* and *Cities of the Flesh*, and C. P. Snow's *The Light and the Dark* (London 1947) is an interesting attempt to reconstruct a Manichean personality in a modern setting.

All serious modern work in this field has been based on the fundamental texts published by Father Antoine Dondaine, and his magisterial expositions of them. In particular his study of 'L'hiérarchie cathare en Italie', though not readily obtainable is not to be missed: it is probably the most influential work on medieval heresy printed in modern times. Important recent publications include:

ANGUELOV, D., *Le bogomilisme en Bulgarie*, trans. J. Duvernoy (Toulouse 1972)
COHN, N., *Europe's Inner Demons* (London 1975)
HAMILTON, B., *The Albigensian Crusade* (Historical Ass. pamphlet G. 84, London 1974)
MUNDY, J. H., 'Une famille cathare: les Maurand', *Annales* 29 (1974)
MUSY, J., 'Mouvements populaires et hérésies au XIe siècle en France', *Revue Historique* CCCLIII (1975)
ROSENWEIN, B. H. and LITTLE, L. K., 'Social meaning in the monastic and mendicant spiritualities' *Past and Present* 63 (1974)
SMALLEY, B., *Historians in the Middle Ages* (London 1974)
TAVIANI, H., 'Naissance d'une hérésie en Italie du Nord au XIe. siècle', *Annales* 29 (1974)
VIOLANTE, C., 'La pauvreté dans les hérésies du XIe siècle en occident' in M. Mollat (ed.) *Etudes sur l'histoire de la pauvreté* (Paris 1974)

Bibliography

An asterisk (*) indicates that the relevant passage from the text has been translated in the introductory note to the document indicated. Bold numbers in square brackets indicate the document number of the translation in this book.

Acta Synodi Atrebatensis, PL 142 [3]

ADHEMAR OF CHABANNES, *Historiarum libri iii* ed. G. Waitz, MGH SS IV [1]

ALEXANDER III, correspondence with Louis VII and Henry, archbishop of Rheims, Bouquet XV [25]

Annales Brunwilarenses ed. G. H. Pertz, MGH SS XVI [22*]

Annales de Margan ed. H. R. Luard, RS (London 1864)

Annales Rodenses ed. G. H. Pertz, MGH SS XVI [23*]

ANSELM OF ALESSANDRIA, *De hereticis* see Dondaine (1950) [40]

ANSELM OF LIÈGE, *Gesta episcoporum Leodicensis* ed. R. Koepke, MGH SS VII [5]

BAKER, D. M. see Studies in Church History

BELPERRON, P., *La croisade contre les Albigeois et la réunion du Languedoc à la France* (Paris 1943)

'BENEDICT OF PETERBOROUGH' see Roger of Hoveden

BENTON, J. F., *Self and Society in Medieval France: the Memoirs of Abbot Guibert of Nogent* (New York 1970)

BERNARD OF CLAIRVAUX, *Epistola 241*, PL 182 [14]
Letters of St Bernard trans. Bruno Scott James (London 1953)
vita Prima, PL 185 [15]
Life and Works of St Bernard trans. S. J. Eales (London 1886–96)

BOLTON, BRENDA M., 'Innocent III's treatment of the *Humiliati*', Studies in Church History 8 (1971), 73–82
'Tradition and Temerity: Papal Attitudes to Deviants 1159–1216', Studies in Church History 9 (1972)
'Mulieres sanctae', Studies in Church History 10 (1973)

BONENFANT, P., 'Un clerc cathare en Lotharingie au milieu de XIIe siècle', Le Moyen Age LXIX (1963)

BORST, A., *Die Katharer* (Stuttgart 1953)

BROOKE, C. N. L., *Europe in the Central Middle Ages* (London 1964)
'Heresy and Religious Sentiment: 1000–1250', Bulletin of the Institute of Historical Research XLI (1968)

BROOKE, Z. N., *Europe, 919–1198* (London 1938)

BROWN, P. R. L., *Augustine of Hippo* (London 1967)
'The Diffusion of Manichaeism in the Roman Empire', Journal of Roman Studies

LXIX (1969), 92–103

Religion and Society in the Age of St Augustine (London 1972)

CAESARIUS OF HEISTERBACH, *Dialogue on Miracles*, trans. H. von E. Scott and C. C. S. Bland (London 1929)

Cahiers de Fanjeaux, 3, *Cathares en Languedoc* (Toulouse 1968)

CAUCHIE, A. H. J., *La querelle de l'investiture dans les diocèses de Liège et Cambrai* I (Louvain 1891)

CHENU, M. D., *La théologie au douzième siècle* (Paris 1957) (trans. L. K. Little and J. Taylor as *Nature, Man and Society in the Twelfth Century*)

Chronica regio Coloniensis, *MHG Script* XVIII [29*]

Chronica universalis anonymi Laudunensis ed. G. Waitz, *MGH SS* XXVI [34]

Chronicon S. Andreae Castri Cameracesii ed. D. L. C. Bethmann, *MGH SS* VII [6]

COHN, N., *The Pursuit of the Millenium* (3rd edn., London 1970)

COLISH, MARCIA L., 'Peter of Bruys, Henry of Lausanne, and the facade of St Gilles', *Traditio* 28 (1972) 451–60

Concilium Lumbariense . . . adversus haereticos qui Boni homines dicebantur, Mansi, XXII [30]

CONGAR, Y. M. J., 'Henry de Marcy, abbé de Clairvaux', *Studia Anselmiana* XLIII, *Analecta monastica* V (1958)

'Arriana haeresis', *Revue des sciences philosophiques et théologiques* XLIII (1959)

CONSTANTINE OF LYONS, *Life of St Germanus* see Hoare

Council of Toulouse, 1119, Mansi, XXI

Council of Rheims, 1157, Mansi, XXI [25*]

COWDREY, H. E. J. 'The Papacy, the Patarenes, and the Church of Milan', *Transactions of the Royal Historical Society* 5th ser., 18 (1968)

CRACCO, G., 'Riforma ed eresia in momenti della cultura Europea tra X e XI secolo', *Rivista di storia e letteratura religiosa* VII (1971), 411–77

De heresi catharorum in Lombardia see Dondaine (1949)

DELARUELLE, E., 'Le catharisme en Languedoc vers 1200: une enquête', *Annales du Midi* 72 (1960) [37]

DONDAINE, A., *Le liber de duobus principiis* (Rome 1939)

'Les actes du concil Albigeoise de St Félix-de-Caraman', *Miscellanea Giovanni Mercati* V (*Studi e Testi* 125), Vatican (1946) [39]

'Aux origines du valdéisme: une profession de foi de Valdès', *AFP* XVI (1946)

'L'hiérarchie cathare en Italie: I, Le *De heresi catharorum*', *AFP* XIX (1949) [37]; 'II, Le *Tractatus de hereticis* d'Anselme d'Alexandrie O. P.', *AFP* XX (1950) [40]

'L'origine de l'hérésie médiévale', *Rivista di storia della chiesa in Italia* VI (1952)

'Durand de Heusca et la polémique anti-cathare', *AFP* XXIX (1959)

DOSSAT, Y. 'Remarques sur un prétendu evêque cathare du Val d'Aran', *Bulletin philologique du comité des travaux historiques et scientifiques* (1955–6)

'A propos du concile cathare de St Félix: les Milingues', *Cahiers de Fanjeaux* 3 (1968)

DOUGLAS, D. C. and GREENAWAY, G. W. *English Historical Documents* II, (London 1953)

ECKBERT OF SCHÖNAU, *Sermones contra catharos PL* 195 [29]

EMERTON, E., see Gregory VII

EUGENIUS III, *Epistola ad clerum et populum Atrebatensem*, Mansi, XXI

EVERSIN OF STEINFELD, Letter to St Bernard, *PL* 182 [22]

FEARNS, J. V., 'Peter von Bruis', *Archiv für Kulturgeschichte* XLVIII (1968)

FLICHE, A. and MARTIN, V., (eds.) *Histoire de l'église:* (Paris): VIII, *La réforme grégorienne et la reconquête chrétienne; IX Du premier Concile du Latran à l'avènement d'Innocent III* (2 vols); X, *La Chrétienté romaine* (1198–1274)

FREDERICQ, P. *Corpus documentorum inquisitionis haereticae pravitatis Neerlandicae* (Ghent 1889–1906) [31–33]

GARSOIAN, N. *The Paulician Heresy* (The Hague and Paris 1967)

'Byzantine Heresy: a reinterpretation', *Dumbarton Oaks Papers* XXV (1971), 101–12

GEOFFREY OF AUXERRE, *see* Bernard of Clairvaux, *Vita Prima* [15]

Gesta Pontificum Cenomannensium, Bouquet XII [11, 13]

Gesta Treverorum, ed. G. Waitz, *MGH SS* VIII [10]

GIBBON, E., *The Decline and Fall of the Roman Empire*

GREENAWAY, G. W., *Arnold of Brescia* (Cambridge 1931)

GREGORY VII, *Registrum*, ed. E. Caspar, *MGH Epist* II [7]

Correspondence of Pope, trans. E. Emerton, (New York 1932)

GRIFFE, E. *Les débuts de l'aventure cathare en Languedoc* (Paris 1969)

GRUNDMANN, H. *Religiöse Bewegungen im Mittelalter* (Berlin 1935; 2nd edn. Darmstadt 1961)

Bibliographie zur Ketzergeschichte des Mittelalters (1900–1966) (Rome 1967)

GUIBERT OF NOGENT *see* Benton, J. F.

GUIRAUD, J., *Histoire de l'inquisition au moyen âge* (Paris, 1935–8)

HAMPE, K., *Germany under the Salian and Hohenstaufen Emperors*, trans. R. F. Bennett (Oxford 1973)

HERBERT OF BOSHAM, *Epistola ad Willelmum Viziliacensem abbatem PL* 190

Hérésies et sociétés see Le Goff

HERIBERT, MONK, *Epistola de hereticis Petragoricis PL* 181 [24]

HERIMAN OF REICHINAU, *Chronicon*, ed. G. H. Pertz, *MGH SS* V [5*]

HILDEBERT OF LAVARDIN, *Epistola PL* 171 [12]

HOARE, F. R., *The Western Fathers* (London 1954)

HUGH OF POITIERS, *Historia Viziliacensis monasterii*, Bouquet XII [27]

JAFFÉ, P. *Bibliotheca Rerum Germanicarum* I (Berlin 1864) [21]

JOHN OF FLEURY, *ad Olibam abbatem epistola*, Bouquet X

JOHN OF ORVIETO, *Vita S. Petri Parentinii*, *Acta Sanctorum* May V [38]

JOHN OF SALISBURY, *Historia Pontificalis*, ed. M. Chibnall, (London 1956) [20]

KNOWLES, D. and OBOLENSKY, D., *The Christian Centuries: II, The Middle Ages* (London 1969)

LANDULF SENIOR, *Historia Mediolanensis* II ed. D. L. C. Bethmann and W. Wattenbach, *MGH SS* VIII [4]

LATOUCHE, R., 'La commune du Mans, 1070', *Mélanges d'histoire du Moyen Age dédiés à la mémoire de Louis Halphen* (Paris 1950) and *Etudes Médiévales* (Paris 1968)

LE GOFF, J., (ed.) *Hérésies et sociétés dans l'Europe pré-industrielle, 11e.–18e. siècles* (Paris and The Hague 1969)

LEA, H. C., *A History of the Inquisition in the Middle Ages.* (London 1888; New York 1955–8)

LEMERLE, P., 'L'histoire des Pauliciens d'Asie mineure d'après les sources grecques' *Travaux et Mémoires* 5 (1973)

LIÈGE, CANONS OF, letter to L., Supreme Pontiff *PL* 179 [23]

LUCHAIRE, A., *Innocent III*: II, *La croisade des Albigeois* (Paris 1905)

MCDONNELL, E. W., *The Béguines and Beghards in Medieval Culture* (New Brunswick 1954)

MAISONNEUVE, H. *Études sur les origines de l'inquisition* (2nd edn. Paris 1960)

MANSELLI, R. *Studi sulle eresie del secolo XII* (Rome 1953)
'Il monaco Enrico e la sua eresia', *Bulletino dell'Istituto storico Italiano per il medio evo* LXV (1953) **[16]**
L'eresia del male (Naples 1963)
'Eckberto di Schönau e l'eresia catara', *Arte e Storia: Studi in onore di Leonello Vincent* (Turin 1965), pp. 311–38

MENS, A., 'Les béguines et les béghards dans le cadre de la culture médiévale', *Le Moyen Age* 64 (1958), 305–15

MOORE, R. I., 'The Origins of Medieval Heresy', *History* LV (1970)
'St Bernard's Mission to the Languedoc in 1145' *Bulletin of the Institute of Historical Research* XLVII (1974).
'Nicetas, émissaire de Dragovitch: a-t-il traversé les Alpes?' *Annales du Midi* 85 (1973)

VON MOOS, P. *Hildebert von Lavardin* (Stuttgart 1965)

MOREAU, E. DE, *Histoire de l'église en Belgique* (2nd edn. Brussels 1945–51)

MORGHEN, R., 'Problèmes sur l'origine de l'hérésie au moyen âge', *Revue Historique* CCCXXXVI (1966)

MUNDY, J. H., *Liberty and Political Power in Toulouse*, 1050–1230 (New York 1954)
Europe in the High Middle Ages, 1150–1309 (London 1973)

MUNZ, P., *Frederick Barbarossa* (London 1969)

NELLI, R. *Le phenomène cathare* (Paris and Toulouse 1964)

NELSON, JANET L., 'Society, Theodicy and the Origins of Heresy' *Studies in Church History*, 9 (1972), 65–77

NIEL, F., *Albigeois et Cathares* (Paris 1955)

NOIROUX, J. M., 'Les deux premiers documents concernants l'hérésie aux Pays-Bas', *RHE* XLIX (1954)

OBOLENSKY, D. *The Bogomils* (Cambridge 1948, repr. Twickenham 1972)

OLDENBOURG, ZOE, *The Massacre at Montsegur* (London 1959)

OTTO OF FREISING, *Deeds of Frederick Barbarossa* trans. C. C. Mierow (New York 1953)

PARTNER, P., *The Lands of St Peter* (London 1972)

PAUL OF ST PÈRE DE CHARTRES, *Gesta synodi Aurelianensis* Bouquet X **[2]**

PETER THE VENERABLE, *Tractatus contra Petrobrusianos* ed. J. V. Fearns, *Corpus Christian-orum, Continuatio Medievalis*, X (1968) **[17]**
Letters ed. G. Constable (Cambridge, Mass. 1967)

PETIT-DUTAILLIS, C., *Les communes françaises* (Paris 1947)

POOLE, R. L., *The Historia Pontificalis of John of Salisbury* (Oxford 1927)

PUECH, H. C., 'Catharisme médiévale et Bogomilisme', Accademia Nazionale dei Lincei . . . *Atti dei convegni* 12: *Oriente ed Occidente nel Medio Evo* (Rome 1957)

PUECH, H. C. and VAILLANT, A., *Le traité contre les Bogomiles de Cosmas le prêtre* (Paris 1945)

RALPH OF COGGESHALL, *Chronicon Anglicanum* ed. J. Stevenson (*RS* London, 1875) **[28]**

RAINIER SACCHONI, *Summa de Catharis* see Dondaine, (1939) **[39]**

ROGER OF HOVEDEN, *Gesta Regis Henrici Secundi* ed. W. Stubbs (*RS* London 1867) **[35, 36]**
Chronica ed. W. Stubbs, (*RS* London 1869)
Annals [*Chronica*]. trans. H. T. Riley (London 1853)

ROUSSEAU, H., 'L'interprétation du catharisme', *Annales* 24 (1) (1969)

ROUSSET, P., 'Recherches sur l'émotivité à l'époque romane', *Cahiers de Civilisation Médiévale* 2, (1959)

RUNCIMAN, S., *The Medieval Manichee* (Cambridge 1947)

RUSSELL, J. B., 'A propos du synode d'Arras', *RHE* LVII (1962)
'Some interpretations of the Origins of Medieval Heresy', *Medieval Studies* XXV (1963)
Dissent and Reform in the Early Middle Ages (Los Angeles 1965)

SETTON, K. M. and BALDWIN, M. (eds.), *A History of the Crusades* II (Philadelphia 1962)

SIGEBERT OF GEMBLOUX, *Continuatio Gemblacensis* ed. D. L. C. Bethmann *MGH SS* VI **[18]**

SOUTHERN, R. W., *The Making of the Middle Ages* (London 1953)
Western Society and the Church in the Middle Ages (London 1970)

STUBBS, W. *Select Charters* (9th edn. Oxford 1913)

Studies in Church History ed. D. M. Baker (Cambridge): 8 (1971), *Councils and Assemblies*; 9 (1972), *Schism, Heresy and Religious Protest*; 10 (1973), *Sanctity and Secularity*

SULPICIUS SEVERUS, *Life of St Martin of Tours* see Hoare.

THOUZELLIER, C., 'Hérésie et croisade au XIIe. siècle', *RHE* XLIX (1954)
Catharisme et valdéisme en Languedoc à la fin du XIIe. et au début du XIIIe. siècle (Paris 1963)
'Les cathares languedociens et le "nichil" ', *Annales* 24 (1) (1969)
Hérésies et hérétiques, Storia e Letteratura 116 (Rome 1969)

TURBERVILLE, A. S., *Medieval Heresy and the Inquisition* (London 1920)

UTRECHT, CANONS OF, letter to Frederick archbishop of Cologne, *Acta Sanctorum* 1 June **[8]**

VACANDARD, E., *Vie de St Bernard* (Paris 1920)

VERMEESCH, A *Essai sur les origines et la signification de la commune dans le nord de la France* (Heule 1966)

VICAIRE, M. H., *St Dominic and his Times* (London 1964)

Vita Norberti ed. R. Wilmans *MGH SS* XII **[9]**

WAKEFIELD, W. L., *Heresy, Crusade and Inquisition in Southern France, 1100–1250* (London 1974)

WAKEFIELD, W. L. and EVANS, A. P., *Heresies of the High Middle Ages* (New York 1969)

WALEY, D. *Medieval Orvieto* (Cambridge 1952)

WHITNEY, J. P., *Hildebrandine Essays* (Cambridge 1932)

WIBALD OF STAVELOT, Correspondence. *See* Jaffe

WIDENGREN, G., *Mani and Manichaeism* (London 1965)

WILLIAM OF NEWBURGH, *Historia rerum Anglicarum: Chronicles of the Reigns of Stephen* etc. ed. R. Howlett (*RS* London 1884–5) **[19, 26]**

WILLIAMS, W. *St Bernard of Clairvaux* (Manchester 1935)

WOLFF, P., *The Awakening of Europe* (Harmondsworth 1968)

Index

Index